BlackBerry® Storm™

FOR

DUMMIES®

2ND EDITION

BlackBerry® Storm™
FOR
DUMMIES®
2ND EDITION

by Robert Kao and Dante Sarigumba

WILEY

Wiley Publishing, Inc.

BlackBerry® Storm™ For Dummies,® 2nd Edition

Published by
Wiley Publishing, Inc.
111 River Street
Hoboken, NJ 07030-5774

www.wiley.com

Copyright © 2010 by Wiley Publishing, Inc., Indianapolis, Indiana

Published by Wiley Publishing, Inc., Indianapolis, Indiana

Published simultaneously in Canada

For general information on our other products and services, please contact our Customer Care Department within the U.S. at 877-762-2974, outside the U.S. at 317-572-3993, or fax 317-572-4002.

For technical support, please visit www.wiley.com/techsupport.

Wiley also publishes its books in a variety of electronic formats. Some content that appears in print may not be available in electronic books.

Library of Congress Control Number: 2009942322

ISBN: 978-0-470-56531-5

Manufactured in the United States of America

10 9 8 7 6 5 4 3 2 1

WILEY

About the Authors

Robert Kao is one well-rounded professional. His ability to translate his technical knowledge and communicate with users of all types led him to cowrite *BlackBerry For Dummies* and *BlackBerry Pearl For Dummies*. He started out as a BlackBerry developer for various financial firms in New York City, that truly global city. Kao is currently the founder of a mobile software start-up. A graduate of Columbia University, with a Computer Engineering degree, he currently lives in South Brunswick, New Jersey.

Dante Sarigumba is a long-time user of BlackBerry and a gizmo enthusiast. He is a cohost of the Mobile Computing Authority biweekly podcast. He works for a major investment bank in New York as a software developer and lives in South Brunswick, New Jersey, with his wife, Rosemarie, and two sons, Dean and Drew.

Dedication

I would like to thank my father (MHK), my mother (SYT), and the rest of the Kao family for everything they've done for me. I wouldn't be here without their kindness and understanding. I would also like to thank my lovely wife, Marie-Claude, and little Jade for all their support. In addition, thanks to Manon Lalancette and the rest of Gamelin family for all your cheers!

—Robert Kao

To Yosma, Dean, and Drew: My greatest treasures. Thank you for your thoughts, understanding, and support.

—Dante Sarigumba

A few thank-yous are in order here. First, to Rob and Dante, for giving me the opportunity to work on this title with them. To Marcus, Diana, Dieter, Joel, Andrew, and the entire Smartphone Experts team, for being the absolute best at everything they do. Thanks also goes to Erika, for putting up with my obsessive CrackBerrying. Lastly, I need to give props to my mother, who at 60 years old recently got her first cell phone, a BlackBerry Bold, read *BlackBerry Bold For Dummies,* and now BBMs me on it daily.

—Kevin Michaluk

Authors' Acknowledgments

Collectively, we'd like to thank the following people:

- Tiffany Ma, for stepping in when Katie was on maternity leave.

- Mary Bednarek, for making sure we were headed in the right direction while Katie was away.

- Katie Mohr, welcome back just in time to help us put things together. Congratulation on the newborn!

- Susan Pink, our editor, for making us look good.

- Robert Hawley, our technical editor, for checking our work.

- Robert Hawley, our editor, for making us look good.

- Carol McClendon, our agent, for presenting our proposal to the right people.

- Victoria Berry, PR of Research In Motion, for getting us access to the proper channels at the right time.

- Steve and Sheila, thanks for everything.

In addition, we thank the rest of the Wiley staff. Without you all, this book would not have been possible.

—Rob and Dante

Publisher's Acknowledgments

We're proud of this book; please send us your comments at http://dummies.custhelp.com. For other comments, please contact our Customer Care Department within the U.S. at 877-762-2974, outside the U.S. at 317-572-3993, or fax 317-572-4002.

Some of the people who helped bring this book to market include the following:

Acquisitions and Editorial

Project Editor: Susan Pink

Acquisitions Editor: Katie Mohr, Tiffany Ma

Copy Editor: Susan Pink

Technical Editor: Robert Hawley

Editorial Manager: Jodi Jensen

Editorial Assistant: Amanda Graham

Sr. Editorial Assistant: Cherie Case

Cartoons: Rich Tennant (www.the5thwave.com)

Composition Services

Project Coordinator: Katherine Crocker

Layout and Graphics: Joyce Haughey, Ronald G. Terry, Timothy C. Detrick

Proofreaders: John Greenough , Kathy Simpson

Indexer: Ty Koontz

Special Help Annie Sullivan

Publishing and Editorial for Technology Dummies

Richard Swadley, Vice President and Executive Group Publisher

Andy Cummings, Vice President and Publisher

Mary Bednarek, Executive Acquisitions Director

Mary C. Corder, Editorial Director

Publishing for Consumer Dummies

Diane Graves Steele, Vice President and Publisher

Composition Services

Debbie Stailey, Director of Composition Services

Contents at a Glance

Introduction 1

Part I: Meet and Greet Your BlackBerry Storm 7
Chapter 1: Your BlackBerry Is Not an Edible Fruit............................9
Chapter 2: Navigating the BlackBerry Storm 17
Chapter 3: Whipping Up a Storm of Your Own 27

Part II: Getting Organized and Online with Your Storm... 41
Chapter 4: Remembering and Locating Your Acquaintances 43
Chapter 5: Keeping Your Appointments 69
Chapter 6: Setting Alarms and Keeping Your Passwords........................83
Chapter 7: You've Got (Lots of) E-Mail 97
Chapter 8: Too Cool for E-Mail...123
Chapter 9: Instant Messaging 143
Chapter 10: Surfing the Internet Wave..157

Part III: Going Multimedia with Your Storm................ 181
Chapter 11: Taking Great Pictures..183
Chapter 12: Satisfying Your Senses with Media Player 197
Chapter 13: Getting around with BlackBerry GPS 221
Chapter 14: Calling Your Favorite Person 227

Part IV: Working with BlackBerry Desktop Manager.... 241
Chapter 15: Syncing the Synchronize Way 243
Chapter 16: Switching Devices..271
Chapter 17: Protecting Your Information 279
Chapter 18: Installing and Managing Third-Party Applications....................291

Part V: The Part of Tens 307
Chapter 19: Ten Great Storm Accessories......................................309
Chapter 20: Ten Fun Games for Your Storm 315
Chapter 21: Ten Important Types of Web Sites 319

Index 325

Table of Contents

Introduction 1

About This Book 2
Who Are You? 2
What's in This Book 3
    Part I: Meet and Greet Your BlackBerry Storm 3
    Part II: Getting Organized and Online with Your Storm 3
    Part III: Going Multimedia with Your Storm 3
    Part IV: Working with BlackBerry Desktop Manager 4
    Part V: The Part of Tens 4
Icons Used in This Book 4
Where to Go from Here...5

Part 1: Meet and Greet Your BlackBerry Storm 7

Chapter 1: Your BlackBerry Is Not an Edible Fruit. 9

How It All Works: The Schematic Approach 10
    The role of the network service provider.......................10
    Connecting to your computer 12
Oh, the Things You Can Do! 12
    All-in-one multimedia center 13
    Internet at your fingertips...13
    Me and my great personal assistant..............................13
    A touch-screen PC in the palm of your hand 14
    Look, Dad, no hands! 14
Chew on a BlackBerry Storm 14
    BlackBerry OS 5.0...15
    Saving power 15
    Putting a sentry on duty 15

Chapter 2: Navigating the BlackBerry Storm .17

Exploring Your BlackBerry's Face...17
Using the SurePress Touch Screen 20
Tapping the Keyboards: QWERTY and SureType.......................20
    Virtual QWERTY keyboard 20
    Virtual SureType keyboard..21
Physical Keys and More...24
    microSD slot 25
    Switching applications 25

Chapter 3: Whipping Up a Storm of Your Own 27

   Making Your BlackBerry Yours 27
      Branding your BlackBerry 28
      Choosing a language, any language...28
      Typing with ease using AutoText 29
      Inserting text shortcuts..31
      Customizing your screen's look and feel....................................31
      Programming the left and right convenience keys......................33
      Choosing themes 34
      Wallpapering 34
      Ringing freedom 35
   Keeping Your BlackBerry Safe 38

Part II: Getting Organized and Online with Your Storm ... 41

Chapter 4: Remembering and Locating Your Acquaintances 43

   Accessing Contacts 44
   Working with Contacts 45
      Creating a contact...45
      Adding contacts from other BlackBerry applications 50
      Viewing a contact...51
      Editing a contact 51
      Deleting a contact 52
   Copying Contacts from Desktop Applications......................................53
   Looking for Someone?..54
   Organizing Your Contacts 57
      Creating a group...57
      Using the Filter feature on your contacts 59
      Setting preferences 61
   Sharing a Contact 62
      Sending a vCard 63
      Receiving a vCard 64
   Searching for Someone Outside Your Contacts 64
   Synchronizing Facebook Contacts 65
      Adding a Facebook friend info to Contacts 66
      Automatic syncing between Facebook profiles and Contacts.......67

Chapter 5: Keeping Your Appointments 69

   Accessing BlackBerry Calendar..69
   Choosing Your Calendar View 70
      Switching Calendar views 71
      Moving between time frames 71
   Customizing Your Calendar 73
   Managing Multiple Calendars...75

All Things Appointment: Adding, Opening, and Deleting.......................76
    Creating an appointment 76
Understanding Appointments versus Meetings 80
    Sending a meeting request 80
    Responding to a meeting request......................................80
    Setting your meeting dial-in number................................81

Chapter 6: Setting Alarms and Keeping Your Passwords 83
    Accessing Clock...83
    Customizing Your Clock 84
    Setting a Wake-Up Alarm 87
    Setting and Exiting Bedside Mode...88
    Using Stopwatch 89
    Using Timer 90
    Using Password Keeper 91
        Setting a password for Password Keeper.....................92
        Creating credentials 92
        Generating passwords randomly..................................93
        Using your password..94
        Seeing Password Keeper options................................95
        Changing your password to Password Keeper.............96

Chapter 7: You've Got (Lots of) E-Mail 97
    Getting Up and Running with E-Mail 97
        Using the BlackBerry Internet Service client 98
        Combining your e-mail accounts into one...................98
        Adding an e-mail account 99
        Using Desktop Redirector: How enterprising!............101
    Configuring Your E-Mail Signature 102
    Enabling Wireless Reconciliation 103
        Enabling wireless e-mail synchronization 103
        Permanently deleting e-mail from your BlackBerry....104
    Automating Replies and Out-of-Office Messages..................105
    Working with E-Mail 105
        Receiving e-mails 106
        Sending e-mail 109
        Spell-checking your outgoing messages 111
        Adding a sender to your Contacts...............................112
        Deleting e-mail...112
        Filtering your e-mail...113
    Searching Messages Like a Pro..116
        Searching by sender or recipient................................116
        Searching by subject 117
        Running a general search...117
        Saving search results...119
        Reusing saved searches 120
    Long Live E-Mail...121

Chapter 8: Too Cool for E-Mail **123**

Sending and Receiving PIN-to-PIN Messages 123
Getting a BlackBerry PIN 125
Assigning PINs to names 127
Sending a PIN-to-PIN message 128
Receiving a PIN-to-PIN message 129
Keeping in Touch the SMS/MMS Way 129
Using shorthand for speedy replies 130
AWHFY? 130
Showing some emotion 132
Sending a text message 133
Viewing a message you receive 135
Always Online Using Instant Messaging 136
Chatting using IM rules 136
Instant messaging on your BlackBerry 137
Taking control of your IM app 141

Chapter 9: Instant Messaging **143**

Accessing BlackBerry Messenger 144
Using BlackBerry Messenger 144
Adding a Contact 147
Having Conversations 150
Starting a conversation 150
Starting a group conversation 150
Sending a file 152
Saving the conversation history 154
Broadcasting a Message 155

Chapter 10: Surfing the Internet Wave **157**

Kicking Up Browser 157
Getting to Browser 158
Hitting the (air) waves 160
Navigating Web pages 161
Saving a Web page address 164
Sending an address by e-mail 166
Saving Web images 166
Bookmarking Your Favorite Sites 166
Adding and visiting a bookmark 166
Modifying a bookmark 168
Organizing your bookmarks 168
Exercising Options and Optimization Techniques 171
Configuring Browser 172
Setting general Browser properties 173
Specifying cache operations 174
Gears settings 176
Installing and Uninstalling Applications from the Web 177

Using Browser in Business 179
   Using Browser on your company's BlackBerry
      Enterprise Server server 179
   Using your network provider's browser............................ 180
   Setting the default browser 180

Part III: Going Multimedia with Your Storm 181

Chapter 11: Taking Great Pictures 183

Saying "Cheese" 183
   Reading the screen indicators 185
   Choosing the picture quality... 186
   Zooming and focusing... 187
   Setting the flash.. 188
   Setting the white balance.. 188
   Setting the picture size... 188
   Geotagging 189
Working with Your Pictures.. 189
   Viewing pictures 189
   Creating a slide show 190
   Trashing pictures.. 191
   Listing filenames versus thumbnails.............................. 191
   Checking picture properties.. 191
   Organizing your pictures 192
   Sharing your pictures.. 194
   Setting a picture as Caller ID 195
   Setting a Home screen image 196

Chapter 12: Satisfying Your Senses with Media Player...........197

Accessing Media 198
Let the Music Play 199
   Creating a playlist 201
   Playing from your playlist.. 203
Now Showing.. 203
Picture This 204
   Viewing in Pictures 205
   Zoom to see details... 205
Lord of the Ring Tones 205
Recording Your Voice..206
Playing Your Voice Notes 207
Turning It Up (or Down) 208
Navigating the Menu 208
   Navigating the menu in Pictures.....................................208
   Navigating the menu in Music, Videos, Ring Tones,
      and Voice Notes 209
Using Explore 209

Memory Use 210
Changing the Media Flavor..210
    Customizing Media 211
    Customizing Pictures 212
Working with Media Files 212
    Using your Storm as a flash drive............................213
    Meet and greet Media Manager...............................214
    Synchronizing with iTunes using BlackBerry Media Sync...........218
    Downloading sounds 219

Chapter 13: Getting Around with BlackBerry GPS...............221

Putting Safety First 221
Getting What You Need 222
Choosing GPS Application Options..................................222
    BlackBerry Maps...223
    Google Maps 224
    TeleNav GPS Navigator 225

Chapter 14: Calling Your Favorite Person 227

Using the BlackBerry Phone Application 227
    Making a call 227
    Getting a call 229
    Muting your call 230
    Turning down the volume..230
Customizing Your Phone 230
    Setting up your voice mail number 231
    Using call forwarding..231
Arranging Conference Calls...233
    Talking privately to a conference participant...............234
    Alternating between phone conversations 234
Communicating Hands Free 235
    Using the speaker phone 235
    Pairing your BlackBerry with a Bluetooth headset......235
    Using your voice to dial 236
Taking Notes While on the Phone 237
    Accessing phone notes 238
    Forwarding phone notes 239

Part IV: Working with BlackBerry Desktop Manager... 241

Chapter 15: Syncing the Synchronize Way 243

Data Synchronization on a Windows PC 244
    Launching BlackBerry Desktop Manager..................245
    Connecting BlackBerry Desktop Manager to your Storm............246
    Running BlackBerry Desktop Manager for the first time.............247

Setting Up Synchronize on a Windows PC 248
    Configuring PIM synchronization 249
    Mapping fields for synchronization..253
    Confirming record changes 255
    Resolving update conflicts..255
    Ready, set, synchronize! 257
Data Synchronization on the Mac 258
    Installing BlackBerry Desktop Manager...259
    Opening BlackBerry Desktop Manager for the first time..............260
Synchronizing, Mac Style..261
    Setting synchronization options...261
    Deleting all music files on your Storm 267
    Doing a manual sync...268
    Configuring an automatic sync 269

Chapter 16: Switching Devices 271

Switching to a New BlackBerry...271
Switching from a Non-BlackBerry Device..274
    Palm device requirements..274
    Windows Mobile device requirements 275
    Run the wizard 275

Chapter 17: Protecting Your Information 279

Accessing Backup and Restore...280
Backing Up BlackBerry Style...281
    Backing up your Storm manually...281
    Setting up automatic backups...283
Restoring Your Data from Backup Information 284
Protecting Your Data Your Way 285
    Backing up your way...286
    Restoring your way..287
    Clearing BlackBerry information your way 288
Backing Up and Restoring Wirelessly 289

Chapter 18: Installing and Managing Third-Party Applications 291

Using BlackBerry App World 291
    Navigating App World 292
    Installing an application using App World 293
Finding and Installing Applications from Other App Stores 294
Accessing Application Loader 296
Installing an Application..297
    Installing, Windows Style...297
    Installing, Mac Style...299
Uninstalling an Application 301
    Uninstalling with Application Loader under Windows PC 301
    Uninstalling with BlackBerry Desktop Manager on the Mac........302
    Uninstalling with the Storm..302

Upgrading the BlackBerry Storm OS...303
    Upgrading the Storm OS, Windows Style............................303
    Upgrading the Storm OS, Mac Style....................................305

Part V: The Part of Tens 307

Chapter 19: Ten Great Storm Accessories 309
Unify AV Solution...309
microSD Card...310
Full Keyboards...310
Stereo Headsets...310
Case and Belt Clip..311
Screen Protector and Skins...311
Extra Battery, Charger, and Charging Pod 312
External Speaker..312
Bluetooth Music Gateway..313
Car Mount..313

Chapter 20: Ten Fun Games for Your Storm 315
Top-Rated Free Games...316
Nintaii..316
Bookworm...316
Crash Bandicoot Mutant Island 317
Air Traffic Control..317
World Poker Tour 2—Texas Hold 'Em..................................317
Bubble Army...317
Aces Mahjong...317
Next Dual Pack...318
Chuzzle..318

Chapter 21: Ten Important Types of Web Sites..................319
Weather...319
News..320
Search Engines, Directories, and Portals 320
Business..321
Travel..321
Sports..322
Advice and Self-Help..322
Social and Virtual Networking 323
Shopping and Shipping Information....................................323
Other Browsing Categories 324

Index 325

Introduction

*H*i there, and welcome to *BlackBerry Storm For Dummies,* 2nd Edition. This book is intended to cover most of what you need to know about the BlackBerry Storm and the BlackBerry Storm2 smart phones. Throughout the book, we're going to use the Storm to describe both smart phones but will point out differences along the way. If you already have a Storm, this is a great book to have around when you want to discover new features or need something to slap open and use as a quick reference. If you don't have a Storm yet and have some basic questions (such as "What is a BlackBerry Storm?" or "How can a BlackBerry Storm help me be more productive?"), you can benefit by reading this book cover to cover. No matter what your current BlackBerry user status — BUS, for short — we're here to help you get the most out of your BlackBerry Storm.

Right off the bat, we can tell you that a BlackBerry Storm isn't a fruit you find at the supermarket, nor is it related to nasty weather patterns. Rather, it's an always-connected smart phone that has e-mail capabilities and a built-in Internet browser. With your BlackBerry Storm, you're in the privileged position of always being able to receive e-mail, message your friends, and browse the Web.

On top of that, a BlackBerry Storm has all the features you expect from a personal organizer, including a calendar, to-do lists, and memos. Oh, and did we mention that a BlackBerry Storm has a built-in mobile phone? Talk about multitasking! Imagine you are stuck on a commuter train. With your BlackBerry Storm by your side, you can compose e-mail while conducting a conference call — all from the comfort of your seat.

That's not all. BlackBerry Storm goes a step further to make it more fun for you to own this device. You can snap a picture with its camera, listen to your music collection, record a funny video, and enjoy watching that video on YouTube.

In this book, we show you all the basics and then go the extra mile by highlighting some of the lesser-known (but still handy) features of the BlackBerry Storm. Your Storm can work hard for you when you need it to and can play hard when you want it to.

And finally, you'll be happy to know that we acquired the help of a well-known BlackBerry enthusiast and co-founder of CrackBerry.com, Kevin Michulak, to provide you with insights and helpful tips scattered throughout the book.

About This Book

BlackBerry Storm For Dummies is a comprehensive user guide as well as a quick user reference. This book is designed so that you can read it cover to cover if you want, but you don't need to read one chapter after the other. Feel free to jump around in the book while you explore the different functionalities of your BlackBerry Storm.

We cover basic and advanced topics, but we stick to those that we consider the most practical and frequently used. If you use or want to use a certain function of your BlackBerry Storm, we likely cover it here.

Who Are You?

In this book, we tried to be considerate of your needs, but because we've never met you, our image of you is as follows. If you find that some of these images are true about you, this might just be the book for you:

- You have a BlackBerry Storm and want to find out how to get the most from it.

- You don't have a BlackBerry Storm yet, and you're wondering what one could do for you.

- You're looking for a book that doesn't assume that you know all the jargon and tech terms used in the smart phone and PDA industry. (*PDA* stands for *personal digital assistant,* by the way. Take that, you jargon, you!)

- You want a reference that shows you, step by step, how to do useful and cool things with a BlackBerry Storm without bogging you down with unnecessary background or theory.

- You're tired of hauling your ten-pound laptop with you on trips, and you're wondering how to turn your BlackBerry Storm into a miniature traveling office.

- You no longer want to be tied to your desktop system for the critical activities in your life, such as sending and receiving e-mail, checking your calendar for appointments, and surfing the Web.

- You like to have some fun, play games, and be entertained from a device but don't want to carry an extra game gadget.

What's in This Book

BlackBerry Storm For Dummies consists of five parts, and each part consists of different chapters related to that part's theme.

Part 1: Meet and Greet Your BlackBerry Storm

Part I starts with the basics of your Storm. You know: what it is, what you can do with it, and what elements make it up with. We describe how you navigate using the innovative touch screen that behaves like multiple buttons and the difference between the QWERTY and SureType keyboard layouts. We also show you how to personalize and express yourself through your BlackBerry Storm. This part wraps up with must-knows about security.

Part II: Getting Organized and Online with Your Storm

Part II deals with the fact that your BlackBerry Storm is also a full-fledged PDA. We show you how to keep your contacts in Contacts as well as how to manage appointments and meetings in Calendar. You also find out how to use the Clock application to set an alarm, use as a timer, and set your device to Bedside mode. You explore the Password Keeper application to centralize your passwords. As you'll see, most BlackBerry applications interconnect, working hard for you.

Part II also shows you what made BlackBerry what it is today: always-connected e-mail. We get into the other strengths of the BlackBerry — Web surfing functionality — but it doesn't stop there. We point out how you can use other forms of messages such as text messaging, instant messaging, PIN-to-PIN messages, and BlackBerry Messenger.

Part III: Going Multimedia with Your Storm

You find the fun stuff in Part III. Rock your world and use your Storm to play music, watch videos, and take pictures. You also get the scoop on how to record videos and sample ring tones. Plus you get timesaving shortcuts on the Media applications. And rest assured that your BlackBerry will be a good companion when you're traveling because we also show you how to use its GPS. Last, Part III describes the phone part of Storm and money-saving tips; it is a smart phone after all.

Part IV: Working with BlackBerry Desktop Manager

In Part IV, we detail BlackBerry Desktop Manager and show you some of the hoops you can put it through with your BlackBerry Storm, including making backups and installing BlackBerry applications from your PC to your Storm. You also find out how to port data from your older devices — BlackBerry or not — to your new Storm. And we didn't forget to cover important topics, such as data-syncing your appointments and contacts with desktop applications such as Outlook. And finally, you'll find all the possible ways you can install third-party applications.

Part V: The Part of Tens

All *For Dummies* books include The Part of Tens, and this book is no different. In Part V, we show you where to get cool BlackBerry Storm accessories, find useful mobile Web sites, and get great applications and games to play on your BlackBerry Storm. In addition, we keep this list up-to-date on our Web site at www.blackberryfordummies.com.

Icons Used in This Book

Scattered through the book are CrackBerry tips brought to you by Kevin Michaluk and the enthusiastic members of the CrackBerry.com member community. These tips represent millions of hours of combined BlackBerry use. Some are short and sweet; others are slightly more in depth. All will help you get the most out of your Storm. And if you ever run into a problem you can't solve or a question you can't find the answer to in this book, look no further than www.crackberry.com.

If a paragraph sports this icon, it means we're talking about BlackBerry Storm smart phones that are provided by your employer.

This icon highlights an important point that you don't want to forget because it just might come up again. We'd never be so cruel as to spring a pop quiz on you, but paying attention to this detail can definitely help you.

 This book rarely delves into the geeky, technical details, but when it does, this icon warns you. Read on if you want to get under the hood a little, or just skip ahead if you aren't interested in the gory details.

 Here's where you can find not-so-obvious tricks that can make you a BlackBerry Storm power user in no time. Pay special attention to the paragraphs with this icon to get the most out of your Storm.

 Look out! This icon tells you how to avoid trouble before it starts.

Where to Go from Here

If you want to find out more about the book or have a question or comment for the authors, please visit us at any of the following:

- www.blackberryfordummies.com
- www.crackberry.com

Give Chapter 1 a quick look to get an idea of where this book takes you and then feel free to head straight to your chapter of choice.

Part I

Meet and Greet Your BlackBerry Storm

The 5th Wave — By Rich Tennant

"He seemed nice, but I could never connect with someone who had a ring tone like his."

In this part . . .

The road to a happy and collaborative relationship with your BlackBerry Storm starts here. Chapter 1 covers all the nuts and bolts: how the Storm works, its look and feel, and connectivity. Chapter 2 describes how you navigate with the virtual keys. Chapter 3 discusses customizing your BlackBerry and also how to take care of your device.

Chapter 1

Your BlackBerry Is Not an Edible Fruit

In This Chapter

▶ Checking out your BlackBerry behind the scenes

▶ Seeing what your BlackBerry can do

▶ Saving power and feeling secure

*B*ecause you're reading this book, you probably have a BlackBerry Storm (and we're pretty sure that you're not eating it). We're just curious, though — what convinced you to buy this particular smart phone? Was it the touch screen? Was it the always-connected e-mail? The multimedia player to replace your iPod or iPhone? Or was it the really good sales pitch? We know; the list could go on and on — and we might never hit on the exact reason you got yours. For whatever reason you got your BlackBerry, congratulations; you made an intelligent choice.

The same smarts that made you buy your BlackBerry Storm are clearly at it again. This time, your intelligence led you to pick up this book, perhaps because your intuition told you there's more to your BlackBerry Storm than meets the eye.

Your hunch is right. Your Storm *can* help you do more than you supposed. For example, your BlackBerry is a whiz at making phone calls, but it's also a computer that can check your e-mail and surf the Web. We're talking *World Wide* Web here, so the sky's the limit. Help is always at your fingertips rather than sitting on some desk at home or at the office:

- ✔ Need to check out the reviews of that restaurant on the corner?

- ✔ Need to know — right now — what's showing in your local movie theaters, or what's coming in the weather tonight, or what's the best place to shop the sales?

- ✔ Need to know your current location and get directions to that cozy bed-and-breakfast, or retrieve news headlines, or check stock quotes?

- ✔ Want to do some online chatting or view some pictures online?

- ✔ Hanker to network with your old classmates?

You can do all these things (and more) by using your BlackBerry Storm.

Storm is also a full-fledged *personal digital assistant (PDA)*. Out of the box, it provides you with the organizational tools you need to set up to-do lists, manage your appointments, take care of your address books, and more.

Being armed with a device that's a phone, an Internet connection, a PDA, and a full-on media player all built into one makes you a powerful person. With your Storm (along with this resourceful book), you really can increase your productivity and become better organized. Watch out, world! BlackBerry Storm–wielding powerhouse coming through!

If you stick with us, you will find out all you need to get the most out of your device or maybe even save a troubled relationship. (Well, the last one is a bit of an exaggeration, but we got your attention, right?)

How It All Works: The Schematic Approach

For those who always ask, "How do they do that?" you don't have to go far; this little section is just for you.

The role of the network service provider

Along with wondering how your BlackBerry Storm works, you might be wondering why you had to get your Storm through a network service provider such as Verizon or Telus rather than directly from RIM (Research In Motion). Why did you need to go through a middleman? After all, RIM makes BlackBerry Storm.

That's an excellent question — and here's the quick-and-dirty answer. RIM needs a delivery system — a communication medium, as it were — for its technology to work. Not in a position to come up with such a delivery system all by its lonesome, RIM partnered (and built alliances across the globe) with what developed into its network service providers — the usual suspects (meaning the big cellphone companies). These middlemen support the wireless network for your BlackBerry Storm so you can connect to the BlackBerry Internet service — and get all those wonderful e-mails (and spend so much valuable time surfing the Internet). See Figure 1-1 for an overview of this process.

Know your BlackBerry history

Your BlackBerry Storm is truly wondrous, boasting many features beyond your ordinary mobile phone. And its "sudden" popularity didn't happen overnight. Like any other good product, BlackBerry Storm has come a long way from its (relatively humble) beginnings.

In the days when the Palm Pilot ruled the PDA world, Research In Motion (RIM, the maker of the BlackBerry) was busy in its lab, ignoring the then-popular graffiti input method and designing a device with a QWERTY keyboard — the kind of keyboard people were used to from working on their computers. RIM didn't stop there, however. It added an always-connected e-mail capability, making this device a must-have among government officials as well as finance and health professionals.

To meet the needs of government officials and industry professionals, RIM made reliability, security, and durability the priorities when manufacturing its devices. Today, BlackBerry Storm comes from the same line of RIM family products, inheriting all the good genes while boosting usability and adding more functions to its core BlackBerry applications. As a result, BlackBerry is popular among not only *prosumers* (professional customers), but also consumers. Starting with BlackBerry Pearl, RIM has been targeting the mainstream consumer market. Clearly, with BlackBerry Storm, RIM is winning the hearts of consumers while maintaining its hold on the enterprise market.

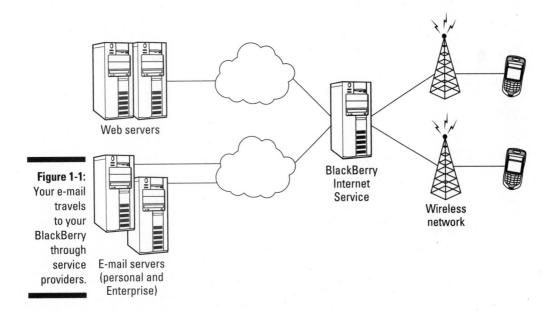

Figure 1-1:
Your e-mail travels to your BlackBerry through service providers.

Web servers

E-mail servers (personal and Enterprise)

BlackBerry Internet Service

Wireless network

Network service providers don't build alliances for nothing, right? In return, RIM gave them the right to brand their names on the BlackBerry they offer for sale. For example, a Verizon BlackBerry Storm looks different from a similar model you get from TELUS Canada.

Do BlackBerry functionalities differ from phone model to phone model? Quick answer: With the core BlackBerry applications (such as Tasks and Contracts), you find no major differences. Other features, such as Instant Messaging, might or might not be supported by the network service provider.

Just to keep the scorecard straight, when we talk about features available from one network service provider that aren't available from others, we point that out.

Connecting to your computer

Nowadays, a personal laptop or net book is a household necessity. People spend so much time on them, and so much information is stored in them. No surprise that BlackBerry works hand-in-hand with your PC. The USB cable that comes with your BlackBerry does more than just charge your device.

Part IV helps you use your PC connection with the help of BlackBerry Desktop Manager and all the utilities that come with it. In Chapter 15, you find how to sync your device with the Personal Information Manager data that you keep in your PC. You can also read Chapter 16 for directions for switching from another device (even a non-BlackBerry device) to a new BlackBerry. For example, you find out how to import your contacts list into your new BlackBerry. Chapter 17 tells you how to protect your data.

If you have a Mac instead of a PC, there is now BlackBerry Desktop Manager for Mac. Check out Chapter 15 for more.

Oh, the Things You Can Do!

In the BlackBerry world, it used to be that always-connected e-mail was the primary factor that made BlackBerry attractive and is likely first in the long list of reasons you got yours.

With Storm you get that, but the touch screen is the center of all attention these days. The touch screen on Storm is a work of art (and science) and a beautiful part of the device. Just hop off your flight, turn on your BlackBerry, and voila: You can receive and send e-mails whether you're in Hong Kong, London, or Paris. Your significant other can get in touch with you wherever you are — just to say hi or to remind you that you promised Aunt Edna a case of Chanel No. 5.

Although e-mail is BlackBerry's strength, it's not the only major benefit of the device, as you find out in this section.

All-in-one multimedia center

Previously, many people hesitated to buy a BlackBerry due to the lack of multimedia functions. They wanted a camera and audio and full video playback. BlackBerry Storm has changed all that and has more features than you may expect. Not only does Storm have a high-resolution camera — 3.2 megapixels, to be exact — but it also has a memory slot for a microSD card (see Chapter 2). What does that mean? Well, it means your BlackBerry can function as the following:

- A music and video player that support all the common file formats
- A portable flash drive
- Your personal photo collection

On top of all that, Storm offers a touch-screen virtual QWERTY keyboard.

Internet at your fingertips

Yup, with the new BlackBerry Web browser on Storm, you can surf the Net nearly as smoothly as you do on a desktop computer. Even better, you can continue chatting with your friends through Instant Messenger, just as though you never left your office. You'll get an alert when your stock is tanking. True, that isn't fun, but you want this information as fast as possible.

Intrigued? Read how Storm can take full advantage of the Web in Chapter 10.

Me and my great personal assistant

You might be saying, "But I'm really a busy person, and I don't have time to browse the Web. What I *do* need is an assistant to help me better organize my day-to-day tasks." If you can afford a personal assistant, by all means go ahead and hire one. The next best thing is a personal *digital* assistant (PDA). Just as people come in many flavors, so do many PDAs.

Whip out that BlackBerry of yours and take a closer look. That's right, your BlackBerry is also a full-fledged PDA, helping you be more productive and much more:

- Remember all your acquaintances (see Chapter 4)
- Manage your appointments (Chapter 5)
- Set alarms and keep your passwords (Chapter 6)

A touch-screen PC in the palm of your hand

Touch screen? Check.

Remarkable communication device? Check.

Full-fledged PDA? Check.

These capabilities are just the tip of the iceberg. Don't underestimate the device because of its size: Your Storm is also a powerful computer.

Need convincing? Here goes. Out of the box, with no fiddling, it comes with a great set of organizational and productivity tools in the form of programs. Software developers outside RIM are taking advantage of this growing market — which means hundreds of applications are available. For example, you can download graphics-intensive games or a mortgage calculator.

Download? Absolutely! BlackBerry Storm comes with BlackBerry App World, which lets you download applications *OTA,* or *over the air.* See Chapter 18 for more

Look, Dad, no hands!

Your Storm is equipped with an earphone that doubles as a mic for hands-free talking. This accessory is your doctor's prescription for preventing the stiff neck that comes from wedging your Storm between your ear and your shoulder. At the minimum, it helps free your hands so you can eat Chinese takeout. Some places require you by law to use an earphone while driving (but only when you're talking on a cellphone, of course).

We don't recommend using your cellphone while driving, hands-free or not.

But RIM didn't stop with just your standard wired earphones. BlackBerry also supports cool wireless earphones based on Bluetooth technology. How could a bizarrely colored tooth help you here? *Bluetooth* is the name for a (very) short-distance wireless technology that connects devices. See Chapter 14 for how to connect your BlackBerry to a Bluetooth headset.

Chew on a BlackBerry Storm

Reliability and quality were probably your main concerns when you decided on BlackBerry Storm. Will the product last? Will it perform like the manufacturer says? Will I regret having bought this item six months down the road?

This section looks at some of the hardware features that make buying the BlackBerry device a wise purchase.

BlackBerry OS 5.0

When the Storm rolled out, there was lots of talk about sluggishness with OS 4.7. With the new OS 5.0, which ships with Storm and Storm2, the user interface has improved greatly, with fast response time and an overall improvement over OS 4.7, true to the BlackBerry reputation.

Saving power

Anyone with BlackBerry experience knows that the BlackBerry is a highly efficient power consumer, but the addition of a colored, high-resolution touch screen has weakened the power efficiency. Power requirements have increased so much that you need to recharge roughly every two days.

We know frequent recharging is a bit of a hassle. but hey, now you have a sweet media player on deck!

Putting a sentry on duty

The virtual world isn't exempt from general human nastiness; in fact, every day a battle is fought between those who are trying to attack a system and those who are trying to protect it. Fortunately, security is a BlackBerry strong point.

A computer connected to the Internet faces an extra risk of being cracked by a hacker or infected by a virus. Viruses try to replicate themselves and generally bug you. Viruses often come as e-mail attachments. However, BlackBerry supports few file types out of the box (mostly images and documents). You won't face threats from e-mails with these attachments. And data that you send to or get from the PDA is *encrypted* (coded) to prevent snooping.

See Chapter 3 for information on setting up a password for your BlackBerry.

Chapter 2

Navigating the BlackBerry Storm

In This Chapter

▶ Checking out the features of your BlackBerry Storm

▶ Introducing the touch screen

▶ Finding out how to type with your BlackBerry Storm's virtual keyboards

You might have heard that the BlackBerry Storm is different from the other BlackBerry smart phones. From the outside, BlackBerry Storm has been completely revamped. Not only is it sleek and slim, but it also has a brighter, bigger, and higher-resolution screen than the older models. But what makes it fundamentally different? It has a *touch screen*.

What? No more trackball? No more QWERTY keyboard? How do you select and scroll with the touch screen? What can you do with it? We answer those questions in this chapter. Bear with us, and you will be master of your BlackBerry Storm in no time.

Exploring Your BlackBerry's Face

In this section we show you all the keys and features on your BlackBerry Storm. You can see them in Figure 2-1.

First, read about the major features:

- ✓ **SurePress touch screen:** This screen is the *graphical user interface (GUI)* on your BlackBerry Storm. It lets you point to things using your finger instead of having to type.

- ✓ **Virtual QWERTY keyboard:** This is available on the Storm while you're typing when you tilt the screen on its side (horizontally). You see all the keys individually as you would on a QWERTY BlackBerry. The QWERTY keyboard can also be shown in portrait mode (when the screen is vertical) by changing the Options.

✔ **Virtual SureType keyboard:** This keyboard layout appears while you're typing with your Storm in portrait mode. Each virtual SureType key contains two letters. If you tweak the Screen/Keyboard Options, the SureType keyboard will not show up.

✔ **Escape key:** This key cancels a selection or returns you to a previous page in an application. The escape key is the arrow key to the left of the end key.

✔ **Menu key (BlackBerry key):** This key displays the full menu of the application you're using. Also, if you press and hold the menu key, it shows you a list of applications currently running. It's like pressing Alt+Tab on a PC. See the "Switching applications" section, at the end of the chapter, for more.

✔ **Convenience keys:** Your BlackBerry Storm has two convenience keys that are, by default, preprogrammed to open an application. In Chapter 3, we show you how to reprogram the convenience keys to display the programs you use the most.

✔ **microSD slot:** You can access the microSD slot by removing the back cover, but without removing the battery. The microSD slot is a crucial element of your BlackBerry media experience.

✔ **Send key:** This key takes you straight to the Phone application, regardless of which application you're currently using. If you're already in the Phone application, the send key starts dialing the number you entered.

✔ **End/Power key:** Use this key to end your call. If you're not on a phone call, this key allows you to jump back to the Home screen from wherever you are. Press and hold this key to turn your BlackBerry on or off.

Most BlackBerry users exit an application to return to the Home screen by pressing the End key. However, this doesn't actually close the application; instead, it leaves it the app running in the background. Yes, your Storm is a multitasking machine! (Holding down the menu key for an extra moment displays all open apps, allowing you to move between them quickly.) Although multitasking is a benefit, leaving an unused app running hogs your Storm's precious memory resources, especially when that app is pulling data in regularly over your wireless connection. Make it a habit to close unused applications. You can do this by pressing the menu key in an open application and touch-pressing Close, which is typically the last choice on an app's menu. You can also back your way out of most open apps by pressing the Escape/Back key repeatedly until you reach the Home screen. Closing unused apps helps keep your Storm running lightning fast.

✔ **Mute key:** Use this key to mutes a call when you're on a call.

✔ **Lock key:** Press this key to quickly lock the BlackBerry screen. You'd use this when you want to put your BlackBerry in your pocket and prevent accidental typing, for instance.

Lock key   Mute key

Notification LED

Volume keys

Left
convenience
key

Right
convenience
key

Figure 2-1:
The main
BlackBerry
Storm
features
are here,
including
a popular
e-mail and
SMS alert
program
called
PeeKaWho.

Touch screen

Send key   End key

Menu key Escape key

With so many combinations of settings available in your Storm, Research
In Motion ships the device with defaults that should be acceptable to most
users, though they may not be ideal for you. One of the first option screens
a new Storm owner should visit is Screen/Keyboard, under Options. At the
bottom is Touchscreen settings. Many people find that setting Sensitivity to
High and the Tap Interval and Hover Period to their lowest setting (100) yields
the best performance, as does setting Key Rate, also found on this screen, to
Fast. Do your own experimenting to see what feels best for you. You'll be using
your touch screen a lot, so you definitely want it dialed in just right.

Using the SurePress Touch Screen

When you first turn on your BlackBerry, the display screen displays the *Home screen,* which is your introduction to your BlackBerry Storm's graphical user interface. The different icons represent the different applications in your BlackBerry.

If you tilt your BlackBerry sideways, the screen follows you.

We use these terms to show you how to interact with your BlackBerry Storm:

- ✔ **Tap** by lightly touching. This action allows you to highlight a choice in a list or place the typing cursor in a particular place. Tapping does not, however, select or confirm a choice.

- ✔ **Touch-press** by firmly touching and pressing on something to select it.

- ✔ **Finger-swipe** by moving your finger from left to right or right to left across the screen. Usually, you use this action to go from one page to another page.

- ✔ **Finger-scroll** by keeping your finger on the touch screen and moving up, down, left, or right on the screen. You scroll to different parts of the screen.

Applications have a row of icons on the bottom of the screen. You can access these shortcuts without using the menu key. If this is your first touch-screen device, play and have fun with it. Trust us; it won't bite.

Tapping the Keyboards: QWERTY and SureType

Surprised by the heading of this section? Just when you thought the term *QWERTY* wasn't going to be part of this book, it is. That's right. In the following sections, we talk about the onscreen — or virtual — keyboards that you use to enter information.

Virtual QWERTY keyboard

You see the virtual QWERTY keyboard appear if you tilt your BlackBerry Storm sideways while entering text into a text field. See Figure 2-2.

Figure 2-2:
This
BlackBerry
Storm
displays
its virtual
QWERTY
keyboard.

You can hide the virtual keyboard by pressing the menu key and touch-pressing Hide Keyboard.

Whether you use your pinky or your index finger, how you type on your BlackBerry is up to you. However, most people find that typing with two thumbs is the most efficient way to type on a BlackBerry Storm. And like the SureType keyboard with its Custom Dictionary, the QWERTY keyboard helps you as you type so you can get the word out (literally) with less keystrokes.

A slight space down the middle divides the right and left sides of the virtual keyboard. Keeping your thumbs on their own sides of the keyboard goes a long way in helping with typing accuracy.

Virtual SureType keyboard

The SureType keyboard appears when you hold your BlackBerry Storm upright (vertical). Many keys share letters, as shown in Figure 2-3. The idea is that SureType is smart enough to figure out what letter you want. Basically, you can type with only one thumb, and your BlackBerry learns the words that you frequently use.

For example, if you want to type the word *hi,* press the GH key and then the UI key. SureType lists the words it thinks you're typing, as shown in Figure 2-3. If the first word is what you want, simply touch the word or the virtual Space key. The word is selected and you can keep typing. If what you want appears a little later in the list, finger-scroll to the word and touch it.

Figure 2-3:
Did you
want to type
hi or *gi?*

These tips can speed up your SureType learning curve:

✔ **Always finish typing a word before correcting it.** This way, SureType learns what you want to type next time.

✔ **If SureType correctly gets the word you're typing (on the first try), use the space key to move on.**

✔ **Take advantage of Custom Dictionary, which is a list of words that you define.** More on this later in this section.

✔ **Type! Type! Type!** Because SureType learns how you type, the more you use it, the faster it adapts.

Multitap

Besides using SureType, you can type in another mode while BlackBerry is upright: *multitap.* The best way to explain multitap is by example. Say you want to type an *h* character on the virtual SureType keyboard. You search out the *h* on your keyboard but notice the key reads GH. What's a person to do? Do you really want to go through life writing *GHello* for *Hello?*

Your problem has a perfectly easy solution. To get the letter *h*, which is the second letter on the key, tap the key twice — hence, the term *multitap.* (To get the letter *g,* you would tap the GH key once.)

Custom Dictionary

BlackBerry Storm keeps all its learned words in a safe place — Custom Dictionary, to be precise. You can review your Custom Dictionary — and even add to it — using the Custom Dictionary option.

Using the Custom Dictionary option to add words or proper names to the list means that SureType doesn't have to learn them when you're typing.

To see or add words by using the Custom Dictionary, follow these steps:

1. **From the Home screen, press the menu key and then touch-press the Options icon (wretch icon).**

2. **Select Custom Dictionary.**

   The Custom Dictionary opens, listing all the words that the Storm has learned. (If you purchased your BlackBerry recently, the list might have only a few words or even no words.)

3. **Press the menu key and then touch-press New.**

4. **To save your changes, press the menu key and then touch-press Save.**

Getting people's names right is tough with SureType, but fortunately, SureType can automatically learn all the names in Contacts as follows:

1. **From the Home screen, press the menu key and then touch-press the options icon.**

2. **Touch-press the Language and Text Input option.**

   The Language option screen appears. This screen is where the handy Input Option button makes its home.

3. **Touch-press the Show Text Input Option button.**

   The Input Options screen appears, with the following options:

   - Auto Word Learning: If this option is on, the Storm learns as you type.
   - Use Contacts as Data Source: If this option is on, the Storm learns all the names in your Contacts.
   - Learn Words from Email Messages: You can choose All Messages or Contacts Only.
   - Predictive: If this option is on, every time you type, the Storm displays possible choices to predict the word you are typing. This can be a timesaver.
   - Include Spell Check Variants: This is related to the Predictive Input option. If turned on, the predictive choice list includes different spelling variants.

  4. Make sure the Use Contacts as Data Source option is selected.

   If it isn't, touch-press the check box to select it.

  5. To save your changes, press the menu key and then touch-press Save.

You'll be most efficient with your Storm if you master all the keyboards available and use the appropriate orientation and layout at the right time. Many people get comfortable with one keyboard layout — for example, using landscape with the full QWERTY — but you'll find you can do everything faster if you mix things up a bit:

   ✔ **Portrait, SureType:** Invest the time to learn the SureType keyboard. Although at first it's weird to see two letters on one key, the predictive text works well, and holding the keyboard in portrait mode and typing with two thumbs allows you to keep your words per minute impressively high. For typing e-mails, this mode is our favorite.

   ✔ **Portrait, full keyboard:** If you have solid dexterity with your thumbs, the full keyboard in portrait orientation most closely approximates the full physical keyboard on other BlackBerry smart phones such as the Bold and Curve. If you can use this keyboard comfortably, it's likely the one you'll grow to like best, but many owners find the spacing a little too tight for two-thumb typing.

   ✔ **Landscape, full keyboard:** When it comes to typing e-mail addresses, Web site URLs, short text messages with slang, or information such as names into the Address Book, we turn the Storm sideways to use the full QWERTY keyboard. Portrait keyboards reduce the physical distance your fingers have to travel, thus allowing you to reduce the time between typing out letters and to go quicker.

   ✔ **Multitap:** With two full keyboards at your disposal, Research In Motion could remove this option and receive no complaints!

Practice makes perfect! Get familiar with the different keyboard options.

Physical Keys and More

Although you will do most of the key entry on the Storm through the onscreen keyboards (see the "Tapping the Keyboards: QWERTY and SureType" section, earlier in this chapter), a few physical keys will help you navigate the user interface of your Storm more quickly:

   ✔ **Escape key:** Simple yet useful, the escape key allows you to return to a previous screen or cancel a selection. The escape key is the arrow key to the left of the end key.

   ✔ **Menu key (BlackBerry key):** The menu key brings up the full menu for the application you are using. When you're on the Home screen, pressing the menu key displays a list of applications installed on your BlackBerry.

✔ **Convenience keys:** Your BlackBerry Storm has two convenience keys, one on the left and one on the right. By default, the right convenience key opens the Camera and the left convenience key opens the voice command application. Think of these two keys as shortcuts to the application you need fast access to. You can program and change these keys to open whatever is installed on your BlackBerry; see Chapter 3 for more info.

microSD slot

Your BlackBerry Storm comes with 1GB of internal memory. If you're a music or video fan, however, you know that 1GB isn't enough to hold anything entertaining. But no need to worry. The folks at Research In Motion incorporated a microSD (external memory card) slot into your BlackBerry Storm so you can add memory and store all the media files you want in your BlackBerry Storm. You can purchase a microSD card separately for a relatively low price these days. At the time of this writing, a 4GB microSD card costs $20.

Switching applications

When you are moving around in an application (such as Browser), an option called Switch Application appears when you press and hold the menu key for 2 seconds. Switch Application, which is similar to Alt+Tab in Windows, lets you multitask between applications. The Switch Application pop-up menu appears in Figure 2-4.

You can program the convenience key so you can get to your favorite application, such as the Tasks application, even more quickly than by using the Switch Application function.

Figure 2-4:
Switch
Application
menu.

Chapter 3

Whipping Up a Storm of Your Own

In This Chapter

▶ Typing using AutoText and shortcuts
▶ Customizing the screen
▶ Programming the convenience keys
▶ Choosing different themes
▶ Changing your profile
▶ Watching your BlackBerry's back

*Y*ou want to have your BlackBerry around as long as you possibly can (or at least until you have the bucks for that way-cool new model that's coming down the pike). And for the time that you *do* have your device, you'll want to trick it out. (C'mon, admit it — your BlackBerry is definitely a fashion statement.)

In addition to customizing, you want to keep your BlackBerry in tip-top shape by watching out for things such as information security. Luckily for you, this chapter fills you in on all you need to know to keep your BlackBerry Storm a finely tuned (and yet quirkily personal) little smart phone.

Making Your BlackBerry Yours

BlackBerry Storm smart phones are increasingly popular — so much so that millions of BlackBerry Storms are out there serving the needs of people like you. Because of this fact, we're certain that finding ways to distinguish your BlackBerry from your colleagues' is high on your list of priorities.

Your wish is our command. Follow the tips and techniques outlined in this section, and you, too, can personalize to your heart's content.

Branding your BlackBerry

Like any number of other electronic gadgets, your BlackBerry Storm comes to you with a collection of settings. This section helps you put your name on your BlackBerry Storm, both figuratively and literally.

You can start by branding your name on your BlackBerry Storm:

1. **Press the menu key and touch-press the options icon.**

2. **Touch-press Owner Options.**

   You see places to enter your owner information.

3. **Enter your name in the Name field and your contact information in the Information field.**

   Phrase a message that would make sense to any possible Good Samaritan who might find your lost BlackBerry and want to get it back to you.

   If you lock or don't use your BlackBerry for a while, the standby screen displays the owner information that you entered. Read how to lock your BlackBerry, either manually or by using an auto setting, as described in the later section, "Keeping Your BlackBerry Safe."

4. **Press the menu key and touch-press Save.**

Choosing a language, any language

Set the language to your native tongue so you don't need to hire a translator to use your BlackBerry. You can also set your input method of choice here, which can affect whether AutoText shows up. Don't worry. We explain what that means in the next section.

Here's how you choose a language:

1. **Press the menu key and touch-press the options icon.**

2. **Touch-press the Language and Text Input option.**

   Here, you can choose the language and input method.

3. **Touch-press the Language field and then select your native (or pre-ferred) tongue.**

   Language choices vary depending on your network provider and region (North America, Europe, and so on). Most handhelds sold in North America default to English or English (United States).

   If your network provider supports it, you can install more languages in your BlackBerry by using Application Loader in BlackBerry Desktop Manager. For more information on Application Loader, see Chapter 18.

4. **Press the menu key and touch-press Save.**

Isn't it great when you can actually read what's on the screen? But don't think you're finished quite yet. You still have some personalizing to do.

Typing with ease using AutoText

Even the most devoted BlackBerry user has to admit that typing on a full keyboard is easier than thumb-typing on a BlackBerry. To even the score a bit, your BlackBerry Storm comes with an AutoText feature, which is a kind of shorthand.

AutoText basically works with a pool of abbreviations that you set up. Then you type an abbreviation to get the word you associated with that abbreviation. For example, after setting up *b/c* as an AutoText word for *because,* any time you type *b/c,* you automatically get *because* onscreen.

The whole AutoText thing works only if you set up your own personal code, mapping your abbreviations to their meanings. (This is why we're discussing AutoText as part of the personalization discussion.)

To set up your own code, do the following:

1. **Press the menu key and touch-press the options icon.**

2. **Touch-press the AutoText option.**

You can choose to see (or search for) existing AutoText words or create new ones.

3. **Press the menu key and touch-press New.**

The AutoText screen appears, as shown in Figure 3-1.

Figure 3-1: Create AutoText here.

4. **In the Replace field, enter the characters that you want to replace.**

5. **In the With field, type what replaces your characters.**

6. **Choose between two options in the Using field:**

   • SmartCase capitalizes the first letter when the context calls for that, such as the first word in a sentence.

   • Specified Case replaces your AutoText with the exact text in the With field.

Say you have the AutoText *cbweb* set up for the term *crackberry.com*, and you want it to appear as is, in terms of letter cases (always lowercase the first *c*). If you choose SmartCase for this AutoText entry, and it's the first word in a sentence, the word is capitalized; that isn't what you want. On the other hand, if you use Specified Case, your AutoText always appears as *crackberry.com* no matter where it is in the sentence.

7. **Scroll to the Language field, and touch-press All Locales.**

   We prefer All Locales because regardless of the language input method (for example, French), any self-created AutoText is available for you to use. In the case of the AutoText *cbweb (crackberry.com)*, you can use this AutoText whether you're typing in French or Chinese. On the other hand, if you select only the French input method for *cbweb* as the Language field, you could use only the *cbweb* AutoText entry if your input method is set to French in the Language option.

   You can choose the input method in the Language options. We go over choosing a language input method next.

8. **Press the menu key and touch-press Save.**

If you specify a language input method other than All Locales, your input method setting in the Language option must match the Language field in AutoText to use your newly created AutoText:

1. **Press the menu key and touch-press the options icon.**

2. **Touch-press Language and Text Input Option.**

   Here, you can choose the language and input method.

3. **Select the Input Language field and then select the input method you need from the list.**

   For your new AutoText setting to work (assuming that you didn't choose All Locales as the language for your AutoText), this option needs to match the input method set in your Language option.

4. **Press the menu key and touch-press Save.**

If Word Completion is enabled, word suggestions appear above your sentence, suggesting the full word you are in the middle of typing. Instead of completing the word, you can select the full word from the list of suggestions. We find Word Completion distracting and prefer to use Auto Correction, which is less invasive and still does an okay job. If Word Completion's pop-up word suggestions bug you, changing to Auto Correction will make them disappear!

Inserting text shortcuts

If you frequently give out your BlackBerry phone number or PIN in e-mails, you'll appreciate what we call *text shortcuts*. Basically, you can use the AutoText feature to add a customized word for preset items — things such as your BlackBerry number, PIN, or just the date — so you don't have to type them all the time.

Keep in mind that we're talking about your BlackBerry PIN here — your device's unique identifying number — and not the PIN someone would use to empty out your checking account with the help of one of those automated tellers. For more on BlackBerry PINs, see Chapter 8.

To add a text shortcut for your phone number, for example, follow these steps:

1. **Display the AutoText screen.**

   AutoText is an option in Options.

2. **Type an appropriate word in the Replace field.**

   mynum would work nicely.

3. **Touch-press the With field and type** "my number is ".

4. **Press the menu key and choose Insert Macro.**

   You're prompted with a list of preset items.

5. **Select the Phone Number (%p) option.**

6. **Press the menu key and touch-press Save.**

7. **Test your AutoText by drafting a simple e-mail and typing** mynum.

Customizing your screen's look and feel

You can get the display font, font size, and screen contrast to your liking. Now we know that some of you don't give a hoot if your fonts are Batang or Bookman as long as you can read the text, but we also know that some of you won't stop configuring the fonts until you get them absolutely right.

For all you tweakers out there, here's how you play around with your BlackBerry's fonts:

1. **Press the menu key and touch-press the options icon.**

2. **Touch-press Screen/Keyboard.**

   The Screen/Keyboard screen appears with various customizable fields, as shown in Figure 3-2.

Figure 3-2: The Screen/ Keyboard screen is waiting for personaliza- tion.

3. **Touch-press the Font Family field and then touch-press a font from the drop-down list.**

4. **Continuing down the Screen/Keyboard screen, touch-press the Font Size field and then touch-press a font size.**

   The smaller the font size, the more you can see onscreen; however, a small font is harder on the eyes.

   Note: As you finger-scroll up and down the list of fonts and font sizes, notice that the text *The quick brown fox jumps over the lazy dog* in the background takes on the look of the selected font and size so that you can preview what the particular text looks like.

5. **Press the menu key and touch-press Save.**

With fonts out of the way, it's time to change the brightness of your screen as well as a few other viewing options, including how to program the conve- nience keys so every time you press it, the convenience key opens the appli- cation that you use most often:

1. **Press the menu key and touch-press the options icon.**

2. **Touch-press Screen/Keyboard.**

3. **Touch-press the Backlight Brightness field and then select the desired brightness from the drop-down list.**

   You can choose 10 to 100, where 10 is the darkest and 100 is the brightest.

4. **Touch-press the Backlight Timeout field and choose an amount of time.**

   You can choose ten seconds up to two minutes. The lower this setting, the less time you'll have backlighting (after you press each key). However, a low setting helps you conserve battery life.

5. **Touch-press the Tap Interval field and decide how sensitive you want the tap to be.**

   You can choose 100 to 500, where 100 is the most sensitive and 500 is the least sensitive.

6. **Touch-press the Hover Period field and decide how sensitive you want your touch on the touch screen to be.**

   Here, 100 is the most sensitive and 1000 is the least sensitive. Keep in mind that if your setting is too sensitive, it might be hard to control.

   When you hover your finger over an icon or link without touch-pressing the screen, a small yellow text box appears, giving you hints at what you can expect by touch-pressing the icon.

7. **To confirm your changes, press the menu key and touch-press Save.**

Programming the left and right convenience keys

The folks at RIM have given the Storm left and right convenience keys as a way for you to quickly get to the programs you use the most often. By default, the left convenience key is set to open the voice dialing app, and the right convenience key opens the Camera app.

If you want to setup your convenience keys differently, here's what you can do:

1. **Press the menu key and touch-press the options icon.**

2. **Touch-press Screen/Keyboard.**

3. **Touch-press Left Side Convenience Key Opens field.**

4. **Touch-press an application that you want the convenience key to open.**

   Typically, we set these keys to open applications we often need, such as the Browser or Task application.

5. **Touch-press Right Side Convenience Key Opens field.**

6. **Touch-press an application you want the Right Convenience key to open.**

7. **To confirm your changes, press the menu key and touch-press Save.**

Choosing themes

Your BlackBerry might be preloaded with different *themes,* which are pre-defined sets of looks (wallpaper, fonts, menu layout) for your BlackBerry. You can download themes from BlackBerry's mobile Web site.

Regardless of what BlackBerry model you have, follow these steps to change your theme:

1. **Press the menu key and touch-press the options icon.**

2. **Touch-press the Theme option.**

   You see a list of available themes; your Storm may come with only one theme, but you can always download more.

3. **Touch-press the theme you want.**

4. **Press the menu key and touch-press Activate.**

   You see the change after a short wait.

You can download other themes. Just remember that you have to use your BlackBerry, not your PC, to access the following URLs:

✔ http://mobile.blackberry.com

✔ http://blackberrywallpaper.com

Wallpapering

Like your desktop PC, the BlackBerry Home screen can be customized with personalized *wallpaper.*

You set an image to be your BlackBerry Home screen background by using the BlackBerry Media application:

1. **From the Home screen, press the menu key and touch-press the Media application.**

   The Media application opens, showing several icons: Music, Videos, Pictures, Ring Tones, Voice Notes, Video Camera, and Voice Notes Recorder.

2. **Touch-press the Picture category.**

   Doing so brings up three options:

   - All Pictures shows you a thumbnail view of all your photos — the ones you took and the ones that came with your BlackBerry Storm.

   - Picture Folders lists the folders that contain photos, as well as a thumbnail list of the photos.

   - Sample Pictures shows you a thumbnail view of the pictures that came with your BlackBerry Storm.

3. **Touch-press All Pictures.**

4. **Touch-press the picture you want to use for your Home screen wallpaper.**

   The selected picture appears in full-screen view.

5. **Press the menu key and touch-press Set As.**

   The picture is now your new Home screen wallpaper.

6. **Press and hold the escape key to return to the Home screen and see the result.**

   If you hold your BlackBerry Storm in its upright (vertical) position, you see your new wallpaper.

You can download free wallpaper here as long as you use your BlackBerry, not your PC, to access the URLs:

- ✔ `http://mobile.blackberry.com`
- ✔ `blackberrywallpapers.com`

After you have your BlackBerry's look and feel just the way you want, do one more thing before you move on: Get your BlackBerry sounding the way you want it to.

Ringing freedom

The whole appeal of the BlackBerry phenomenon is the idea that this little electronic device can make your life easier. One of the ways it accomplishes this is by acting as your personal reminder service — letting you know when an appointment is coming up, a phone call is coming in, an e-mail has arrived, and so on. Basically, your BlackBerry is set to bark at you if it knows something it thinks you should know too. Figure 3-3 lists the kinds of things your BlackBerry considers bark-worthy, ranging from Message alerts to Calendar reminders.

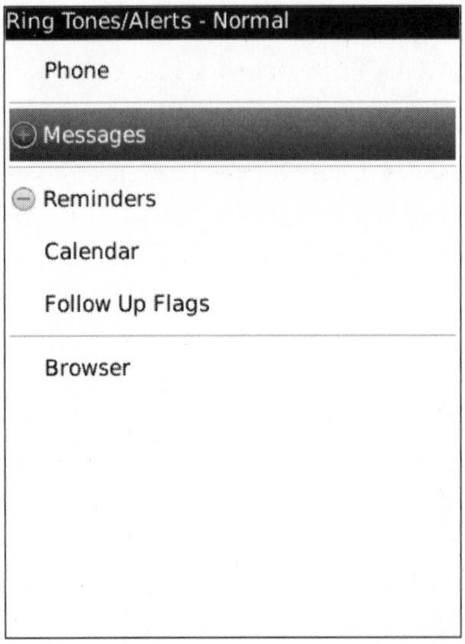

```
┌────────────────────────────────────────┐
│ Ring Tones/Alerts - Normal               │
│     Phone                                │
│ ⊕  Messages                              │
│ ⊖  Reminders                             │
│     Calendar                             │
│     Follow Up Flags                      │
│     Browser                              │
│                                          │
│                                          │
└────────────────────────────────────────┘
```

Figure 3-3:
Set
attention-
needy
applications
here.

Different people react differently to different sounds. Some BlackBerry barks would be greatly appreciated by certain segments of the population, whereas other segments might react to the same sound by pitching their BlackBerry under the nearest bus. The folks at Research In Motion are well aware of this fact and have devised a great way for you to customize how you want your BlackBerry to bark at you; they call it your *profile*.

You can jump right into things by using a predefined profile.

Checking out the different profiles

Each profile is divided into four categories that represent the application for which you can define alerts:

- ✔ **Phone:** Alerts you if there is an incoming call or a new voice mail.
- ✔ **Messages:** Alerts you when a new e-mail (see Chapter 8), PIN message, or SMS message is in your inbox.
- ✔ **Reminders:** Alerts you when you have upcoming calendar appointments or to-do reminders.
- ✔ **Follow Up Flags:** Alerts you when you have e-mail or phone calls to follow up on.
- ✔ **Browser:** Alerts you when you receive a new channel *push,* which is a Web page sent to your BlackBerry as an icon on your Home screen.

You can personalize the alert on all listed applications. Because the way you customize them is similar, we use one application (Messages) as an example in the text that follows, as we customize a predefined profile that comes with your BlackBerry.

Customizing a predefined profile

If you're okay with customizing a predefined, factory-loaded profile, just do the following:

1. From the BlackBerry Home screen, touch-press the Sounds application.

A screen lists different sound profiles: Normal (Active), Loud, Medium, Vibrate Only, Silent, Phone Calls Only, or All Alerts Off. See Figure 3-4.

Figure 3-4: A Profile application helps you personalize.

2. Touch-press Set Ring Tones/Alerts.

A screen lists different applications. Note that you are setting the ring tones/alerts for whatever sound profile is currently selected. For example, if you're currently using Normal, when you touch-press Set Ring Tones/Alerts, you are modifying the Normal profile's setting.

3. Touch-press Messages to expand the category.

If you have multiple e-mail accounts routed to your BlackBerry, you can set settings for each. Note that SMS and PIN messages are also listed in the Message category.

4. Touch-press one of your e-mail accounts.

5. Touch-press the Ring Tone field and then touch-press a tune from the drop-down list.

Doing so enables sound when e-mail arrives for this e-mail account. If you want any sounds to play, you can choose this in the Volume field.

6. **Touch-press the Volume field and then touch-press to select the volume level you desire.**

   You can choose options ranging from silent to 10 for loudest.

7. **Touch-press the Vibration field and then touch-press Custom.**

   This displays more options for vibration. You can control how many vibrations each e-mail triggers, the vibration duration, and whether you want the vibration to happen when your Storm is in its holster.

8. **Press the menu key and touch-press Save.**

   As mentioned earlier, you can follow these same steps to personalize other applications listed in each profile.

Maybe you get a lot of e-mail. You probably don't want your BlackBerry sounding off 200 times a day. Set your BlackBerry Storm to notify you only if an e-mail is marked urgent, requiring your immediate attention.

Keeping Your BlackBerry Safe

The folks at Research In Motion take security seriously, and so should you. Make sure you set up a password on your BlackBerry. If your BlackBerry hasn't prompted you to set up a password, you should immediately do so.

Follow these steps to set up a password:

1. **From the BlackBerry Home screen, touch-press the options icon.**

2. **Touch-press Password.**

3. **Touch-press Disable Settings and select Enabled.**

4. **Touch-press Security Timeout and select a time.**

   Choose anywhere from 1 minute up to 1 hour.

5. **Press the menu key and touch-press Save.**

   You're prompted for a password.

6. **Type a password and then type it again for verification.**

   From this point on, whenever you lock your BlackBerry and want to use it again, you have to type the password. If you don't use your BlackBerry, it locks according to Security Timeout setting.

Setting up your password is a good first step, but just having a password won't help much if you don't take the further step of locking your BlackBerry when you're not using it. (You don't want people at the office or sitting at the next table at the coffee shop checking out your e-mails or phone history when you take a bathroom break, do you?) How do you lock your BlackBerry? Press the lock key, which is on the top left of your Storm.

You can customize your Storm to use different alerts (such as ring tones or vibrations) for different events (e-mail, SMS, and so on) in different situations (Normal profile, Loud profile, and so on). You can even set unique ring tone alerts for individuals when they call or message you. However, some people want even more control. One application, BerryBuzz, has proved to be extremely popular, allowing you to take your notifications to the next level of customization by setting unique LED colors for incoming events. You can find it in the CrackBerry App Store under BerryBuzz or in App World under BeBuzz.

Part II

Getting Organized and Online with Your Storm

The 5th Wave   By Rich Tennant

@RICHTENNANT

Seven presentations in as many days, and still no investors.

Ready? Here they come...

TD RESEARCH INC.
Smert Phone Technology
○ DYNAMIC
○ INNOVATIVE
○ COST EFFICIEN

In this part . . .

This is where you find out how to use your BlackBerry Storm to its fullest to get you — and keep you — organized. Peruse the chapters here to find out how to use Contacts, keep appointments, set alarms, use the timer and Bedside mode, and keep your passwords safe and easy to retrieve.

This chapter also describes the good stuff — using your BlackBerry for e-mail, text messaging, messaging using BlackBerry Messenger, as well as going online and Web surfing.

Chapter 4

Remembering and Locating Your Acquaintances

· ·

In This Chapter

▶ Exploring BlackBerry Contacts

▶ Adding, viewing, editing, and deleting contacts

▶ Copying a contact for a desktop app

▶ Finding a contact in Contacts

▶ Organizing contacts

▶ Sharing BlackBerry Storm's contacts

▶ Looking for someone outside your contacts

▶ Synchronizing your Facebook contacts

· ·

*A*ddress books were around long before the BlackBerry was conceived. Your BlackBerry Storm Contacts feature serves the same function as any other: to record and organize information about people. It also gives you a central place to reach your contacts by landline phone; cellphone; e-mail; or the speedy messaging of PIN, SMS, MMS, or BlackBerry Messenger.

You can benefit from using BlackBerry Contacts if any of the following fits you and your lifestyle:

✔ You travel.

✔ You meet clients frequently.

✔ You spend a lot of time on the phone.

✔ You ask people for their phone number or e-mail address more than once.

✔ You carry around a paper day planner.

✔ Your wallet is full of important business cards, with phone numbers written on the backs, that you can never find.

If you're one of those stubborn folks who insist that they don't need an address book — "I'm doing just fine without one, thank you very much!" — perhaps you need to think of it another way. You've been using a virtual address book all the time: the one buried in your cellphone. And that address book often isn't even a very good one! Read this chapter to see how to transfer all that good contact info from an old phone into your new BlackBerry-based Contacts.

Accessing Contacts

The Contacts icon looks like an old-fashioned address book. (Remember those? Maybe not.) If you have a hard time locating it, check out Figure 4-1. Opening Contacts couldn't be simpler: Just touch-press the Contacts icon.

Figure 4-1:
The
Contacts
icon.

You can access Contacts from Phone, Messages, BlackBerry Messenger, and Calendar. Say you're in Calendar, and you want to invite people to one of your meetings. Look no further — Invite Attendee (essentially, displays Contacts) is on the menu, ready to lend a helping hand.

Because the Storm does not have a physical keyboard, you lose the speed inherent in keyboard shortcuts. App developer NikkiSoft introduced QuickLaunch for the original BlackBerry Storm, and it remains a must-have app. QuickLaunch enables you to set shortcuts for common tasks, such as calling your significant other, e-mailing your boss, or visiting a specific Web site. Setting a convenience key to open QuickLaunch allows you to access these shortcut commands immediately, saving time and touch-screen presses.

Working with Contacts

Getting a new gizmo is always exciting; your new toy is full of features you're dying to try out. Calling someone was probably the first thing you wanted to do with your new BlackBerry Storm. But wait a second. You'll have to type the phone number not just this time, but each time you want to call. What a hassle.

Most people — social creatures that we are — keep a list of contacts somewhere such as in an e-mail program, in an old cellphone, or on a piece of paper (tucked away in a wallet). We're pretty sure you have some kind of list somewhere. The trick is getting that list into your BlackBerry Storm so you can access the info more efficiently. The good news is that getting the information into your BlackBerry Storm isn't hard.

Often, the simplest way to get contact information into your BlackBerry Storm is to enter it manually. However, if you've invested a lot of time keeping the information updated on your desktop computer, you might want to hot-sync that data into your BlackBerry Storm. For more on synchronizing data, check Chapter 15.

Creating a contact

Imagine you've just run into Jane, an old high-school friend you haven't seen in years. Jane wants to give you her number, but you don't have a pen handy. Are you forced to chant her phone number to yourself until you can scare up a writing implement? Not if you have your handy BlackBerry Storm on you.

With BlackBerry Storm in hand, follow these steps to create a new contact:

1. **On the Home screen, touch-press the Contacts icon.**

   Contacts opens. You can also access Contacts from different applications. For example, check Chapter 7 on how to access Contacts from Messages.

2. **Touch-press the plus icon located at the bottom of the screen.**

   The New Contact screen appears, as shown in Figure 4-2.

3. **Enter the contact information in the appropriate fields.**

   Use your BlackBerry Storm virtual keyboard to enter contact information. Hold the device sideways (landscape) to get the full QWERTY keyboard. When entering an e-mail address, press the Space key to insert an *at* symbol (@) or a period (.).

   We don't think you can overdo it when entering a person's contact information. Enter as much info as you possibly can. Maybe the benefit won't be obvious now, but when your memory fails or your boss needs a critical piece of data that you happen to have, you'll thank us for this advice.

To create another new, blank e-mail field for the same contact, press the menu key and touch-press Add Email Address. You can have up to three e-mail addresses per contact.

BlackBerry Storm can dial an extension after the initial phone number. When entering the phone number, type the primary phone number, touch-press P on the virtual keyboard, and add the extension number.

4. **Press the menu key and touch-press Save.**

Jane is added to the list, as shown in Figure 4-3.

Here's something slick to know when you're entering phone information for a contact: BlackBerry Storm can also dial an extra number after the initial phone number. That extra number can be someone's extension, a participant code on a conference number, or simply your voice mail PIN. When you're entering the contact's phone number, type the primary phone number, enter X, and then add the extension number. Say you enter 11112345678X1111; when you tell your Storm to call that number, it will dial 11112345678 first. Then you'll see a prompt asking you to continue or skip dialing the extension.

The menu is always available through the menu key. The application is smart enough to figure out which items are more relevant based on what you're doing. You can always touch-press the full menu listing.

Taking notes

The Notes field in the New Contact screen (you might need to scroll down a bit to see it) is useful for adding a description about your contact. For example, use the field to jog your memory with tidbits such as *Knows someone at ABC Corporation* or *Can provide introduction to a Broadway agent.* Or perhaps your note is something personal, such as *Likes golf; has 2 children: boy, 7 & girl, 3; husband's name is Ray.* It's up to you. Again, the more useful the information, the better it serves you.

Adding your own fields

Perhaps your contact information doesn't fit into any of the available fields. Although you can't create fields from scratch, you can commandeer one of the User fields for your own purposes.

The User fields are at the bottom of the screen; you have to scroll down to see them. Use these fields any way you want; you can even change the field's name. For example, you can rename User fields to capture suffixes (such as MD, PhD, and so on) or things such as

✔ Profession

✔ Hobbies

✔ School

✔ Nickname

Figure 4-2:
Create a
new contact
here.

Figure 4-3:
The
Contacts
screen
shows your
new
contact.

Keep in mind that changing the User field name for a particular contact changes it for *all* your contacts.

Follow along to rename a User field:

1. **While editing a contact, scroll to the bottom of the screen to navigate to one of the User fields.**

2. **Press the menu key and touch-press Change Field Name.**

   Note: The Change Field Name selection on the menu appears only if the cursor is in a User field.

3. **Use the virtual keyboard to type the new name.**

4. **Touch-press the enter key.**

5. **Press the menu key and touch-press Save.**

   You're all set.

Adding a picture to a contact

Most phones can display a picture of whoever's calling; BlackBerry Storm is no stranger to this neat feature:

1. **Have a picture of the person.**

   See Chapter 11 for more about taking photos with your BlackBerry Storm.

2. **Get the photo to your BlackBerry Storm.**

   You can send it via e-mail, copy it to the microSD card, or copy it to the built-in memory of Storm. If you don't know how to use a microSD card, Chapter 12 is your gateway to media satisfaction.

3. **From the Home screen, touch-press the Contacts icon.**

4. **Touch a contact.**

   The contact is highlighted.

5. **Press the menu key and touch-press Edit.**

   The Edit screen appears.

6. **Press the menu key and touch-press Add Picture; see Figure 4-4.**

Figure 4-4: Add a picture here.

7. **Navigate to the drive and folder that has the picture.**

   You can use multiple locations for storing media files (including pictures). Chapter 12 gives you the scoop.

8. **Touch-press the picture you want.**

   The picture appears on the screen with a rectangle over it.

9. **Slide the picture to position the rectangle over the face.**

   Contacts uses a tiny image, just enough to show the face of a person. The rectangle you see here indicates how the application crops the image.

10. **Press the menu key and touch-press Crop and Save.**

11. **Press the menu key and touch-press Save.**

Assigning a tone

Oh, no — your ringing BlackBerry has woken you. Ring tones help you decide whether to ignore the call or get up. We hope you can easily switch yourself to sleep mode if you ignore the call.

Follow these steps to assign a ring tone to one of your contacts:

1. **While editing a contact, scroll to the Custom Ring Tones/Alerts section.**

   Under the Ring Tones/Alerts section, you see Phone and Messages. You can customize the ring tone when you receive a call and when you have a new message such as an e-mail or an SMS.

2. **Touch-press Phone and customize the ring tone on the screen that follows.**

   You can change the following options:

   • Ring Tone: Select from a list of ring tones here.

   • Volume: Control the volume. Values are Active Profile (the default) and 1 to 10 (loudest).

   • Play Sound: Control in what state to play the tone. Values are Active Profile (the default), In Holster, Out of Holster, and Always.

   • LED: Use the LED to indicate a call.

   • Vibration: Enable vibration as a way of notification. Choices are Active Profile (the default), Off, On, and Custom. Custom enables you to control how long you want the vibration to last.

   • Vibrate with Ring Tone: Choose between vibration and play the tone. Choices are Active Profile (the default), On, and Off.

3. **Press the escape key and touch-press Save.**

   You're back to the Edit Contact screen.

4. **Touch-press Messages.**

   You are presented with the Messages screen, allowing you to customize the ring tone when you receive a message. You can do all the customizations listed in Step 2 plus the following:

   • Notify Me During Calls: Toggle notification while you are actively on a call. Your choices are Yes and No (the default).

   • Count: Set the number of times the ring tone repeats. Choices are Active Profile (the default), 1, 2, and 3.

5. **Press the escape key.**

6. **Press the menu key and then touch-press Save.**

Spend a little time adding your own contact records. We recommend adding at least one record for your business contact info and one for your personal contact info. This saves you time having to type your own contact information every time you want to give it to someone. You can share your contact record by sending it as an attachment to an e-mail. (See the later section "Sharing a Contact.")

Adding contacts from other BlackBerry applications

When you get an e-mail message, it's a logical time to add the e-mail address information into Contacts. The same is true when you get a phone call, which gives you a phone number within the Phone application. You might have noticed that Phone lists only *outgoing numbers*. That's half of what you need. Oddly enough, you can access incoming phone calls in Messages:

1. **Touch-press Messages from the Home screen.**

   Messages opens.

2. **Press the menu key and touch-press View Folder.**

3. **Touch-press Phone Call Logs.**

A phone log entry stays as long as you have free space in your BlackBerry Storm. When BlackBerry runs out of space (which could take years, depending on how you use it), it deletes read e-mails and phone logs, starting from the oldest.

You can view device memory info; touch-press Memory from the Home screen, touch-press Options, and then touch-press Memory. The screen displays three types of memory: Application Memory, Device Memory, and Media Card. Pay close attention to Application Memory, because this is where your applications are installed, including data from out-of-the-box applications such as Contacts, Messages, Calendar, and Web Browser cache. Your Storm has limited Application Memory (128MB for the original Storm and 256MB for the Storm2). If free Application Memory drops below 10MB, your device might begin to slow down a bit, and if it approaches 0MB, you may experience lag. At this point, you need to free some space. Pulling the battery will immediately net some space, because applications that were running and using persistent memory will now be closed. Deleting unused applications helps, as does removing unnecessary bloatware that comes preloaded on the device (such as movie trailers and sample photos). You can visit www.crackberry.com for step-by-step tutorials on freeing up application memory.

Creating a contact from an existing e-mail address or phone number in Messages is easy:

1. **Touch-press Messages from the Home screen.**

   Messages opens.

2. **Touch the e-mail address or the phone number.**

   A menu appears.

3. **Touch-press Add to Contacts.**

   A New Contact screen appears, filled with that particular piece of information.

4. **Enter the rest of the information you know.**

5. **Press the menu key and touch-press Save.**

This is just one more sign of BlackBerry's ongoing attempt to make your life easier.

Viewing a contact

You just entered your friend's name into your BlackBerry, but you have this nagging thought that you typed the wrong phone number. You want to quickly view the information. Here's how you do it:

1. **On the Home screen, touch-press the Contacts icon.**

   Contacts opens.

2. **Scroll to and touch-press the contact name you want.**

   Touch-pressing the name is the same as opening the menu and choosing View — just faster.

   View mode displays only information that's been filled in, as shown in Figure 4-5. It doesn't bother showing fields that have no information.

Editing a contact

Change is an inevitable part of life. If you want to keep current the information you diligently put in your contacts list, you'll have to do some updating now and then.

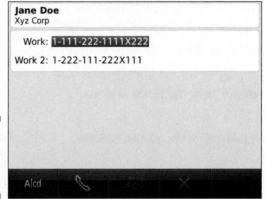

Jane Doe
Xyz Corp

Work: 1-111-222-1111X222
Work 2: 1-222-111-222X111

A|cd

Figure 4-5:
View mode
for a
contact.

To update a contact, follow these steps:

1. **On the BlackBerry Storm Home screen, touch-press the Contacts icon.**

   Contacts opens.

2. **Scroll to and highlight a contact name and press the menu key.**

3. **Touch-press Edit.**

   The Edit Contact screen appears.

   In any BlackBerry Storm application, including Contacts, you can display a menu by pressing the menu key. You see the Edit option in the menu right below View.

4. **Edit the contact information as you see fit.**

   Hold the device sideways to get the full QWERTY keyboard.

5. **Press the menu key and touch-press Save.**

   The edit you made for this contact is saved.

When you're editing information and want to replace the entry, clear the contents. When you're in an *editable field* (as opposed to a selectable field), just press the menu key and touch-press Clear Field. This feature is always available for an editable field.

Deleting a contact

It's time to get rid of someone's contact information in your contacts list. Maybe it's a case of duplication or a bit of bad blood. Either way, BlackBerry Storm makes it easy to delete a contact:

1. **On the Home screen, touch-press the Contacts icon.**

   Contacts opens.

2. **Scroll to and highlight the contact name you want to delete.**

3. **Touch-press the Delete (x) icon at the bottom of the screen.**

   A confirmation screen appears, as shown in Figure 4-6.

4. **Touch-press Delete.**

   The contact disappears from your contacts list.

Figure 4-6:
The con-
firmation
screen
when you're
about to
delete a
contact.

 Dealing with the confirmation screen can be a pain if you want to delete several contacts in a row. If you're *100 percent* sure you want to ditch a number of contacts, you can suspend the Confirmation feature by setting the Confirm Delete option to No in the Contacts Options screen. Check the "Setting preferences" section, later in this chapter, for more on Contacts options.

Copying Contacts from Desktop Applications

Most people maintain their contacts by using desktop applications — you know, Microsoft Outlook, IBM Lotus Notes, or Novell GroupWise. A word to the wise: You don't want to maintain two address books. That's a recipe for disaster. Luckily for you, RIM makes it easy to get your various address books — BlackBerry, desktop, laptop, whatever — in sync.

Your BlackBerry Storm comes with BlackBerry Desktop Manager, a collection of programs, one of which is Synchronize. Synchronize allows you to synchronize the data between your device and the PC software. It also allows you to set up and configure the behavior of the program, including how the fields in the desktop version of Address Book map to Contacts fields in your BlackBerry.

Check out Chapter 15, which details using the Synchronize feature of the BlackBerry Desktop Manager application.

Looking for Someone?

Somehow — usually through typing and shuttling data between devices — you've created a nice long contacts list. Nice enough, we suppose — but useless unless you can find the phone number of Rufus T. Firefly at the drop of a hat.

That's where the Find screen comes in. In fact, the first thing you see in Contacts when you open it is the Find screen, as shown in Figure 4-7.

Find:
New Contact:
ABC Headquarters
Daniel
Dante Sarigumba
Global Support
Jane Doe Xyz Corp
Joe Blow

Figure 4-7: Your search starts here.

You can conveniently search through your contacts by following these steps:

1. **In the Find field, enter the letters that start the name you're searching for.**

   Your search criterion is the person's name. You can enter the last name, first name, or both. The list is usually sorted by first name, last name. As you type the letters, the list shrinks based on matches. Figure 4-8 illustrates how this works.

Figure 4-8:
Enter more
letters to
shorten the
potential
contacts list
search.

2. **Scroll and highlight the name from the list of matches.**

   If you have multiple matches, slide the screen to scroll through the list to find the person's name.

3. **Press the menu key and touch-press one of the possible actions shown in Figure 4-9.**

   Here are the actions you can choose the menu items and what each one leads to:

   - Activity Log: Opens a screen listing e-mails, calls, and SMS messages you've made to the contact.

   - View Work Map: Appears only if you have filled in the work address information. This allows you to map the location using Maps.

   - Email: Starts a new e-mail message. See Chapter 7 for more information.

   - PIN: Starts a new PIN-to-PIN message, which is a messaging feature unique to BlackBerry. With it, you can send a quick message to someone who has a BlackBerry. See Chapter 8 for more details about PIN-to-PIN messaging.

   - Call: Uses Phone to dial the number.

   - SMS: Starts a new *SMS,* or *Short Message Service,* message, which is used in cellphones. See Chapter 8 for more details about SMS.

   - MMS: Starts a new *MMS,* or *Multimedia Messaging Service,* message. MMS is an evolution from SMS that supports voice and video clips. See Chapter 8 for details about MMS. The MMS item appears on the menu only if you have filled in the contact's Mobile field.

- SIM Phone Book: Allows you to view contacts saved on the SIM card. This menu option is not in context with the selected contact.

- Send as Attachment: Starts a new e-mail message attaching the contacts. See Chapter 7 for more information.

- Forward to Messenger Contact: Allows you to add this contact to your contacts list in BlackBerry Messenger. This option appears only if BlackBerry Messenger is installed.

You can attach a contact, a security certificate, or a file. Those three choices are in the menu displayed after you press the menu key.

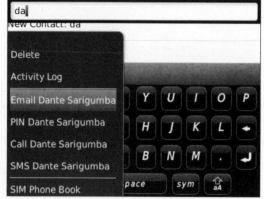

Figure 4-9: You get action options for the selected contact.

If you have a finger fumble and press a key in error, press the escape key once to return to the original list (the one showing all your contacts), or press the menu key and touch-press View All.

You're not hallucinating: Sometimes Email *<contact name>* or Call *<contact name>* appears on the menu, and sometimes it doesn't. Contacts knows when to show those menu options. If a contact has a phone number, Call *<contact name>* and SMS *<contact name>* show up, and the same is true for e-mail and the *personal identification number (PIN)*. In fact, this list of actions is a convenient way to find out whether you have certain information — a phone number or an e-mail address — for a particular contact.

In a corporate environment, your BlackBerry Enterprise Server administrator might disable PIN-to-PIN messaging because it doesn't go to the corporate e-mail servers and, therefore, can't be monitored. If this is the case, the menu option PIN*<contact name>* won't appear even though you entered PIN information for your contacts. Note that you can still receive a PIN-to-PIN message, but you can't send one.

Organizing Your Contacts

You've been diligent by adding your contacts to the BlackBerry Contacts app, and your list has been growing at a pretty good clip. It now has all the contact information for your business colleagues, clients, and (of course) family and friends. In fact, you now have hundreds of contacts, and it's taking more time to find someone.

Imagine that you've just seen an old acquaintance, and you want to greet the person by name. You know that if you saw the name, you'd recognize it. The trouble is that your list has 300-plus names, which would take so long to scroll through that this acquaintance would surely come up to you in the meantime, forcing you to hide the fact that you can't remember his name. (How embarrassing.) In this scenario, the tried-and-true Find feature wouldn't be much help. What you need is a smaller pool of names to search through.

This isn't rocket science. You'll want to do one of the following or both:

- ✔ **Organize your contacts into groups.** Using groups (as every kinder- garten teacher could tell you) is a way to arrange something (in your case, contacts) to make them more manageable. How you arrange your groups is up to you. You should base the principle on whatever makes sense to you and fits the group you set up. For example, you can place all your customer contacts within a Clients group and family members in a Family group.

- ✔ **Set up your contacts so you can filter them.** Use the Filter feature with BlackBerry's Categories. (Categories is labeling your contacts to make it easy to filter them.) The Filter feature narrows the contacts list to such an extent that you have only to scroll down and find your contact — no need to type search keywords, in other words.

Whether you use the Group feature, Filter feature, or both is up to you. You find out how to use these methods in the next sections of this chapter.

Creating a group

A BlackBerry *group* in Contacts — as opposed to any other kind of group you can imagine — is just a simple category. In other words, when you create a group, you arrange your contacts into subsets without affecting the contact entries themselves. In Contacts itself, a group shows up in the contacts list just like any other contact. The only wrinkle here is that when you select the group, the contacts associated with that group — and only the contacts asso- ciated with that group — appear onscreen.

Need some help visualizing how this works? Go ahead and create a group, following these steps:

1. **On the Home screen, touch-press the Contacts icon.**

   Contacts opens.

2. **Press the menu key and touch-press New Group.**

   A screen similar to that in Figure 4-10 appears. The top portion of the screen is where you type the group name, and the bottom portion is where you add members.

Figure 4-10:
An empty
screen,
ready for
creating a
group.

3. **Type the name of the group in the New Group field.**

   You can name it anything.

4. **Press the menu key and touch-press Add Member.**

   The main contacts list shows up in all its glory, ready to be pilfered.

5. **Touch-press the contact you want to add to your new Group list.**

   You can associate only a single piece of contact information from a member, either an e-mail address or a phone number. Why? Because a group is used as a distribution list, which means you simply add the group to the To, Cc, or Bcc field when you compose an e-mail or MMS. If you're adding a member with more than one piece of contact information — say, an e-mail address and a phone number — you'll be prompted to choose either of the two pieces of information.

6. **(Optional) Touch-press a phone number or an e-mail address.**

   If you simply want to group your contacts and not necessarily need to use it as a distribution list, you must follow a rule. The contact needs to have at least an e-mail address or a phone number before you can add it as a member of a group. (Contacts is strict on this point.) Skirt this roadblock by editing that contact's information and putting in a fake (and clearly inactive) e-mail address, such as notareal@emailaddress.no.

7. **Press the menu key and touch-press Continue.**

   The name you just entered appears in your group list, as shown in Figure 4-11.

Figure 4-11: Your new group has one member.

8. **Repeat Step 4 to add more friends to your list.**

9. **Press the menu key and touch-press Save Group.**

   Your group is duly saved, and you can now see it listed on your main contacts list.

Groups is a valuable tool for creating an e-mail distribution list. When adding members to the group, make sure that you select an e-mail address field for your members instead of a phone number. Use a naming convention to easily distinguish your group in the list. Appending *-DL* or *-Distribution List* to the group name can quickly indicate that it is a distribution list.

Using the Filter feature on your contacts

Are you a left-brainer or a right-brainer? Yankees fan or Red Sox fan? Innie or outie? Dividing the world into categories is something everyone does (no divisions there), so it should come as no surprise that BlackBerry divides your contacts into distinct categories as well.

By default, two categories are set for you on the BlackBerry:

✔ Business
✔ Personal

Why stop at two? BlackBerry makes it easy to create more categories. In this section, you first find out how to categorize a contact; then you see how to filter your contacts list. Finally, you find out how to create categories.

Categorizing your contacts

Whether you're creating or editing a contact, you can categorize a particular contact as long as you're in Edit mode.

If the trick is getting into Edit mode, it's a pretty simple trick. Here's how to do that:

1. **On the Home screen, touch-press the Contacts icon.**

   Contacts opens.

2. **Highlight the contact.**

3. **Press the menu key and touch-press Edit.**

   Contacts is in Edit mode for this particular contact, which is exactly where you want to be.

4. **Press the menu key and touch-press Categories.**

   A Categories list appears. By default, the list contains only the Business and Personal categories.

5. **Touch-press the Personal check box.**

6. **Press the menu key and touch-press Save.**

   You're back at the Edit screen for this contact.

7. **Press the menu key and touch-press Save.**

You now have one — count 'em, one — contact with Personal as its category, which means you can filter your contacts list by using a category. Here's how:

1. **On the Home screen, touch-press the Contacts icon.**

2. **Press the menu key and touch-press Filter.**

   Your Categories list appears. If you haven't added any categories in the meantime, you see only the default Business and Personal categories.

3. **Touch-press the Personal check box.**

   A mark appears in the check box, and your contacts list shrinks to the contacts in the Personal category, as shown in Figure 4-12.

As you add contacts to a category, you can use Find. Enter the first few letters of the name to further narrow the contact search. If you need a refresher on how Find works, see the "Looking for Someone?" section, earlier in this chapter.

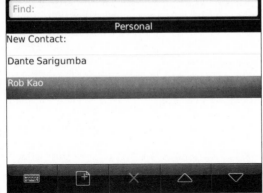

Figure 4-12:
The contacts list after you apply a filter.

Adding a category

Whoever thought the default categories — Business and Personal — were enough for the complexities of the real world probably didn't know many people. BlackBerry makes it easy to add categories, so you can divide your world as much as you like:

1. **On the Home screen, touch-press Contacts.**

2. **Press the menu key and touch-press Filter.**

   You get a view of the default categories (Business and Personal).

3. **Press the menu key and touch-press New.**

   A pop-up screen asks you to name the category.

4. **Type a name for your category in the Name field.**

5. **Touch-press Enter (bottom rightmost key on the virtual keyboard).**

   The category is automatically saved. The Filter screen lists all the categories, including the one you just created.

6. **Press the escape key to get back to the Contacts main screen.**

Setting preferences

Vanilla, anyone? Some days you'll wish that your contacts list were sorted differently. For example, there's the day when you need to find the guy who works for ABC Company but has a foreign name that you can hardly pronounce, let alone spell. What's a body to do?

You're in luck. Contacts Options, shown in Figure 4-13, navigates some out-of-the-ordinary situations. To get to the Contacts Options screen, touch-press Contacts from the Home screen, press the menu key, and touch-press

Options. Despite the Contacts Options screen's simplicity, it provides you with three important options that change the behavior of Contacts:

- **Sort By:** Changes the way the list is sorted. You can use First Name, Last Name, or Company. Touch-press the field to view and select one of the possible choices. Remember that guy from ABC Company? You can use the Sort By option to sort by Company. Then all contacts from ABC Company would be listed next to one another, and with any luck, the guy's name will jump out at you. Choices you have are First Name (the default), Last Name and Company.

- **Separators:** Allows you to change the dividers on the contacts list. It's purely aesthetics, but check it out; you might like the stripes.

- **Allow Duplicate Names:** Self-explanatory. If you turn this on, you can have multiple people in your Contacts who happen to have the same name. If you disable this option, you get a warning when you try to add a name that matches one already on your list. Maybe you're just tired and mistakenly try to add the same person twice to your list. Then again, sometimes people just have the same name. We recommend keeping the default value of Yes, allowing you to have contacts with the same names.

- **Confirm Delete:** Displays a confirmation screen for all contact deletions.

Always keep this feature turned on for normal usage. Because there are many ways you could delete someone from your contacts, this feature is a good way of minimizing accidents.

Contacts Options	
Views	
Sort By:	First Name ▼
Separators:	Lines ▼
Actions	
Allow Duplicate Names:	Yes ▼
Confirm Delete:	Yes ▼

Figure 4-13: Choose your sort type here.

Sharing a Contact

Suppose that you want to share your contact information with a friend who also has a BlackBerry. A *vCard* — virtual (business) card — is your answer and can make your life a lot easier. In BlackBerry Land, a vCard is a contact in your contacts that you send to someone as an attachment to an e-mail.

At the receiving end, the BlackBerry (being the smart device that it is) recognizes the attachment and informs the BlackBerry owner that she has the option of saving it, making it available for her viewing pleasure in Contacts.

Sending a vCard

Because a vCard is nothing more than a Contacts contact attached to an e-mail, sending a vCard is a piece of cake. (Of course, you do need to make sure that your recipient has a BlackBerry device to receive the information.)

Here's how you go about sending a vCard:

1. **On the Home screen, touch-press the Messages icon.**

   Messages opens.

2. **Press the menu key and touch-press Compose Email.**

   The new message screen appears, allowing you to compose a new e-mail.

3. **In the To field, start typing the name of the person you want to receive this vCard.**

4. **When you see the name in the drop-down list, touch-press it.**

   You see an e-mail screen with the name you just selected as the To recipient.

5. **Type the subject and message.**

6. **Press the menu key and touch-press Attach Contact.**

   Contacts opens.

7. **Touch-press the name of the person whose contact information you want attached.**

   The e-mail composition screen reappears, and an icon that looks like a book indicates that the e-mail now contains your attachment. Now all you have to do is send your e-mail.

8. **Press the menu key and touch-press Send.**

   You just shared the specified contact information. (Don't you feel right neighborly now?)

Receiving a vCard

If you get an e-mail that has a contact attachment, here's how to save it to your contacts:

1. On the Home screen, touch-press the Messages icon.

2. Touch-press the e-mail that contains the vCard.

The e-mail with the vCard attachment opens.

3. Touch-press the attachment.

4. Press the menu key and touch-press View Attachment.

The vCard appears.

5. Press the menu key and touch-press Add to Contacts.

The vCard is saved and is available in your BlackBerry Storm Contacts.

Searching for Someone Outside Your Contacts

Does your employer provide your BlackBerry Storm? Do you use Outlook or Lotus Notes on your desktop machine at work? If you answer yes to both of these questions, this section is for you.

BlackBerry Contacts allows you to search for people in your organization, basically through this software:

✔ Microsoft Exchange (for Outlook)

✔ IBM Domino (for Notes)

✔ Novell GroupWise

Exchange, Domino, and GroupWise serve the same purposes: namely, to facilitate e-mail delivery in a corporate environment and to enable access to a database of names.

For you techies out there, these databases are called Global Address Lists (GAL) in Exchange, Notes Address Books in Domino, and GroupWise Address Books in GroupWise.

If you want to search for someone in your organization through a database of names, simply follow these steps:

1. On the Home screen, touch-press the Contacts icon.

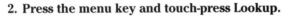

2. Press the menu key and touch-press Lookup.

Some corporations might not enable the Lookup feature. Please check with your IT department for more information.

3. Type the name you're searching for.

4. Press the enter key.

You could enter the beginning characters of either a person's last or first name. You aren't searching your contacts but your company's database, so this step might take some time.

For big organizations, we recommend being more precise when searching. For example, searching for *Daniel* yields fewer hits than searching for *Danl*. The more precise your search criteria, the fewer hits you'll get and the faster the search will be.

While the search is in progress, you see the word *Lookup* and the criteria you put in. For example, if you enter *Daniel,* the top row reads *Lookup: Daniel.* After the search is finished, BlackBerry displays the number of hits or matches — for example, *20 matches: Daniel.*

5. Touch-press the matches count.

The matches appear. A header at the top of this screen details the matches displayed in the current screen as well as the total hits. For example, if the header reads *Lookup Daniel (20 of 130 matches),* 130 people in your organization have the name *Daniel,* and BlackBerry is displaying the first 20. You have the option of fetching more by pressing the menu key and touching Get More Results on the menu that appears.

You can add the listed name(s) to your contacts list by using the Add command (for the currently highlighted name) or the Add All command for all the names on the list. (As always, press the menu key.)

6. Touch-press the person whose information you want to review.

The person's contact information is displayed on a *read-only* screen, which means you can read it but not change it. You might see the person's title, e-mail address, work number, mobile number, fax number, and street address at work. Any of that information gives you confirmation about the person you're looking for. Of course, what shows up depends on the availability of this information in your company's database.

Synchronizing Facebook Contacts

Do you network like a social butterfly? You must be using one of the popular social networking applications, such as MySpace or Facebook. You must have tons of friends from these networking sites and want to copy their contact information to your Storm. Individual networking sites may or may not have a way of copying contacts to and from your BlackBerry. But if you're in Facebook, you're in luck.

With the latest Facebook application (version 1.6 as of this writing), it's much easier to get Facebook contacts into your Storm. The Facebook app also allows you to synchronize information between your Storm and your friend's information in Facebook.

Adding a Facebook friend info to Contacts

Pulling down your friend's information from Facebook to your contacts list is quite easy:

1. **Touch-press the Facebook icon from the Home screen.**

   The Facebook application is filed under the Downloads folder.

2. **Touch-press the Friends icon, which is at the top of the screen.**

   Your friends list appears, similar to the one on the left in Figure 4-14.

3. **In the Find field, start typing your friend's name.**

   This narrows the list, as shown on the right in Figure 4-14.

Figure 4-14: Select Facebook friends to add to Contacts.

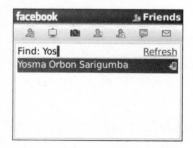

4. **Highlight the friend you want to add to Contacts, press the menu key, and touch-press Connect to BlackBerry Contact.**

   A dialog box appears, as shown in Figure 4-15, allowing you to choose whether to connect this Facebook friend to an existing contact or add the friend as a new contact to your Storm. In this case, you want to add.

   If the same person exists in Storm and Facebook, you can simply link the contact here. Also, see the next section, "Automatic syncing between Facebook profiles and Contacts," to get an automatic update on your BlackBerry whenever your friend changes his or her profile in Facebook.

Figure 4-15:
Connect a
Facebook
friend to
an existing
contact or
add a new
contact.

facebook
This friend is not currently connected with your BlackBerry Contact list. Select the BlackBerry contact you want to connect this friend to.
Select Contact | New Contact

The term *connect* in Facebook means telling the app which contact is associated with a Facebook friend. Once the app records this linkage, it knows which contact to update when information in Facebook changes.

5. **Touch-press New Contact.**

   A progress screen appears momentarily, telling you that it's getting the contact information from Facebook. When the process is finished, a new contact is added to your Storm, and the contact info appears on the screen.

6. **Press the escape key.**

   The Facebook app displays a prompt, asking you whether to ask for a phone number. This is a default behavior even if the phone number is already in your BlackBerry.

7. **Touch-press Yes or No to the prompt requesting a phone number.**

   You're back to the previous Facebook screen, where an Address Book icon has been added to the right of your friend's name to indicate that this friend is now connected, or linked, to a BlackBerry contact.

Automatic syncing between Facebook profiles and Contacts

When running the Facebook application for the first time, you're asked to enable synchronization. You can choose among the following Facebook and BlackBerry connections:

✔ **BlackBerry Calendar application:** When this option is enabled, a calendar item is automatically created in your Storm whenever you have a new Facebook event.

✔ **BlackBerry Message application:** When this option is enabled, you'll see new Facebook notifications in your Messages application.

✔ **BlackBerry Contacts application:** When this option is enabled, your Storm contacts are periodically updated with the latest Facebook information, including the profile pictures. Your Storm contacts also will be sent to Facebook.

If you opted out of these options the first time you ran Facebook, you can still enable them from the Facebook Options screen. The following steps enable Contacts synchronization:

1. **Touch-press the Facebook icon from the Home screen.**

   The Facebook application is filed under the Downloads folder.

2. **Press the menu key and then touch-press Options.**

   The Options screen appears, with lots of information, so you have to scroll down to see all the options. Feel free to check other options, but for synchronizing contacts, refer to the first two pages of the screen, which look like the one shown in Figure 4-16.

Figure 4-16: Synchronize Facebook friends.

3. **Touch-press the BlackBerry Contacts application check box.**

   If you scroll down, you see another check box (Figure 4-16, right), which allows you to synchronize Facebook profile photos with Contacts photos.

4. **Touch-press the check box titled Update Existing Photos in Your BlackBerry Contacts List with Facebook Friend Profile Photos.**

5. **Press the escape key and touch-press Yes on the Save Changes prompt.**

   Your contacts will now be periodically updated with Facebook friends.

Chapter 5

Keeping Your Appointments

In This Chapter

▶ Seeing your schedule from different time frames

▶ Making your calendar your own

▶ Scheduling a meeting

▶ Making and breaking appointments

To some folks, the key to being organized and productive is mastering time management (and we're not just talking about reading this book while you're commuting to work). Many know that the best way to organize their time is to use a calendar — a daily planner tool. Those who prefer digital to paper use a planner program on their PC — either installed on their hard drive or accessed through an Internet portal (such as Yahoo!). The smartest of the bunch, of course, use their BlackBerry Storm because it has the whole planner thing covered with its Calendar.

In this chapter, we show you how to keep your life (both personal and work) in order by managing your appointments with your BlackBerry Calendar. What's great about managing your time on a BlackBerry Storm? Your Storm is always with you.

Just remember that you won't have excuses anymore for forgetting that important quarterly meeting or Bertha's birthday bash.

Accessing BlackBerry Calendar

BlackBerry Calendar is one of the BlackBerry Storm's core applications, such as Contacts or Phone (read more about the others in Chapter 1), so it's easy to get to. From the Home screen, press the menu key and touch-press the Calendar icon onscreen. Voilà! You have Calendar, as shown in Figure 5-1.

Figure 5-1:
Day view in
Calendar.

Choosing Your Calendar View

The first time you open Calendar, Day view appears by default (refer to
Figure 5-1). However, you can change the Calendar view to one that works
better for your needs:

- **Day:** A summary of your appointments for the day. By default, it lists all
  your appointments from 9 a.m. to 5 p.m.

- **Week:** This view shows you a seven-day summary view of your appointments. By using this view, you can see how busy you are in a particular
  week.

- **Month:** The Month view shows you every day of the month. You can't
  tell how many appointments have in a day, but you can see on which
  days you have appointments.

- **Agenda:** The Agenda view isn't a time-based view like the others. It lists
  your upcoming appointments, including details of the appointments,
  such as where and when.

Different views (like the month view shown in Figure 5-2) offer a different
focus on your schedule. Select the view you want based on your scheduling
needs and preferences. If your life is a little more complicated, you can even
use a combination of views for a full grasp of your schedule.

Figure 5-2:
Change your
Calendar
view to fit
your life.

Switching Calendar views

To switch between Calendar views, simply follow these steps:

1. **From the Home screen, touch-press the Calendar icon.**

   The Calendar application is called up in its default Day view (more than likely).

2. **Press the menu key and then touch-press the view of your choice on the menu that appears.**

   If you start from Month view, your choices are View Day, View Week, and View Agenda (see Figure 5-3).

Moving between time frames

Depending on what Calendar view you're in, you can easily move to the previous or next day, week, month, or year. For example, if you're looking at September in Month view, you can move to August or October See Figure 5-4.

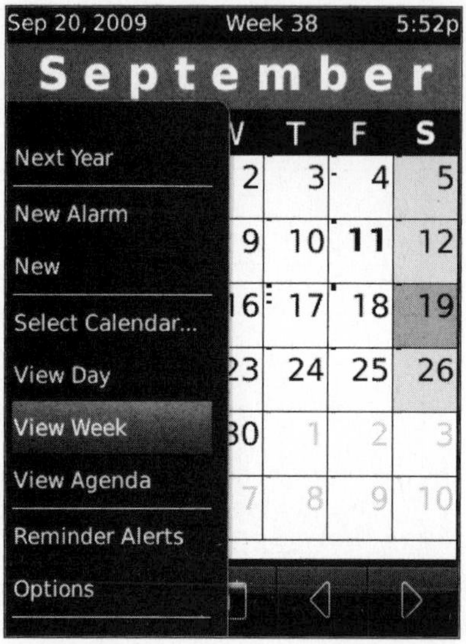

Figure 5-3:
The
Calendar
menu lets
you select
different
views.

Figure 5-4:
Move
between
months or
years in
Month view.

Without using the menu, you can quickly move to the next "page." The bottom-right corner of the screen has back and forward arrows; try them in each time frame view (Day view, Week view, Month view). Moreover, without touch-pressing any key, you can finger-flick between timeframes. For example, in Month view, you can flip to the next day with a finger-flick.

You have similar flexibility when it comes to the other Calendar views. See Table 5-1 for a summary of what's available.

Table 5-1	Moving between Views
Calendar View	*Move Between*
Day	Days and weeks
Week	Weeks
Month	Months and years
Agenda	Days

You can always go to today's date regardless of what Calendar view you're in. Just press the menu key and touch-press the Today menu item. Alternatively, at the bottom of the screen, the icon that looks like a number 1 in a calendar pad (next to the left arrow) gets you back to today. Also, you can jump to any date by pressing the menu key and touch-pressing Go to Date. To change the date, type the desired day, month, and year, as shown in Figure 5-5.

Figure 5-5:
Go to any
date you
want.

Customizing Your Calendar

To change the default view in Calendar — from Day to Month, for example — Calendar Options is the answer.

To get to Calendar Options, follow these steps:

1. Open Calendar.

2. **Press the menu key and touch-press Options.**

3. **Touch-press General Options.**

   You see choices similar to the ones shown in Table 5-2.

4. **To make a choice, touch-press the choice.**

5. **When you have Calendar just the way you like it, press the menu key and touch-press Save.**

Table 5-2	Calendar Options
Option	*Description*
Formatting	
First Day of Week	The day that first appears in Week view.
Start of Day	The time of day that defines your start of day in Day view. The default is 9 a.m. If you change this to 8 a.m., for example, your Day view starts at 8 a.m. instead of 9 a.m.
End of Day	The time of day that defines the end of day in Day view. The default is 5 p.m. If you change this to 6 p.m., for example, your Day view ends at 6 p.m. instead of 5 p.m.
Views	
Initial View	Specify the Calendar view that you see when opening Calendar.
Show Free Time in Agenda View	If Yes, this field allows an appointment-free date to appear in the Agenda view. If No, the Agenda view doesn't show days you don't have appointments.
Show End Time in Agenda View	If Yes, this field shows the end time of each appointment in the Agenda view. If No, the Agenda view shows only the start time of each appointment.
Actions	
Snooze	The delay before a reminder appears. The default is 5 minutes.
Default Reminder	How long before your appointment you're notified. The default is 15 minutes.
Enable Quick Entry	Day view only. Make a new appointment by typing characters.
Confirm Delete	Determines whether you're prompted for confirmation upon appointment deletion.
Keep Appointments	The number of days your Calendar item is saved. We recommend Never.
Show Tasks	A scheduled task appears on your calendar just like a Calendar event. *Note:* A scheduled task is a task with a due date.
Show Alarms	You can see alarms in your calendar if you set this option to Yes.

Managing Multiple Calendars

You might have multiple calendars, just as you might have several e-mail accounts. Do you have multiple calendars? How can you have multiple calendars? It's easy: For each e-mail that you "hook" into your BlackBerry (see Chapter 7), your BlackBerry automatically adds a new calendar. Why is having multiple calendars useful? Consider this example: You might have a calendar from your day job and a calendar from your personal life or a softball club that you belong to. Whatever the reason, your BlackBerry Storm has a great way for you to manage this.

You can assign different color squares to represent different calendars. This color-coding gives you a better view of which event belongs to which calendar, as shown in Figure 5-6. For example, you can have your day job calendar as red and your softball club calendar as green. When two events conflict, the color helps you see the conflict and prioritize. (It's okay to admit that it's all about your softball club!)

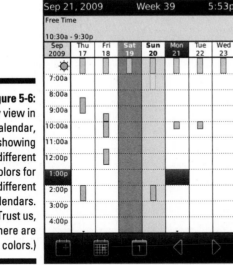

Figure 5-6: Day view in Calendar, showing different colors for different calendars. (Trust us, there are colors.)

Follow these steps to change the color of each calendar:

1. **Open Calendar.**

2. **Press the menu key and touch-press Options.**

   You see a list of calendars here, in addition to a few options.

3. **Touch-press a calendar of your choice.**

   The Calendar Properties screen opens.

4. **Touch-press the colored square and then touch-press the desired color.**

5. **Press the menu key and touch-press Save.**

All Things Appointment: Adding, Opening, and Deleting

After you master the different Calendar views (and that should take you all of about two minutes), and you have Calendar customized to your heart's content (another three minutes, tops), it's time (pun intended) to set up, review, and delete appointments. We also show you how to set up a meeting with clients or colleagues.

Creating an appointment

Setting up a new appointment is easy. You need only one piece of information: when your appointment occurs. Of course, you can easily add related information about the appointment:

- The meeting's purpose
- The location
- Additional notes

In addition to your standard, one-time, limited-duration meeting, you can set all-day appointments. The BlackBerry can assist you in setting *recurring* (repeating) meetings as well as reminders. Sweet!

Creating a one-time appointment

To add a new one-time appointment, follow these steps:

1. **Open Calendar.**

2. **Press the menu key and touch-press New.**

The New Appointment screen appears, as shown in Figure 5-7.

You can also touch-press the bottom-left icon with a plus sign to open the New Appointment screen.

3. Fill in the appointment information.

Type the information regarding your appointment in the appropriate spaces. You should at least enter the time and the subject of your appointment.

4. Press the menu key and touch-press Save.

Your appointment is now available from any Calendar view.

You can have more than one appointment in the same time slot. BlackBerry lets you decide which appointment you should go for and which one you conveniently forget.

Creating an all-day appointment

If your appointment is an all-day event — you're in corporate training or have an all-day doctor's appointment — touch-press the All Day Event check box in the New Appointment screen.

Setting your appointment reminder time

You can associate any Calendar appointment with a reminder alert either a vibration or a beep, depending on how you set things up in your profile. (For more on profiles, see Chapter 3.) You can have *no* reminder for an appointment.

Create a reminder this way: From the New Appointment screen, simply scroll to the Reminder field and select a reminder time anywhere from none to 1 week before your appointment time.

Profile is simply another useful feature that allows you to customize how your BlackBerry alerts you when an *event* occurs. Examples of events are an e-mail, a phone call, or an appointment reminder.

By default, whatever reminder alert you set goes off 15 minutes before the event. But you don't have to stick with the default. You can choose your own default reminder time:

1. **Open Calendar.**

2. **Press the menu key and touch-press Options.**

   A few Calendar options appear, along with a list of calendars.

3. **Touch-press General Options and then touch-press Default Reminder.**

4. **Touch-press a default reminder time anywhere from none to 1 week before your appointment.**

   From now on, any new appointment has the reminder you set up. Assuming a reminder time other than none (you're on your own, then!), a dialog box like the one in Figure 5-8 appears, letting you know that an appointment is coming up.

Figure 5-8:
You get a
reminder
dialog box if
you want.

Creating a recurring appointment

Everyone has some repeating appointments: birthdays, anniversaries, taking out the trash every Thursday at 7:30 a.m. You can set up recurring appointments based on daily, weekly, monthly, or yearly recurrences.

You can define an Every field for all types. Say you have an appointment that recurs every nine days. Set the Recurrence field to Daily, and set the Every field to 9 (see Figure 5-9).

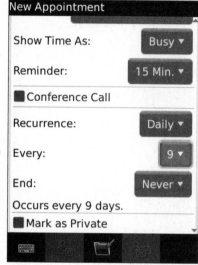

Figure 5-9:
An appointment recurring every nine days.

Depending on what you select in the Recurrence field, you have the option to fill in other fields:

- ✔ **Weekly:** You can fill in the Day of the Week field.
- ✔ **Monthly or Yearly:** The Relative Date check box is available. With this checked, you can ensure that your appointment recurs relative to today's date. For example, if you choose the following, your appointment occurs every two months on the third Sunday until July 31, 2012:

  Start: Sunday, June 17, 2010 at 12 p.m.

  End: Sunday, June 17, 2010 at 1 p.m.

  Recurrence: Monthly

  Every: 2

  Relative Date: Selected

  End: Saturday, July 31, 2012

On the other hand, if all options in our example remain the same but you don't select Relative Date, your appointment occurs every two months, on the 18th of the month, until July 31, 2012. If all this "relative" talk has you dizzy, don't worry: Most of your appointments won't be as complicated as this.

Understanding Appointments versus Meetings

Technically, any event is an appointment, whether it's your friend's birthday or a doctor's appointment. However, when you invite people or are invited to a meeting (face-to-face or via phone), that appointment becomes a *meeting*.

Sending a meeting request

Sending a meeting request to others is similar to creating a Calendar appointment:

1. **Open Calendar.**

2. **Press the menu key and then touch-press New.**

3. **Fill in the key appointment information.**

4. **Press the menu key and touch-press Invite Attendee.**

   You're taken to Address Book to select your meeting attendee.

5. **From Address Book:**

   - If you have contacts in your Address Book: Touch-press the contact you want to invite.

   - If you don't yet have contacts or the one you want isn't in your Address Book: Choose the Use Once option to type the appropriate e-mail address in Calendar.

   You see the attendees in your Calendar meeting notice.

6. **Press the menu key and touch-press Save.**

   Your meeting attendees receive an e-mail inviting them to your meeting.

Responding to a meeting request

You've likely received a meeting request by e-mail, whether for work or for a casual event. (If it's from your boss for an all-staff meeting, and it's close to bonus time, that's an Accept.)

You can accept any meeting request from your managers or colleagues on your BlackBerry just as you would on your desktop PC. Upon reading the e-mail on your BlackBerry, choose one of the following in the Messages application: Accept, Tentative, or Decline.

Your response is sent in an e-mail. We go into more detail about the Messages application in Chapter 8.

If you choose Accept or Tentative, the meeting is added to your calendar automatically. If you have a change of heart and want to delete the event, go back to the calendar event, press the menu key, and touch-press Delete from the menu.

Do you use Google to manage your Calendar and contacts on the Web? Then Google Sync for BlackBerry is what you need! You can download it by visiting http://m.google.com/sync from your BlackBerry's Browser. Google offers a variety of other applications for BlackBerry users, including Google Maps; Google Voice; Google Search App; and the newly released Enhanced Gmail plug-in, which adds more Gmail functionality to the native BlackBerry e-mail client. The BlackBerry native e-mail client is e-mail that comes with your carrier and ends with *blackberry.com* or *blackberry.net*. For Verizon, the native BlackBerry e-mail is username@vzw.blackberry.net.

Setting your meeting dial-in number

In this global economy, many of us have colleagues and friends who are located in another country or even on another continent. So many meetings are through a phone conference that involves a dial-in number, a moderator code (if you are the moderator), and a participation code. Your BlackBerry Storm makes storing and displaying these numbers easy when you're creating a new appointment in Calendar.

To set your phone conference dial-in details, follow these steps:

1. **Open Calendar.**
2. **Press the menu key and touch-press Options.**
3. **Touch-press Conference Call Options.**

   A screen similar to Figure 5-10 appears.
4. **Enter the appropriate numbers.**
5. **Press the menu key and touch-press Save.**

The next time you create a new appointment with a conference call, the conference number shows up.

Figure 5-10:
Setting up
Conference
Call dial-in
details.

Chapter 6

Setting Alarms and Keeping Your Passwords

. . . .

In This Chapter

▶ Getting to know the Clock application

▶ Modifying your clock

▶ Setting alarms

▶ Setting Bedside mode

▶ Using the BlackBerry stopwatch

▶ Setting the BlackBerry timer

▶ Making your life easier with Password Keeper

. . . .

*I*n this chapter, we introduce you to the Clock application, which not only tells you the time, but also allows you to set alarms and a timer. In addition, you can use the application as a stopwatch. And in keeping with one of the key themes of this book — making your life easier — the Clock app has a feature called Bedside mode that turns your Storm into a quiet bedside companion.

To continue with the theme of making your life a little easier, we make sure that you get the scoop on keeping your passwords in a single location safely by using the Password Keeper application.

Accessing Clock

Clock can be found on the Home screen, as you can see on the left side of Figure 6-1. Just look for the icon of an alarm clock. After you find the Clock icon, simply touch-press it, and you see a screen similar to the one on the right side of Figure 6-1.

Figure 6-1:
Launch
Clock (left)
and view
your clock
(right).

If you've changed themes, different icons might be displayed (refer to Chapter 3 for more on themes). Just remember that the Clock application is always located on the Home screen.

Customizing Your Clock

If the default analog clock doesn't fit your taste, you can change it. Customizing your clock is easy and doesn't take much time.

You customize the clock in the Options screen. Follow these steps:

1. **Touch-press Clock from the Home screen.**

   The Clock application opens.

2. **Press the menu key and touch-press Options.**

   The Clock Options screen appears, as shown in Figure 6-2, ready and willing to be customized. We discuss every customization field you see on these screens following the steps.

3. **Move to each field and choose the option you want.**

   Each of these fields is described shortly.

4. **Press the escape key and then touch-press Save from the prompt.**

Figure 6-2:
Customize
your clock
here.

The Clock Options screen is divided into five sections, as follows:

✔ **Clock section:** This is where you choose the type of clock, time zone, time, and whether to show the clock when charging.

• Clock Face: Set the type of clock. The options are Analog (the default; refer to the right side of Figure 6-1), Digital, Flip Clock, and LCD Digital. Digital looks like the clock shown on the left side of Figure 6-3, and Flip Clock is shown on the right side of Figure 6-3.

• Home Time Zone: Select your time zone from the list.

• When Charging: Control the behavior of the clock when you connect your Storm to the charger. Possible choices are Do Nothing, Display Clock (the default), and Enter Bedside Mode.

• Set Time: Click this button, and you see a Date/Time screen that displays the current time in edit mode, allowing you to change the time. You can also change the time zone as well as synchronize your BlackBerry's time to the network carriers' time.

✔ **Alarm section:** Navigate here if you want to customize the behavior of the alarm.

• Alarm Tune: Choose from a list of ring tones you want to play. This setting applies only if you have Tone or Tone + Vibrate selected for the Alert Type. The default tone is Alarm_Antelope.

- Snooze Time: Just like with your ordinary alarm clock, you have the option to hit the snooze. You can choose 30, 15, 10, 5 (the default), 1 minute, or None.

- Volume: You can set the volume of the tone to Silent, 1 to 10 (the default is 8), or Escalating.

- Vibration: You can enable or disable vibration. Choose Off, On (the default), or Custom. If you choose Custom, two new fields appear. The first, Length, enables you to choose the duration of the vibration: Short, Medium (the default), or Long. The second field, Count, vibrates your Storm as your alarm. Choices are 1, 2 (the default), 3, 5, and 10 repetitions.

Figure 6-3:
Digital (left)
and Flip
(right) clock.

✔ **Bedside Mode section:** This section allows you to set the behavior of your Storm when it is in Bedside mode.

- Disable LED: Allows you to disable LED notifications during Bedside mode. Choices are Yes (the default) and No.

- Disable Radio: Allows you to disable the radio during Bedside mode. Choices are Yes and No (the default).

Disabling the radio means that all communication-related applications — such as e-mail, SMS, BlackBerry Messenger, instant messaging clients, and Phone — cannot receive incoming signals.

- Dim Screen: Choose Yes (the default) or No to control the dimming of the screen in Bedside mode.

- Sound Profile: Use for anything that requires sound notification. You have several profiles to choose among: Active Profile (the default), Normal, Loud, Medium, Vibrate Only, Silent, Phone Calls Only, and All Alerts Off. Remember that you can always add a custom profile (see Chapter 3 for details).

✔ **Stopwatch section:** A section to change the face of the stopwatch.

- Stopwatch Face: Choose between an Analog (the default) or a Digital stopwatch.

✔ **Countdown Timer section:** Navigate here if you want to customize the behavior of the timer.

- Timer Face: Your choices are Analog (the default) and Digital.

- Timer Tune: Choose the ring tone you want to play when the timer reaches the time you set.

- Volume: You can select Mute or set the volume of the tone to Low, Medium, High, or Escalating. Escalating means that the tone starts Low and gradually goes to High. The default is Medium.

- Vibration: Choose Yes if you want Storm to vibrate when the timer reaches the time set; otherwise, choose No (the default).

Setting a Wake-Up Alarm

The Clock application is also your bedside alarm clock. You can set it to wake you up once or on a regular basis.

Here's how you tell your wake-up buddy to do the work for you:

1. **Touch-press Clock from the Home screen.**

   The Clock appears.

2. **Touch-press anywhere on the screen and then touch-press Set Alarm.**

   A time field appears in the middle of the screen, as shown in Figure 6-4. The time defaults to the previous set alarm time or, if you haven't used the alarm before, the current time. If the default time isn't your intended alarm time, proceed to Step 3 to change the time.

Figure 6-4:
Set your
alarm time
here.

3. **Tap the specific portion of the time that you want to change, and slide up or down to choose one of the possible values.**

   Any highlighted portion of the time is editable. You can change the hours; minutes; AM/PM; and whether the alarm is ON, OFF, or only WEEKD (weekdays). Setting a value doesn't create an entry in Calendar or Tasks. Finger-scroll up or down to choose a possible value.

4. **Touch-press the OK button to accept all your changes.**

Setting and Exiting Bedside Mode

You can use a setting in the Clock application called Bedside mode to minimize disturbances by your Storm. With Bedside mode, you can dim the screen, disable the LED, and even turn off the radio, all of which pretty much make your Storm behave like a brick. Bear in mind that when you turn off the radio, you won't get incoming phone calls or any type of messaging. If you want a refresher on how to set these options, see "Customizing Your Clock," previously in this chapter.

To set your BlackBerry Storm in Bedside mode:

1. **Touch-press Clock from the Home screen.**

2. **Touch-press anywhere on the screen and then touch-press Enter Bedside Mode (Figure 6-5, left).**

   That's it. Your Storm should now behave like a good bedside companion.

Figure 6-5:
Enter and
exit Bedside
mode here.

Buy a charging pod from shop.blackberry.com or shop.crackberry.com. Then you can put your Storm on a bedside table in an upright position while the charging pod is adding juice to your device. Make sure the Clock setting (not just the Storm) is in Bedside mode when charging. (To do so, touch-press Clock from the Home screen. Press the menu key and then touch-press Options. Under the Clock section, change When Charging to Enter Bedside Mode.)

To exit Bedside mode:

1. **Touch-press Clock from the Home screen.**

2. **Touch-Press anywhere on the screen and then touch-press Exit Bedside Mode, as shown on the right side of Figure 6-5.**

Using Stopwatch

In case you ever need a stopwatch, you need look no further than your BlackBerry Storm. Here's how to run the stopwatch:

1. **Touch-press Clock from the Home screen.**

2. **Touch-Press anywhere on the screen and then touch-press Stopwatch.**

    You see a screen similar to Figure 6-6. Two buttons are at the bottom of this screen:

    • Stopwatch button: Touch-press this button to start and stop the stopwatch.

- **Lap and Reset button:** The image on this button looks like a circular arrow initially. After you start the stopwatch, this button becomes a lap button, and the image changes to a connected arrow with an oval shape. This Lap button is useful when someone is doing laps in a swimming pool or on a track field and you want to record how long each lap takes. Touch-press the button to record the completion of a single lap. The lap and the lap time will be listed on the screen. A lap is labeled as Lap 1 for the first lap, Lap 2 for the second lap, and so on.

3. **To start the stopwatch, touch-press the Stopwatch button.**

4. **To stop the stopwatch, touch-press the Stopwatch button again.**

Figure 6-6:
Start (left) and stop (right) your stopwatch.

Using Timer

Have you overcooked something? Not if you have a good timer to warn you:

1. **Touch-press Clock from the Home screen.**

2. **Touch-Press anywhere on the screen and then touch-press Timer.**

   A screen similar to the left side of Figure 6-7 appears. The left button with the stopwatch image is the start and pause button. You can use the right button with the circular arrow image to stop and reset the timer. The default time for your timer is based on what you set earlier. If you haven't set a time or you want to set a new time, proceed to the next step.

Figure 6-7:
Start and
set the time
of the timer.

3. **Touch-press anywhere on the screen above the buttons.**

   A screen similar to the right side of Figure 6-7 appears.

4. **Lightly touch the portion of the time that you want to change and finger-scroll up or down to choose a possible value.**

   From left to right, the time is based on hours, minutes, and seconds. All are editable.

5. **Touch-press the OK button to accept the time.**

6. **Touch-press Start button (the stopwatch image).**

   Your timer starts ticking. After it reaches the time, it notifies you.

You can customize the type of timer notification to a tone, a vibration, or both. To do so, touch-press Clock from the Home screen. Press the menu key and then touch-press Options. In the Countdown Timer section, make your selections.

Using Password Keeper

Suppose that you're in front of an Internet browser, trying to access an online account. For the life of you, you just can't remember the account password. It's your third login attempt, and if you fail this time, your account will be locked. Then you have to call the customer hotline and wait hours before you can speak to a representative. Argghh! It's happened to all of us. Luckily, BlackBerry Storm gives you an application to avoid this headache.

Password Keeper is the simple yet practical BlackBerry Storm application that makes your life that much easier. Password Keeper is filed in Applications (as shown in Figure 6-8).

Setting a password for Password Keeper

The first time you access Password Keeper, you're prompted to enter a password. *Be sure to remember the password you choose,* because this is the password to all your passwords. Forgetting this password is like forgetting the combination of your safe. There is no way to retrieve a forgotten Password Keeper password. You are prompted to enter this master password every time you access the application.

Trust us: One password is much easier to remember than many passwords.

You can enter any characters or numbers as your password, and there is no length requirement as long as you enter something. However, we recommend that you choose a password combining letters and numbers.

Figure 6-8:
Password
Keeper
in the
Applications
folder.

Creating credentials

Okay, so you're ready to fire up your handy-dandy Password Keeper application. Now what kinds of things does it expect you to do for it to work its magic? Obviously, you'll need to collect the pertinent info for all your various password-protected accounts so that you can store them in the protected environs of Password Keeper. So when creating a new password entry, be sure you have the following information (see Figure 6-9):

 ✔ **Title:** This one's straightforward. Just come up with a name to describe the password-protected account — My Favorite Shopping Site, for example.

 ✔ **Username:** This is where you enter the username for the account.

 ✔ **Password:** Enter the password for the account here.

 ✔ **Website:** Put the Web site address (its URL) here.

 ✔ **Notes:** Not exactly crucial, but the Notes field does give you a bit of room to add a comment or two.

Figure 6-9:
Set your
password
here.

The only required field is Title, but a title alone usually isn't much use to you. We suggest that you fill in as much other information here as possible, *but at the same time, be discreet about those locations where you use your username and password* — so don't put anything in the Website field or use My eBay Account as a title. That way, in the unlikely case that someone gains access to your password to Password Keeper, the intruder will have a hard time figuring out where exactly to use your credentials.

Generating passwords randomly

If you're the kind of person who uses one password for everything but knows deep in your heart that this is just plain wrong, wrong, wrong, random password generation is for you. When creating a new password for yet another online account (or when changing your password for an online account you already have), fire up Password Keeper, press the menu key, touch-press New, press the menu key, and then touch-press Random Password, as shown in Figure 6-10. Voilà! A new password is automatically generated for you.

Figure 6-10: Generate a random password.

Using random password generation makes sense in conjunction with Password Keeper because you don't have to remember the randomly generated password that Password Keeper came up with for any of your online accounts; that's Password Keeper's job.

Using your password

The whole point of Password Keeper is to let your BlackBerry Storm's electronic brain do your password remembering for you. Imagine this scenario: You can no longer live without owning a copy of the CD *A Chipmunk Christmas,* so you surf over to your favorite online music store and attempt to log in. You draw a blank on your password, but instead of seething, you take out your Storm, open Password Keeper, and do a find.

Type the first letters of your account title in the Find field to search for the title of your password. After you find the title, simply touch-press it, and the screen for your account appears, conveniently listing the password. All you have to do now is enter the password in the login screen for the online music store, and Alvin, Simon, and Theodore will soon be wending their way to your address, ready to sing "Chipmunk Jingle Bells."

Yes, you *can* copy-and-paste your password from Password Keeper to another application — BlackBerry Browser, for instance. Just tap the entry from the Password Keeper list, press the menu key, and touch-press Copy Password on the menu that appears. Then navigate to where you want to enter the password, press the menu key, and touch-press Paste on the menu. Keep in mind that for the copy-and-paste function to work for passwords from Password Keeper, you need to enable the Allow Clipboard Copy option in the Password Keeper options (see the upcoming Table 6-1). You can copy-and-paste only one password at a time.

After you paste your password in another application, clear the Clipboard by pressing the menu key and choosing Clear Clipboard. The Clipboard keeps your last copied password until you clear it.

Seeing Password Keeper options

Password Keeper's Options menu, accessible by pressing the menu key while in Password Keeper, allows you to control how Password Keeper behaves. For example, you can set what characters can make up a randomly generated password. Table 6-1 describes all the options in Password Keeper.

Table 6-1	Password Keeper Options
Option Name	*Description*
Random Password Length	Select 4 to 16 characters for the length of your randomly generated password.
Random Includes Alpha	If Yes, a randomly generated password includes alphabetic characters.
Random Includes Numbers	If Yes, a randomly generated password includes numbers.
Random Includes Symbols	If Yes, a randomly generated password includes symbols.
Confirm Delete	If Yes, all deletions are prompted with a confirmation screen.
Password Attempts	Select 1 to 20 attempts to successfully enter the password to Password Keeper.
Allow Clipboard Copy	If Yes, you can copy-and-paste passwords from Password Keeper.
Show Password	If Yes, the password is displayed; otherwise, asterisks take the place of the password characters.

Changing your password to Password Keeper

If you want to change your master password to Password Keeper — the password for opening Password Keeper itself — follow these steps:

1. **Touch-press Password Keeper.**

   The initial login screen for the Password Keeper application appears.

2. **Enter your old password to access Password Keeper.**

3. **In Password Keeper, press the menu key and then touch-press Change Password.**

   Doing so calls up the Password Keeper screen that allows you to enter your new password, as shown in Figure 6-11.

4. **Enter a new password, confirm it by entering it again, and then touch-press OK.**

Figure 6-11: Change your Password Keeper password here.

Chapter 7

You've Got (Lots of) E-Mail

In This Chapter

▶ Linking your e-mail accounts to your BlackBerry

▶ Adding your own e-mail signature

▶ Reconciling e-mails on your Storm and PC

▶ Sending automatic replies and messages

▶ Receiving and sorting messages

▶ Viewing attachments

▶ Sending and forwarding messages

▶ Spell-checking e-mails

▶ Mastering other e-mail basics

▶ Deleting and filtering your e-mails

▶ Searching your e-mail

▶ Saving messages

*Y*our BlackBerry Storm brings a fresh new face to the convenience and ease of use that are associated with e-mail. You can direct mail to your BlackBerry from up to ten e-mail accounts, including the likes of Yahoo! and Gmail. You can set up an e-mail signature, configure e-mail filters, and search for e-mail messages.

In this chapter, we show you how to use and manage your BlackBerry's mail capabilities to its full potential. From setup to sorts, we have you covered here.

Getting Up and Running with E-Mail

Regardless of your network service provider (such as Verizon, Telus, or Vodafone), you can set up your BlackBerry to receive mail from at least one of your current e-mail accounts. Thus, with whatever address you use to send and receive e-mail from your PC (Yahoo!, Gmail, and so on), you can hook up your BlackBerry to use that same e-mail address. Instead of checking your Gmail at the Google site, for example, you can get it on your BlackBerry. Is your company running a BlackBerry Enterprise Server and MS Exchange server but didn't think to give you a company BlackBerry? No worries; you can still get your e-mail via BlackBerry Desktop Redirector. Keep reading.

Most network service providers allow you to connect up to ten e-mail accounts to your BlackBerry. This capability provides you with the convenience of one central point from which you get all your e-mail.

Using the BlackBerry Internet Service client

You can pull together all your e-mail accounts into one by using the *BIS (BlackBerry Internet Service) client*. The BIS client allows you to

- ✔ **Manage up to ten e-mail accounts:** See the next section, "Combining your e-mail accounts into one."

- ✔ **Use wireless e-mail reconciliation:** No more trying to match your BlackBerry e-mail against e-mail in your combined account(s). Just turn on wireless e-mail reconciliation, and you're good to go. For more on this, see the upcoming section "Enabling Wireless Reconciliation."

- ✔ **Create e-mail filters:** You can filter e-mails to get only those messages that you truly care about on your BlackBerry. See the "Filtering your e-mail" section, near the end of this chapter.

Think of the BIS client (also known simply as *BIS*) as an online e-mail account manager that doesn't keep your messages. Instead, it routes the e-mails from your other accounts to your BlackBerry (because it's directly connected to your BlackBerry).

Combining your e-mail accounts into one

To start herding e-mail accounts onto your BlackBerry, you must first run a setup program from the BIS client.

You can access the BIS client from your BlackBerry or from your desktop computer. To do so on the PC, you need the URL that is specific to your network service. Contact your network service provider (such as Verizon or Telus) directly to get that information.

We cover accessing the BIS client from the BlackBerry Storm, but just remember that you can do all these functions from a Web browser as well.

To get started with BIS client from your BlackBerry:

1. **From the BlackBerry Home screen, touch-press the Setup folder.**
2. **Touch-press the Email Settings icon.**

   You are prompted with a login screen similar to Figure 7-1. If you haven't created your account, click the Create button to create your BIS account.

Figure 7-1:
The BIS
client login
screen
on the
BlackBerry.

After you've logged in, you see a list of e-mail accounts that have been set up, as shown in Figure 7-2. If you haven't set up any e-mail accounts yet, you see an Add button. We show you how to add accounts in the next section.

Adding an e-mail account

You can set up your BIS account directly from your Storm. (As we mention earlier in this chapter, you can have up to ten e-mail accounts on your BlackBerry.) To add an e-mail account to your BlackBerry account, follow these steps on your BlackBerry Storm:

1. **From your BlackBerry Home screen, touch-press the Setup folder.**

2. **Touch-press the Person E-mail Setup icon.**

   You are prompted with a login screen similar to Figure 7-1. If you haven't created your account, click the Create button to create your BIS account.

3. **After you log in, touch-press Add.**

   A screen with different e-mail domains (Yahoo!, Google) appears, as shown in Figure 7-3.

Figure 7-2: The BIS client screen after login.

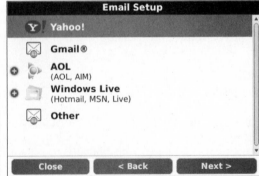

Figure 7-3: Select an e-mail domain.

4. **Touch-press an e-mail domain.**

5. **Enter the e-mail address and password, and then touch-press Next.**

   If you entered your e-mail credentials correctly, you see the setup confirmation screen.

As we mention earlier in this chapter, you can also add an e-mail account to your BlackBerry from your desktop PC or Mac via a Web browser. Just follow these steps.

1. **From the BIS client, click Setup Account.**

   Contact your network carrier for the URL to access the BIS client on your PC or Mac Web browser.

2. **Enter the address and login credentials for that e-mail address.**

   - The e-mail address is the address from which you want to receive e-mail — for example, myid@yahoo.com.

   - The account login is the one you use to log in to this particular e-mail account.

   - The password is the one you use with the login.

3. **Click the Next button.**

   You're finished. It's that easy!

Want to log in to the BIS Web site for your carrier? Here's a list of login addresses for some of the popular North American carriers:

✔ Bell: https://bis.na.blackberry.com/html?brand=bell

✔ Telus: https://bis.na.blackberry.com/html?brand=telus

✔ Verizon: https://bis.na.blackberry.com/html?brand=vzw

✔ Vodafone: https://bis.eu.blackberry.com/html?brand=vodauk

If ever in doubt, simply go to Google and enter **carrier-name BIS login**, and the first result returned will almost always be the BIS login page for your carrier.

Using Desktop Redirector: How enterprising!

If you're a sole proprietor or consultant who works in a corporation that runs Exchange or Lotus and want to get enterprise (corporate) e-mails on your own BlackBerry, this section is for you.

Normally, to get enterprise e-mail, your BlackBerry has to be configured with the BlackBerry Enterprise Server (BES). This is typical if your employer hands you a BlackBerry. However, if you work for a large company as a contractor, you probably won't get a BlackBerry from the company you work for.

When you want to get enterprise e-mail to avoid falling behind (especially if you don't work five days a week), you need Desktop Redirector. To use Desktop Redirector, you first need to install BlackBerry Desktop Manager, which you can find out how to do in Chapter 15.

After you've installed Desktop Manager with Redirector, make sure that Redirector starts every time you boot your PC.

Some corporations allow Desktop Redirector, but some don't. Contact your IT department for proper setup.

Just a few caveats when using the Desktop Redirector:

✔ You get enterprise e-mail as long as your PC is turned on and has a connection to the Internet.

✔ When someone sends you an attachment, you can't retrieve it from your BlackBerry.

✔ When someone sends you a meeting notice, you can see the notice, but you can't accept or reject it.

Configuring Your E-Mail Signature

By default, your e-mail signature is something like *Sent via My BlackBerry,* which can be cool the first week, showing off to people that you're à la mode with your BlackBerry. But sooner or later, you might not want people to know that you are out and about while answering e-mail. Or you might want something more personal.

Follow these steps to configure your e-mail signature by using the BIS client on your BlackBerry:

1. **From your BlackBerry Home screen, touch-press the Setup folder.**

2. **Touch-press the Email Setting icon.**

   You are prompted with a login screen similar to Figure 7-1, earlier in this chapter. If you haven't created your account, click the Create button to create your BIS account.

3. **Log in to the BIS client on the BlackBerry.**

    You see the BIS main screen (refer to Figure 7-2, earlier in this chapter).

4. **Touch-press the e-mail account for which you want to set up an e-mail signature.**

5. **In the Signature field, type the text for your e-mail signature.**

6. **Touch-press Save.**

Enabling Wireless Reconciliation

With wireless reconciliation, you don't need to delete the same e-mail in two places. The two e-mail inboxes reconcile with each other — hence, the term *wireless reconciliation.* Convenient, huh?

Enabling wireless e-mail synchronization

You can start wireless e-mail synchronization by configuring your BlackBerry:

1. **From the Home screen, touch-press Messages.**

    The Messages application opens, and you see the message list.

2. **In the message list, press the menu key and touch-press Options.**

3. **Touch-press Email Reconciliation.**

    The Email Reconciliation screen opens, with the following options:

    • Delete On: Configures how BlackBerry handles e-mail deletion.

    • Wireless Reconciliation: Turns on or off the wireless sync function.

    • On Conflict: Controls how BlackBerry handles any inconsistencies between e-mail on your BlackBerry and the BIS client.

    You can choose who "wins" via the Email Reconciliation option: your BlackBerry or the BIS client.

4. **For the Delete On option, touch-press one of the following:**

    • Handheld: A delete on your BlackBerry takes effect on your BlackBerry only.

    • Mailbox & Handheld: A delete on your BlackBerry takes effect on both your BlackBerry and your inbox on the BIS client.

    • Prompt: This option makes BlackBerry ask you to confirm at the time of deletion.

5. **For Wireless Reconciliation, touch-press On.**

   The changes you make on the device will match the ones on your e-mail account.

6. **For On Conflict, touch-press one of the following in the drop-down list:**

   • Handheld Wins: The e-mail messages in your e-mail account will match the ones on the handheld.

   • Mailbox Wins: The e-mail messages on your handheld will match the ones in your e-mail account.

Next, you need to enable Synchronize Deleted Item on the BIS client:

1. **From your BlackBerry Home screen, touch-press the Setup folder.**

2. **Touch-press the Email Setting icon.**

   You are prompted with a login screen similar to Figure 7-1, earlier in this chapter. If you haven't created your account, click the Create button to create your BIS account.

3. **Log in to the BIS client on the BlackBerry.**

   You see the BIS main screen (refer to Figure 7-2, earlier in this chapter).

4. **Touch-press an e-mail account for which you want to enable Synchronize Deleted Item.**

5. **Touch-press Synchronization Options to expand the options.**

6. **Make sure that the Deleted Items check box is selected.**

7. **Touch-press Save.**

Unfortunately, some e-mail accounts might not work well with the e-mail reconciliation feature of the BlackBerry, so you might have to delete an e-mail twice.

Permanently deleting e-mail from your BlackBerry

When you delete e-mail on your BlackBerry, the same message in that e-mail account is placed in the Deleted folder. You can set up your BlackBerry to permanently delete e-mail, but use this option with caution — after that e-mail is gone, it's gone.

To permanently delete e-mail on the BIS client from your BlackBerry, follow these steps:

1. **Open the Messages application.**

2. **Press the menu key and touch-press Options.**

   The Options screen opens.

3. **Touch-press E-mail Reconciliation.**

   The E-mail Reconciliation screen opens.

4. **Press the menu key and touch-press Purge Deleted Items.**

   You see a listing of all your e-mail accounts.

5. **Choose the e-mail account from which you want to purge deleted items.**

   A screen warns that you are about to purge deleted e-mails on your service client.

6. **If you're sure you want to never see these messages again, touch-press Yes.**

   Deleted e-mails in the selected e-mail account are purged.

Unfortunately, some e-mail accounts might not work with the Purge Deleted Items feature.

Automating Replies and Out-of-Office Messages

Unfortunately, BlackBerry Internet Service doesn't have the "out-of-office" message feature, but that doesn't mean you can't work around it.

One way to set your out-of-office message is to go to your e-mail service account (Gmail, Yahoo!, Hotmail, and so on) and set the out-of-office message from there. If you have more than one e-mail account routed to your BlackBerry, you have to do this for each. Not ideal, but it works.

Working with E-Mail

From Messages, you send and receive your e-mails and also configure wireless e-mail reconciliation with your e-mail account(s).

To access Messages, touch-press the Messages icon on the Home screen.

The message list appears. Your message list can contain e-mail, voice mail messages, missed-phone-call notices, Short Message Service (SMS) messages, and even saved Web pages.

Receiving e-mails

Whether you're concerned about data security or delivery speed, with BlackBerry's up-to-date secured network, you're in good hands.

And whether you've combined accounts or use the plain-vanilla BlackBerry e-mail account, you receive your e-mail the same way. When you get an e-mail message, your BlackBerry notifies you by displaying a number next to a mail icon (an envelope) at the top of the screen. This number represents how many new, unread e-mails you have. The asterisk next to the envelope indicates new mail that you haven't opened in the Messages application.

Your BlackBerry can also notify you of new e-mail by vibration, a sound, or both. You can customize this from the Profile application, as detailed in Chapter 3.

Retrieving your e-mail is simple:

1. **From the Home screen, touch-press the Messages icon.**

   Doing so allows you to view your message list.

2. **Touch-press the e-mail message you want to read.**

   You can tell whether an e-mail is unopened by the small unopened envelope icon on the left side of the e-mail. A read e-mail bears an opened envelope icon; a sent e-mail has a check mark as its icon; and a document icon represents a draft e-mail.

3. **After you finish reading the message, press the escape key to return to the message list.**

Sorting the message list

The BlackBerry lists items by the date and time you received them, but you can sort by different criteria. You can search your e-mail by the sender's name or by keywords. Or you could run a search as broad as looking through all the e-mail that has been sent to you. See the later section "Searching Messages Like a Pro" for more on searching and sorting. For more predefined hot keys, see the upcoming section "Reusing saved searches."

Saving a message to the saved folder

You can save any important e-mail in a folder so you can find it without sorting through tons of e-mail. To do so, touch-press the e-mail you want to save, press the menu key, and touch-press Save. A pop-up message confirms that your e-mail has been saved. *Note:* Your saved e-mail remains in the message list.

To retrieve or view a saved e-mail, follow these steps:

1. **Open the Messages application.**
2. **Press the menu key and touch-press View Saved Messages.**

   You see the list of all the messages you saved.
3. **Touch-press the message you want to view.**

Viewing attachments

Your BlackBerry Storm lets you view most e-mail attachments just like you can on a desktop PC. And we're talking sizeable attachments, too, such as JPEG photo files and Microsoft Word docs, Microsoft PowerPoint slides, and Microsoft Excel spreadsheets. Table 7-1 has a list of supported attachments viewable from your BlackBerry.

Table 7-1	BlackBerry-Supported Attachments
Supported Attachment Extension	*Description*
.bmp	BMP image file format
.doc, .docx	MS Word document
.dot	MS Word document template
.gif	GIF image file format
.htm, .html	HTML Web page
.jpg	JPEG image file format
.mp3	Compressed music file format
.pdf	Adobe PDF document
.png	PNG image file format
.ppt, .pptx	MS PowerPoint document
.tif	TIFF image file format
.txt	Text file
.wav	Music file format
.wpd	Corel WordPerfect document
.xls, .xlsx	MS Excel document
.zip	Compressed file format

To tell whether an e-mail has an attachment, look for the standard paper-clip icon next to your e-mail in the message list.

You retrieve all the different types of attachments the same way. This makes retrieving attachments an easy task. To open an attachment, follow along:

1. **With an e-mail open, press the menu key and touch-press Open Attachment.**

   A dialog box appears, asking if you want to view or edit with Documents to Go.

2. **Touch-press View.**

   You see a screen containing the name of the file, a Table of Contents option, and a Full Contents option.

   - For Word documents, you can see different headings in outline form with the Table of Contents option.

   - For picture files, such as a JPEG, you can simply go straight to the Full Contents option to see the graphic.

   - For all supported file types, you see Table of Contents and Full Contents options. Depending on the file type, use your judgment on when you should use the Table of Contents option.

3. **Scroll to Full Contents, press the menu key, and touch-press Retrieve.**

   Your BlackBerry attempts to contact the BIS client to retrieve your attachment. This action retrieves only part of your attachment. BlackBerry retrieves more as you scroll through the attachment.

Editing attachments

Your BlackBerry Storm comes with Documents to Go, a feature that enables you to not only view, but also edit Word and PowerPoint documents. You can even save the documents to your BlackBerry and later transfer them to your PC.

As an example, we show you how to edit a Word document attached to an e-mail:

1. **Open the Messages application.**

2. **In the message list, open an e-mail with a Word document attached.**

   The e-mail opens for you to read. Notice the little paper clip, indicating that it has an attachment.

3. **Press the menu key and touch-press Open Attachment.**

   You are asked whether you want to view the Word document or edit with Documents to Go.

4. **Touch-press Edit with Documents to Go.**

   You can view your documents.

5. **Press the menu key and touch-press Edit Mode.**

   With Edit Mode, you can edit your document. When you finish editing, you can save the doc on your BlackBerry Storm or e-mail it. For these steps, you will e-mail it.

   If you want to save the attachment on your BlackBerry, go to the folder structure on your BlackBerry. For documents, the default folder structure is usually in the Document folder.

6. **Press the menu key and touch-press Send via E-mail.**

   An e-mail message opens with the Word document attached. Follow the steps in the next section to send this e-mail.

Sending e-mail

The first thing you probably want to do when you get your BlackBerry is write an e-mail to let your friends know all about it. Follow these steps:

1. **Open the Messages application.**

2. **Press the menu key and touch-press Compose Email.**

   You're prompted with a blank e-mail that you need to fill out as you would on your PC.

3. **In the To field, type the recipient's name or e-mail address.**

   You see a list of your contacts matching the name or address you're typing. You can make a selection from this list.

4. **Type your message subject and body.**

5. **When you're finished, press the menu key and touch-press Send.**

   Your message has wings.

Forwarding e-mail

When you need to share an important e-mail with a colleague or friend, you can forward that e-mail. Simply do the following:

1. **Open the e-mail.**

2. **Press the menu key and touch-press Forward.**

3. **Type the recipient's name or e-mail address in the appropriate space.**

   When you start typing your recipient's name, a drop-down list of your contacts appears, and you can choose the recipient from it.

   4. Type a message if needed.

   5. Press the menu key and touch-press Send.

   Your message is on its way to your recipient.

One frustrating feature lacking in the Storm e-mail experience is the ability to edit an e-mail you are forwarding to another recipient. Don't believe me? Try it! When you forward an e-mail, the original e-mail remains as is and you can add new text only above the original message. Luckily, third-party applications such as Forward with Edit and Forward, Reply, and Edit add this functionality. A quick search in App World or the CrackBerry App Store will find these titles.

Sending e-mail to multiple people

When you need to send an e-mail to more than one person, just keep adding recipient names as needed. You can also add recipient names to receive a CC (carbon copy) or BCC (blind carbon copy). Here's how:

   1. Open the e-mail.

   2. Press the menu key and touch-press Compose Email.

   3. Specify the To field for the e-mail recipient and then press the enter key.

   Another To field is added below the first. The CC field works the same way.

   4. To add a BCC recipient, press the menu key and touch-press Add BCC.

   You see a BCC field. You can specify a blind carbon-copy (BCC) recipient the same way you do To and CC recipients.

Whether you're writing a new e-mail, replying to an e-mail, or forwarding an e-mail, the way you add new CC and BCC fields is the same.

Saving a draft e-mail

Sometimes the most skillful wordsmiths find themselves lacking. Don't fret, fellow wordsmith; you can save that e-mail as a draft until your words come to you. Just press the menu key and touch-press Save Draft.

Your e-mail is saved as a draft. When you're ready to send your message, choose the draft from the message list. You can tell which messages are drafts because they sport a tiny document icon; finished messages have an envelope icon.

Attaching any file to your e-mail

Many people are surprised that you can attach any document on your BlackBerry Storm or in the microSD card (in your Storm). When we say *any* file type, we mean Word, Excel, and PowerPoint documents, as well as pictures, music, and videos. Follow these steps:

1. **Open the Messages application.**

2. **Press the menu key and touch-press Compose.**

   You're prompted with a blank e-mail.

3. **In the To field, type the recipient's name or e-mail address.**

   You see a list of your contacts matching the name or address that you're typing. You can make a selection from this list.

4. **Type your message subject and body.**

5. **Press the menu key and touch-press Attach File.**

   You're prompted with folders. Think of them as the folders on your PC.

6. **Touch-press the folders until you get to the file you want to send and then touch-press that file.**

   You see the file in the e-mail message.

7. **Press the menu key and touch-press Send.**

   Your message has wings.

Spell-checking your outgoing messages

Whether you're composing an e-mail message or an SMS text message (see Chapter 8), you can always check your spelling with the built-in spell checker. Simply press the menu key and touch-press Check Spelling.

When it finds an error, the BlackBerry spell checker makes a suggestion. If you want to skip that word and go on to the next, press the escape key. If you want to skip spell checking altogether for an e-mail, press and hold the escape key. (Your Storm does the same type of dotted-underlining as Microsoft Word.)

By default, the spell checker doesn't kick in before you send your message, but you can change that:

1. **Open the Messages application.**

2. **Press the menu key and touch-press Options.**

3. **Touch-press Spell Check.**

4. **Make sure Spell Check EMail Before Sending is checked.**

5. **Press the menu key and touch-press Save.**

Adding a sender to your Contacts

You can add a message sender's contact info to your BlackBerry Contacts directly from Messages. You don't even have to copy or write down the person's name and e-mail address on paper.

To add a sender to your Contacts, follow these steps:

1. **From the Home screen, press the menu key and touch-press Messages.**

2. **Touch-press the e-mail whose sender you want to add to your Contacts list.**

3. **From the opened e-mail, scroll to the sender's name, press the menu key, and then touch-press Add to Contacts.**

   The New Contacts screen opens. The sender's first name, last name, and e-mail address are transferred automatically to your Contacts list.

4. **If needed, add information (such as phone number and mailing address).**

5. **Press the menu key and touch-press Save.**

Deleting e-mail

Keeping your message list tidy can help you stay organized and reduce the amount of memory your e-mail takes.

Cull those messages you no longer need by following these steps:

1. **From the Home screen, touch-press Messages.**

2. **Tap the e-mail you want to delete and touch-press the Delete Message icon at the bottom of the screen.**

   A deletion-confirmation screen appears.

3. **Touch-press Delete to confirm your deletion.**

   The deleted e-mail is toast.

To delete more than one e-mail, tap the first e-mail you want to delete and, while your finger is on that first e-mail, tap the last e-mail you want to delete. This highlights the range of e-mails to delete. When you are happy with your deletion selection, touch-press the Delete Message icon at the bottom of the screen.

You can delete anything listed in the message list (such as an SMS or a voice mail) the same way you delete an e-mail message.

If you want to really clean up your old e-mails and don't want to scroll through tons of messages, you can do the following:

1. **Open the Messages application.**

2. **Tap a horizontal date mark, press the menu key, and touch-press Delete Prior.**

   The *date mark* is simply a horizontal bar with dates. Just as you can highlight e-mails in the message list, you can highlight the date marks.

   A pop-up window prompts you for delete confirmation. Before you take the plunge, remember that going ahead will *delete all the e-mails before the particular date mark.* There is no way to retrieve deleted items from your BlackBerry.

3. **Touch-press Delete to confirm your deletion.**

   All e-mails prior to the date mark are history.

Filtering your e-mail

Most of your e-mail messages aren't urgent. Instead of receiving them on your BlackBerry — and wasting both time and effort — filter them out. While in the BIS client, set up filters to make your BlackBerry mailbox receive only those e-mails that you care about. (Don't worry; you'll still receive them on your main computer.)

The following example creates a simple filter that treats work-related messages as urgent and forwards them to your BlackBerry:

1. **From your BlackBerry Home screen, touch-press the Setup folder.**

2. **Touch-press the Email Settings icon.**

   You are prompted with a login screen similar to Figure 7-1, earlier in this chapter. If you haven't created your account, click the Create button and create your BIS account.

3. **Log in to the BIS client on the BlackBerry.**

   You see the BIS main screen (refer to Figure 7-2, earlier in this chapter).

4. **Touch-press the e-mail account for which you want to set up filters.**

5. **Press the menu key and touch-press Filters.**

   You see a list of filters, if any, and an Add Filter button, as shown in Figure 7-4.

6. **Touch-press the Add Filter button.**

The Add Filter screen appears, as shown in Figure 7-5.

7. Enter a filter name.

The filter name can be anything you like. In Figure 7-5, we entered **To Me**.

Figure 7-4: Filter list screen.

Figure 7-5: Create a filter for your e-mail here.

8. **From the Filter On drop-down list, choose the condition to place on the filter:**

   - High-Priority Mail Email: Select this option if the filter applies only to urgent e-mail.

   - Subject: When this option is selected, the Contains field is enabled and you can type text in it. Specify what keywords the filter will look for in the subject field, separating each entry with a semicolon (;).

   - From Address: When this option is selected, the Contains field is enabled and you can type text in it. Type a full address or part of an address. For example, you can type *rob@robkao.com* or just *kao*. Separate each entry with a semicolon (;).

   - To Address: This option is similar to the From Field Contains option.

   - CC Address: This option is similar to the From Field Contains option.

   This example selects From Address.

9. **Specify the text in the Contains field.**

   See details in the preceding step for what to enter in the Contains field. This example types the domain of your work e-mail address. For example, if your work e-mail address is myName@XYZCo.com, enter **XYZCo.com**.

10. **Select one of the following options for the Action field:**

    Forward Messages to the Device: You can select either or both of the following two check boxes:

    - Header Only: Choose this if you want only the header of the e-mails that meets the condition(s) you set in Steps 7–9 to be sent to you. (A *header* doesn't contain the message — just who sent it, the subject, and the time it was sent.) Choose this if you get automated alerts, for which receiving only the subject is sufficient.

    - Level1 Notification: Level1 notification is another way of saying *urgent e-mail*. A Level1 e-mail is bold in Messages.

    Do Not Forward Message to the Device: Any e-mail that meets the conditions you set in Steps 7–9 doesn't go to your BlackBerry.

11. **Confirm your filter by touch-pressing the Save button.**

    You return to the Filter screen, where you can see your newly created filter in the list.

If you have a hard time setting the criteria for a filter, guesstimate and then check it by having a friend send you a test e-mail. If the test e-mail isn't filtered correctly, set the conditions until you get them right.

Searching Messages Like a Pro

Searching is one of those functions you probably won't use every day — but when you do run a search, you usually need the information fast. Take a few minutes here to familiarize yourself with general searching.

The BlackBerry Messages application provides three ways to search through your messages. Two of the three ways are specific, and one is a broad search:

- **Search by sender or recipient:** Specific. This method assumes that you already know the sender or recipient.
- **Search by subject:** Specific. This approach assumes that you already know the subject.
- **General search:** Broad. You don't have a specific assumption.

You can search through anything listed in the messages list. This means you can search through SMS and voice mail as well as e-mail.

Searching by sender or recipient

Search by sender or recipient when you're looking for a specific message from a specific person. Suppose that your brother constantly sends you e-mail (which means your message list has many entries from him). You're trying to locate a message he sent you about two weeks ago regarding a fishing-trip location. You've scrolled down the message list, but you just can't find that message.

To find a message when you know the sender or recipient, follow these steps:

1. **Open the Messages application.**

2. **Tap a message that you sent to or received from that particular person.**

   The choice you get in the next step depends on whether you highlighted a sent message or a received message.

3. Press the menu key and touch-press one of these options:

- From Someone Specific: Because that certain someone sent you the message, choose Search Sender.

- To Someone Specific: Because you sent that certain someone the message, choose Search Recipient.

The search starts. Any results appear onscreen.

You can shortcut search by sender or recipient by tapping and holding the name in the message list. You can also search by the subject of an e-mail if you tap and hold the subject.

Searching by subject

Search by subject when you're looking for a specifically titled e-mail. As when you're searching by sender or recipient, first scroll to an e-mail bearing the same subject you're searching for. Then follow these steps:

1. Open the Messages application.

2. Highlight an e-mail titled by the subject you're searching for.

3. Press the menu key and touch-press Search Subject.

The search starts, and the results appear onscreen.

You can shortcut search by subject by tapping and holding the subject that you want to search in the message list.

Running a general search

A general search is a broad search from which you can perform keyword searches of your messages. To run a general search:

1. Open the Messages application.

2. Press the menu key and touch-press Search.

The Search screen appears.

3. Fill in your search criteria (see Figure 7-6).

The criteria for a general search follow:

- Name: This is the name of the sender or recipient to search by.

- In: This is related to Name. Use this menu to indicate where the name might appear. Your choices are From, To, Cc, Bcc, and any address field.

- Subject: This is where you type some or all the keywords that appear in the subject.

- Message: Enter keywords that appear in the message.

- Service: If you set up your BlackBerry to receive e-mail from more than one e-mail account, you can specify which e-mail account to search.

- Folder: This is the folder you want to look in. Generally, you should search all folders.

- Show: This list specifies how the search result will appear (namely, whether you want to see only e-mails that you sent or e-mails that you received). Your choices are Sent and Received, Received Only, Sent Only, Saved Only, Draft Only, and Unopened Only.

- Type: This list specifies the type of message you're trying to search for. Your choices are All, EMail, EMail with Attachments, PIN, SMS, Phone, and Voice Mail.

You can set multiple search criteria or a single criterion; it's up to you.

4. **Press the menu key and touch-press Search to launch your search.**

The search results appear onscreen.

Figure 7-6:
The Search screen in Messages.

You can narrow the search results by performing a second search on the initial results. For example, you can search by sender and then narrow those results by performing a second search by subject.

You can also search by sender or recipient when you're looking for a specific message from a specific person. To do so, finger-scroll to an e-mail bearing the specific sender or recipient. Press the menu key and touch-press Search Sender or Search Recipient. If the e-mail you highlighted is an incoming e-mail, you'll see Search Sender. If the e-mail is outgoing, you'll see Search Recipient.

Saving search results

If you find yourself searching with the same criteria over and over, you might want to save the search and then reuse it. Here's how:

1. **Open the Messages application.**

2. **Press the menu key and touch-press Search.**

   The Search screen appears.

3. **Fill in your search criteria.**

   Refer to the "Running a general search" section, earlier in this chapter, for option explanations.

4. **Press the menu key and touch-press Save.**

   The Save Search screen appears (see Figure 7-7). In this screen, you can name your search and assign it a shortcut key.

Figure 7-7:
Name your
search and
assign it a
shortcut
key.

5. **In the Title field, enter a name.**

   The title is the name of your search, which appears in the search result screen.

6. **Touch-press the Shortcut Key field and then touch-press a letter in the drop-down list.**

   You have 20-plus letters to choose among.

7. **Confirm your saved search by pressing the menu key and touch-pressing Save.**

Reusing saved searches

Your BlackBerry comes with five saved search results. Any new saved result makes your search that much more robust.

You can see all saved search results:

1. **Open the Messages application.**
2. **Press the menu key and touch-press Search.**
3. **Press the menu key and touch-press Recall.**

   The recall screen opens, and you can see the seven preloaded search shortcuts, as shown in Figure 7-8.

To reuse one of the saved search results, choose a search from the list (shown in Figure 7-8), press the menu key, and touch-press Search.

To access all your incoming e-mail via shortcut key combination Alt+I, do the following:

1. **Open the Messages application.**
2. **Press the menu key and touch-press Show Keyboard.**
3. **Touch-press the Alt key.**

   The Alt key on the virtual keyboard looks like !?123.

4. **Touch-press the I key.**

   The Messages application will now show only incoming e-mails.

Figure 7-8:
The recall
screen
shows
default
search hot
keys.

Long Live E-Mail

No closet has unlimited space, and your BlackBerry e-mail storage has limits, too. You've likely pondered how long your e-mails are kept in your BlackBerry. (The default is 30 days. Pshew.)

You can choose several options, ranging from 15 days to forever, and because your BlackBerry Storm comes with 1GB of internal memory, it should last you a while!

Because any message you save is kept for as long as you want, saving a message is a good way to make sure you don't lose an important one.

To change how long your e-mails live on your BlackBerry, follow these steps:

1. **Open the Messages application.**

2. **Press the menu key and touch-press Options.**

3. **Touch-press General Options.**

4. **Touch-press Keep Messages and then touch-press Forever.**

   • Forever: If you choose Forever, you'll seldom need to worry about your e-mails being automatically deleted.

   A good way to archive your e-mail is to back up your e-mails by using BlackBerry Desktop Manager. See Chapter 15 for more on backing up your BlackBerry on your PC.

   • Time Option: If you choose a set time option, any message older than that time frame is automatically deleted from your BlackBerry the next time you reboot your BlackBerry. However, it will be deleted only on your BlackBerry — even if you turn on e-mail reconciliation — because these deletions are not completed manually by you.

5. **Confirm your changes by pressing the menu key and touch-pressing Save.**

Chapter 8

Too Cool for E-Mail

In This Chapter

▶ Sending PIN-to-PIN messages

▶ Using SMS and MMS

▶ Setting up and using IM

▶ Figuring out messaging etiquette

*Y*our BlackBerry is primarily a communication tool, with e-mail messages and phone conversations as the major drivers. It's a wonderful technology, but sometimes, another means of communication is more appropriate. For instance, e-mail isn't the tool of choice when you want to send a message instantly or when you want to alert someone to something.

Your BlackBerry offers some less-obvious ways to communicate — ways that may serve as the perfect fit for a special situation. In this chapter, you get the scoop on PIN-to-PIN messaging and text messaging (also known as *Short Message Service,* or *SMS*). We also give you tips on how to turn your BlackBerry into a lean (and not-so-mean) instant messaging (IM) machine.

Sending and Receiving PIN-to-PIN Messages

PIN-to-PIN messaging is based on the technology that underpins two-way pager systems. Unlike sending a standard e-mail, when you send a BlackBerry PIN-to-PIN message, the message doesn't venture outside the RIM infrastructure in search of an e-mail server and (eventually) an e-mail inbox. Instead, it stays solidly in the RIM world, where it is shunted through the recipient's network provider until it ends up in the recipient's BlackBerry.

A little bit of RIM history

Sometime during the last millennium, Research In Motion (RIM) wasn't even in the phone business. Before BlackBerry became all the rage with smart phone features, RIM was doing a tidy little business with its wireless e-mail.

Back then, RIM's primitive wireless e-mail service was served by network service providers on a radio bandwidth: DataTAC and Mobitex networks. These were separate from a typical cellphone infrastructure's bandwidth.

RIM devices at that time already had PIN-to-PIN messaging. This type of messaging is akin to a pager, where a message doesn't live in a mailbox but is sent directly to the BlackBerry with no delay. (No one wants a paging system that moves at turtle speed when you can get one that moves like a jackrabbit, right?)

Several interesting facts followed from RIM's initial decision. Of note, most cellphone users in New York City were left without service during the 9/11 disaster. The entire cellphone infrastructure in New York and surrounding areas was overwhelmed with too many people trying to use the available bandwidth. However, one communication device continued to work during that stressful time: RIM's PIN-to-PIN messaging kept the information flow going.

So when you use PIN-to-PIN messaging, that's another way of saying *sending a message from one BlackBerry to another BlackBerry.*

PIN stands for *personal identification number* (familiar to anyone who's ever used an ATM) and refers to a system for uniquely identifying your device.

Here's the neat part. According to RIM, the message isn't saved anywhere in this universe *except* on the one device that sends the PIN message and the other device that receives it. Compare that with an e-mail, which is saved in at least four locations (both the sender and recipient's e-mail clients and e-mail servers), not to mention all the system's redundancies and backups employed by the server. Think of it this way: If you whisper a little secret in someone's ear, only you and that special someone know what was said. In a way, PIN-to-PIN messaging is the same thing, with one BlackBerry whispering to another BlackBerry. Now, that's discreet.

If you tend to read the financial newspapers — especially the ones that cover corporate lawsuits extensively — you'll know that there's no such thing as privacy in e-mail. PIN-to-PIN messaging, in theory at least, is as good as the old Code of Silence. Now, is such privacy an advantage? You can argue both sides of the issue, depending on what you want to use PIN-to-PIN messaging for.

Basically, if you like the idea that your communications can be kept discreet, PIN-to-PIN messaging has great curb appeal. If you don't care about privacy issues, you still may be impressed by PIN-to-PIN messaging's zippy nature. (It really is the Ferrari of wireless communication — way faster than e-mail.)

The Code of Silence in an enterprise environment has always been a thorny issue in companies with strict regulatory requirements. As expected, RIM addressed this issue with a new feature in later operating systems allowing BlackBerry Enterprise Server administrators to flip a flag, forcing the device to forward all PIN-to-PIN messages to the BlackBerry Enterprise Server. A company can also install on the device third-party applications to report PIN-to-PIN messages.

Getting a BlackBerry PIN

When you try to call someone on the telephone, you can't get far without a telephone number. As you may expect, the same principle applies to PIN-to-PIN messaging: no PIN, no PIN-to-PIN messaging.

In practical terms, you need the PIN of any BlackBerry to which you want to send a PIN message. (You also need to find out your own PIN so that you can hand it out to folks who want to PIN-message you.)

The cautious side of you may wonder why on earth you'd give your PIN to someone. Here's the difference: Unlike a PIN for an ATM account, this PIN isn't your password. In fact, this PIN doesn't give anyone access to your BlackBerry or do anything to compromise security. It's simply an ID; think of it like a phone number.

Here are two quick paths to PIN enlightenment:

 ✔ **From the Message screen:** Send your PIN from the Message screen with the help of a keyword. When you type a preset word, your BlackBerry replaces what you type with a bit of information specific to your device.

 Sound wacky? It's easier than it sounds:

   a. **Compose a new message.**

   If you need a refresher on the whole e-mail message and messaging thing, visit Chapter 7.

   b. **In the subject or body of your message, type** Mypin **and add a space.**

   See the left side of Figure 8-1. As soon as you type the space, `Mypin` is miraculously transformed into your PIN in the format `pin:your-pin-number`, as shown on the right side of Figure 8-1. Isn't that neat? ***Note:*** Case doesn't matter here.

Mypin isn't the only keyword that RIM predefines for you. mynumber and myver give you the phone number and OS version, respectively, of your BlackBerry Storm.

✔ **From the Status screen:** You can also find your PIN on the Status screen. From the Home screen, touch-press Options and then touch-press Status. Figure 8-2 shows a typical Status screen. (The PIN is fourth in the list of items.)

 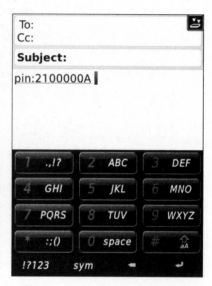

Figure 8-1: Type a keyword (left) and add a space, and the keyword is translated (right).

Figure 8-2: Find your PIN on the Status screen.

Assigning PINs to names

So you convince your BlackBerry-wielding buddies to go to the trouble of finding out their PINs and passing said PINs to you. Now the trick is finding a convenient place to store those PINs so you can use them. Luckily for you, you have an obvious choice: BlackBerry Contacts. And RIM, in its infinite wisdom, makes storing such info a snap. To add a PIN to someone's contact info in Contacts, do the following:

1. **From the BlackBerry Home screen, touch-press Contacts.**

   Contacts opens.

2. **Touch a contact name, press the menu key, and then touch-press Edit.**

   The Edit Contact screen for the contact name you touch-pressed makes an appearance.

3. **On the Edit Contact screen, slide up to scroll down to the PIN field (as shown in Figure 8-3).**

4. **Type the PIN.**

5. **Press the menu key and then touch-press Save.**

   The edit you made for the contact is saved.

It's that simple. Of course, it's even easier if you think ahead and enter the PIN information you have when you set up your initial contact info (by using the New Contact screen), but we understand that a PIN isn't the kind of information people carry around.

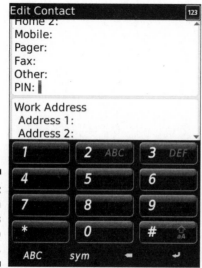

Figure 8-3:
Add a
contact's
PIN info
here.

If all this talk about New Contact screens and Edit Contact screens doesn't sound familiar, check out Chapter 4, which covers the Contacts application in more detail.

Sending a PIN-to-PIN message

PIN-to-PIN just means *from one BlackBerry to another.*

Sending a PIN-to-PIN message is no different from sending an e-mail. Here's how:

1. **From the BlackBerry Home screen, touch-press Contacts.**

2. **Touch a contact name and then press the menu key.**

   If a contact has a PIN, you see a menu item titled PIN *<contact name>*. Say, for example, you have a contact named Rob Kao. When you touch Dante Sarigumba in the list and then press the menu key, the menu item PIN Rob Kao appears as an option, as shown in Figure 8-4.

3. **Touch-press PIN *<contact name>* on the menu.**

   You see the ever-familiar New Message screen.

4. **Enter the rest of the text fields — subject, message, and signature text — just as you would with an e-mail.**

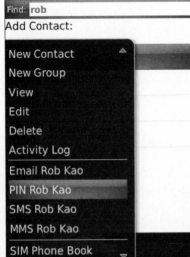

Figure 8-4:
Send a PIN
message
via your
Contacts.

Find: **rob**

Add Contact:

New Contact
New Group
View
Edit
Delete
Activity Log
Email Rob Kao
PIN Rob Kao
SMS Rob Kao
MMS Rob Kao
SIM Phone Book

Alternatively, if you know the PIN, you can type it directly. Here's how:

1. **From the BlackBerry Home screen, touch-press Messages.**

   The Messages application opens.

2. **Press the menu key and touch-press Compose PIN.**

   The New Message screen makes an appearance.

3. **Type the PIN in the To field.**

4. **Add a subject line, the message, and signature, just like you would in an e-mail.**

Unlike when you send an e-mail, when you send a PIN-to-PIN message, you can tell almost instantly whether the recipient got your message. In the Messages list, the letter *D* (for *delivered*) appears on top of the check mark next to the PIN-to-PIN message you sent.

Because of the nature of PIN-to-PIN messaging (the conspicuous lack of a paper trail, as it were), companies can disable PIN-to-PIN messaging on your BlackBerry device. (No paper trail can mean legal problems down the road — can you say *Sarbanes-Oxley?*)

Receiving a PIN-to-PIN message

Receiving a PIN-to-PIN message is no different from receiving a standard e-mail. You get the same entry in your Messages list for the PIN-to-PIN message, and the same screen appears when you open the message.

By default, your BlackBerry vibrates to alert you, but you can change this behavior by changing your profile. (Check out Chapter 3 for details.) When you reply to the message, the reply is a PIN-to-PIN message as well.

Keeping in Touch the SMS/MMS Way

Short Message Service (also known as *SMS,* or *text messaging*) is so popular that you've probably seen TV shows asking for your feedback via SMS. Multimedia Messaging Service (MMS) is a much later evolution of SMS. Rather than sending a simple text message, you can also send someone an audio or a video clip.

How short is *short?* The maximum size per message is about 160 characters. If you send more than that, it gets broken down into multiple messages.

SMS is an established technology (not a new and unproven thing, in other words) that's been popular for years in Europe and Asia.

Text messaging does pose a challenge for beginners. It isn't tough; it's just cumbersome to type the letters on a small virtual keyboard and keep up with the conversation. Also, you need to know the trends and options for text messaging. In-the-know folks use abbreviations that may be difficult for you to understand in the beginning, so don't dive in without your oxygen tank.

A quick preparation goes a long way toward avoiding being labeled uncool when it comes to your SMS syntax. The upcoming sections help smooth your path a bit by filling you in on the basics of SMS-speak.

Using shorthand for speedy replies

On a regular cellphone, three letters share a single key. Typing even a single paragraph can be a real pain.

Human ingenuity prevails. Abbreviations cut down on the amount of text you need to enter. *Texting* (short for *text messaging)* language is fashionable, especially among the 14–18-year-old set. Veteran text messagers (the hip ones, at least) can easily spot someone who's new to SMS technology by how that person doesn't use the right lingo — or uses such lingo incorrectly.

AWHFY?

In text messaging, the challenge lies in using abbreviations to craft a sentence with as few letters as possible. Because text messaging has been around for a number of years, plenty of folks have risen to this challenge by coming up with a considerable pool of useful abbreviations. Don't feel that you have to rush out and memorize the whole shorthand dictionary at once, though.

As with mastering a new language, start with the most commonly used words or sentences. When you become familiar with those, slowly gather in more and more terms. In time, the language will be second nature.

Table 8-1 gives you our take on the most common abbreviations, which are enough to get you started. With these under your belt, you can at least follow the most important parts of an SMS conversation. Feel free to check out the Web site associated with this book (www.blackberryfordummies.com) for a more comprehensive list of shorthand abbreviations.

Table 8-1		SMS Shorthand and Its Meanings	
Shorthand	*Meaning*	*Shorthand*	*Meaning*
2D4	To die for	CUL8R	See you later
2G4U	Too good for you	CUS	See you soon
2L8	Too late	F2F	Face to face
4E	Forever	FC	Fingers crossed
4YEO	For your eyes only	FCFS	First come, first served
A3	Any time, anywhere, anyplace	FOAF	Friend of a friend
AFAIK	As far as I know	FWIW	For what it's worth
ASAP	As soon as possible	GAL	Get a life
ASL	Age, sex, location	GG	Good game
ATM	At the moment	GR8	Great
ATW	At the weekend	GSOH	Good sense of humor
AWHFY	Are we having fun yet?	H2CUS	Hope to see you soon
B4	Before	IC	I see
BBFN	Bye-bye for now	IDK	I don't know
BBL	Be back later	IMHO	In my honest opinion
BBS	Be back soon	IMO	In my opinion
BCNU	Be seeing you	IOU	I owe you
BG	Big grin	IOW	In other words
BION	Believe it or not	KISS	Keep it simple, stupid
BOL	Best of luck	LOL	Laughing out loud
BOT	Back on topic	OIC	Oh, I see
BRB	Be right back	RUOK	Are you okay?
BRT	Be right there	W4U	Waiting for you
BTW	By the way	W8	Wait
CMON	Come on	WTG	Way to go
CU	See you	TOM	Tomorrow

Showing some emotion

Written words can get folks into trouble every now and then; the same words can mean different things to different people. A simple example is the phrase "You're clueless." When you speak such a phrase with the appropriate facial and hand gestures, your friend knows that you're teasing and that it's all a bit of fun. Write that same phrase in a text message, and . . . well, you may get a nasty reply — which you then have to respond to, which prompts another response, and soon enough, you've just ended a seven-year friendship.

SMS is akin to chatting, so *emoticons* show what you mean when you write "You're clueless." (I'm joking! I'm happy! I'm mad!) These cutesy codes help you telegraph your meaning in sledgehammer-to-the-forehead fashion.

We're talking smileys here — those combinations of keyboard characters that, when artfully combined, resemble a human face. The most popular example — one that you've probably encountered in e-mails from especially chirpy individuals — is the happy face, which (usually at the end of a statement) conveys good intentions or happy context, like this :). (Tilt your head to the left to see the face.)

Table 8-2 shows you the range of smiley choices. Just remember that smileys are supposed to be fun. They could be the one thing you need to make sure that your "gently teasing remark" isn't seen as a hateful comment. Smileys help, but if you aren't sure if what you're about to send can be misconstrued even with the help of the smileys, just don't send it.

Your BlackBerry Storm also comes with a handful of smileys. While you're on the conversation or chat screen, press the menu key and touch-press Add Smiley to choose an available smiley.

Table 8-2	Smileys and Their Meanings		
Smiley	*Meaning*	*Smiley*	*Meaning*
:)	Happy, smiling	:(	Sad, frown
:-)	Happy, smiling, with nose	:-(	Sad, frown, with nose
:D	Laughing	:-<	Super sad
:-D	Laughing, with nose	:'-(	Crying

Smiley	Meaning	Smiley	Meaning
:'-)	Tears due to laughter	:-0	Yell, gasped
:-)8	Smiling with bow tie	:-@	Scream, what?
;)	Winking	:-(o)	Shouting
;-)	Winking, with nose	|-0	Yawn
0:-)	I'm an angel (male)	:----(	Liar, long nose
0*-)	I'm an angel (female)	%-(	Confused
8-)	Cool, with sun- glasses	:-|	Determined
:-!	Foot in mouth	:-()	Talking
>-)	Evil grin	:-ozz	Bored
:-x	Kiss on the lips	@@	Eyes
(((H)))	Hugs	%-)	Cross-eyed
@>--;--	Rose	|@@|	Face
:p	Tongue out	#:-)	Hair is a mess
;b	Tongue out with a wink	&:-)	Hair is curly
:-&	Tongue tied	$-)	Yuppie
-!-	Sleepy	:-($)	Put your money where your mouth is
<3	Heart, or love	<(^(oo)^)>	Pig

Shorthand and smileys may not be appreciated in business. Use them appropriately.

Sending a text message

After you have the shorthand stuff and smileys under control, get your fingers pumped up and ready for action: It's message-sending time! Whether it's SMS or MMS, here's how to do it:

1. **From the BlackBerry Home screen, touch-press Contacts.**

2. **Touch-press a contact that has a mobile phone number.**

   SMS works only on mobile phones.

3. **Press the menu key and touch-press SMS (or MMS) *<contact name>*.**

   The menu item for SMS or MMS knows enough to display the name of the contact. For example, if you choose John Doe, the menu item reads `SMS John Doe` or `MMS John Doe`, as shown in Figure 8-5.

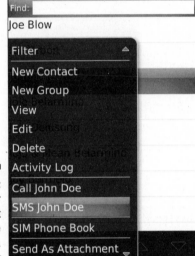

Figure 8-5:
Start your
text
message
here.

4. **If you choose MMS, browse your multimedia folders, and touch-press the audio or video file you want to send.**

   When you're choosing MMS, this extra step allows you to choose the multimedia file, which is the only difference from composing an SMS message.

5. **Type your message.**

   Remember that shorthand business? You should start taking advantage of it the first chance you get. (Practice makes perfect.)

6. **Press the menu key and then touch-press Send.**

   Your message is sent on its merry way.

Messaging etiquette and a few words of caution

Here are some commonsense messaging rules as well as a few words of caution. Even if you're new to messaging, being a neophyte doesn't give you license to act like a jerk. Play nice and take the following pointers to heart:

✔ **Use smileys to avoid misunderstandings.** Read more about emoticons and smileys in this chapter.

✔ **Don't ever forward chain letters.** We mean it. Never.

✔ **If you need to forward a message, check the entire message content first.** Make sure nothing offends the recipient.

✔ **Some things in this world need to be said face to face, so don't even think of using messaging for it.** Ever try dumping your girlfriend or boyfriend over the phone? Guess what? Using messaging is far worse.

✔ **Keep your tone gender neutral.** Some messages that are forwarded through e-mails are inappropriate to the opposite sex.

✔ **Capital letters are as rude as shouting, so _DON'T USE THEM._**

✔ **Know your recipient.** A newbie might not easily grasp smileys and shorthand at first, so act accordingly. (Read more about shorthand in this chapter.)

✔ **Don't reply to any message when you're angry.** You can't unsend a sent message. It's better to be prudent than sorry.

✔ **Don't gossip or be rude.** Beware! Your messages can end up in the wrong hands and haunt you in the future.

✔ **Easy does it.** No documented evidence reveals the deleterious effects (physical or psychological) of too much texting. However, don't text as if you want to enter the books as the first recorded case of Instantmessagingitis. As your great-grandma would tell you, too much of anything is bad for you. It's easy to lose track of time when IMing.

✔ **Drive safely.** Tuck away your BlackBerry whenever you're in the driver's seat.

Viewing a message you receive

If you have an incoming SMS or MMS message, you get a notification just like you do when you receive an e-mail. Also like e-mail, the e-mail icon at the top of the Home screen indicates a new message. Viewing an SMS or MMS message is the same as reading an e-mail. The basic run-through is as follows:

1. **Touch-press Messages from the Home screen.**

2. **Touch-press the unread message.**

   Bob's your uncle: The message appears onscreen.

Customize how your BlackBerry notifies you when you receive an SMS message. See Chapter 3 for more details.

You can tell your BlackBerry to separate SMS messages from e-mail messages:

1. **Touch-press Messages from the Home screen.**
2. **Press the menu key and touch-press Options.**
3. **Touch-press General Options.**
4. **Touch-press the SMS and Email Inboxes selections.**
5. **Touch-press Separate.**
6. **Press the escape key and touch-press Save.**

    An icon for SMS appears on the Home screen.

Always Online Using Instant Messaging

Real-time (as they happen) conversations with your friends over the Internet are possible with IM (instant messaging). IM enables two or more people to send and receive messages over the Internet. Instant messaging started with pure text messages and evolved into a rich medium involving voice and even video conversation in real time.

IM may not be available on your BlackBerry Storm. Service providers choose whether to include it. However, you can add IM to your BlackBerry:

1. **Touch-press Browser from the home screen.**
2. **Press the menu key and touch-press Go To.**
3. **Enter** `http://mobile.blackberry.com` **and touch-press Go.**
4. **Navigate to IM and Social Networking.**

    Here, you'll find download links for all the free applications for the popular IM networks and also a download link for BlackBerry Messenger. (Chapter 9 covers BlackBerry Messenger.)

Chatting using IM rules

When you're IMing — that's right; it's a verb — you can tell lots of things:

- When someone's typing a message to you
- Whether your buddies are online

✔ When your buddies are away from their computers

✔ When your buddies are simply too busy to be interrupted at the moment

IM adds a totally different slant on long-distance communication, opening a wide array of possibilities — possibilities that can be used for good (team collaboration) or ill (mindless gossip), depending on the situation.

As you may expect, IM is great for both personal and business applications. Whether you're maintaining friendships or working to create new ones, IM is definitely one powerful tool to consider adding to your social-skills toolbox.

Instant messaging on your BlackBerry

Most network providers dish out the three most popular IM services to their BlackBerry customers:

✔ Google Talk

✔ Yahoo! (Y!) Messenger

✔ Windows Live Messenger

Those three IM programs aren't the only popular ones. Here are a few more:

✔ AOL Instant Messenger (AIM)

✔ ICQ Instant Messenger

✔ iChat AV (on the Macintosh)

✔ Jabber (open source)

If you're using an IM network that isn't preloaded, you can always check the RIM Web site to download the applications at `mobile.blackberry.com`. On this page, go to IM and Social Networking. The list of IM applications should be listed on the next page with a link for download.

IM basics: What you need

Assuming that you have the IM application available on your BlackBerry, you need just two things to start using the standard five IM programs:

✔ User ID

✔ Password

Getting a user ID/password combo is a breeze. Just go to the appropriate registration Web page (from the following list) for the IM application(s) you want to use. Note that it's easier and faster to use your desktop or laptop to sign up.

- ✔ Google Talk: `www.google.com/accounts/NewAccount?service=talk`
- ✔ AOL Instant Messenger (AIM): `https://reg.my.screenname.aol.com/_cqr/registration/initRegistration.psp`
- ✔ ICQ Instant Messenger: `www.icq.com/register`
- ✔ Windows Live Messenger: `http://messenger.msn.com/download/getstarted.aspx`
- ✔ Yahoo! Messenger: `http://edit.yahoo.com/config/eval_register?.src=pg&.done=http://messenger.yahoo.com`

Given the many IM network choices available, your friends are probably signed up on a bunch of different networks. You might end up having to sign up for multiple networks if you want to reach them all via IM.

Although Twitter may not fall under the umbrella of instant messaging services in the traditional sense, it is quickly becoming the communication medium of choice for millions of people. Several free and premium Twitter clients have emerged. TwitterBerry was the first and maintains a loyal user base, but I recommend checking out UberTwitter, TweetGenius, or SocialScope for your Twitter needs. When you're all set up, be sure to send me a tweet at `@crackberrykevin` and say hi!

Going online with IM

After you obtain the user ID/password combo for one (or more) IM services, you can use your BlackBerry to start chatting with your buddies by following these steps:

1. **From the BlackBerry Home screen, touch-press the IM application of your choice.**

   To illustrate how to do this, we use Google Talk. An application-specific login screen appears for you to sign on, similar to the one in Figure 8-6. It's straightforward, with the standard screen name (also called a user name or ID) line and password line.

2. **Enter your screen name/ID and password.**

Google Talk

Google
talk BETA

Username:

Password:

Sign In

☑ Remember password
☑ Automatically sign me in

Need an account?
Go to google.com/accounts on your computer.
Forgot your password?

Figure 8-6:
Login
screen for
Google Talk.

3. **If you want, touch-press the Remember Password check box. Also if you want, touch-press the Automatically Sign Me In check box.**

   When the Remember Password check box is enabled, the ID/password information is preentered the next time you come back to this screen. (Um, that is, you don't have to type this stuff every time you want to IM.)

   We recommend that you touch-press this check box to save time but also set your smart phone password to Enabled so that security isn't compromised. Refer to Chapter 3 if you need a refresher on how to enable passwords on your BlackBerry.

   The Automatically Sign Me In check box turns on and off sign-in when your BlackBerry Storm is powered up. This is helpful if you have a habit of turning off your BlackBerry periodically.

4. **Press the menu key and touch-press Sign In.**

   At this point, IM tries to log you in. This can take a few seconds, during which time the screen reads `Sending request to AOL` or something similar while it's in this phase. After you're logged in, a simple listing of your contacts, or buddies, appears onscreen.

5. **Touch-press the person you'd like to chat with.**

   A menu appears, listing various things you can do. Features could differ a bit for each IM application, but for Google Talk, here's a sample of what you can do: Start Chat, Send File, Add a Friend, Rename, Remove, and Block.

6. **Touch-press the action you'd like to take.**

Adding a contact, buddy, or friend

A contact may be referred to as contact, buddy, or friend in the IM app. But before you can start chatting with your contacts, you need to know their user IDs. See Table 8-3.

Table 8-3	Getting a Friend's Credentials
Provider	*Where You Get Someone's User ID*
AOL Instant Messenger	Your friend or by searching AOL's directory
Google Talk	The text before the @ sign in his or her Google e-mail address
ICQ Instant Messenger	Your friend's e-mail or the ICQ Global Directory
Windows Live Messenger	MSN Passport ID or Hotmail ID
Yahoo! Messenger	The text before the @ sign in his or her Yahoo! e-mail address

Luckily for you, you don't need to search for an ID every time you want to IM someone. You can store IDs as part of a contacts list. Follow these steps:

1. **Starting within the IM service of your choice, press the menu key.**

2. **Touch-press the Add a Friend option, which is shown in Figure 8-7.**

   The Add a Friend screen appears.

3. **Enter the user ID of your contact on the Add a Friend screen.**

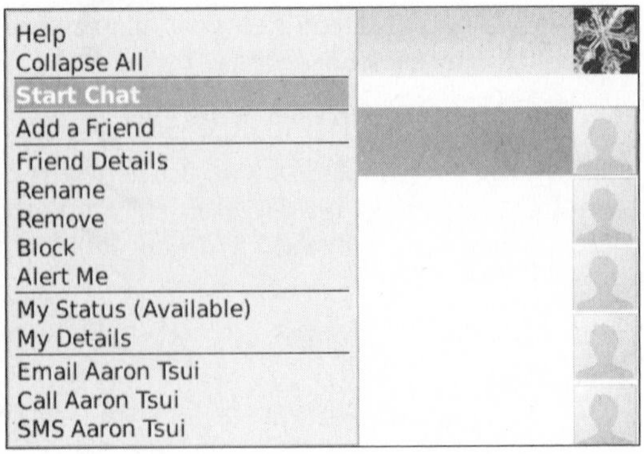

Figure 8-7: Adding a friend.

Help
Collapse All
Start Chat
Add a Friend
Friend Details
Rename
Remove
Block
Alert Me
My Status (Available)
My Details
Email Aaron Tsui
Call Aaron Tsui
SMS Aaron Tsui

4. **Touch-press OK.**

   IM is smart enough to figure out whether this contact has a valid user ID. If the ID is valid, the application adds the ID to your list of contacts. The buddy goes either to the Online or Offline section of your list, depending on whether he or she is logged in. If the ID you entered isn't valid, you are warned.

Doing the chat thing

Suppose you want to start a conversation with one of your contacts (a safe assumption, we think). When you send a message within the IM application, you're initiating a conversation. Here's how:

1. **Log in to the IM application of your choice.**

2. **Touch-press the person you want to contact.**

   A typical online chat screen shows up. The top portion lists old messages sent to and received from this contact. You type your message at the bottom part of the screen.

3. **Type your message.**

4. **Touch-press the enter key.**

   Your user ID and the message you just sent show up in the topmost (history) section of the chat screen. When you get a message, it's added to the history section so that both sides of your conversation stay in view.

Sending your smile

You can quickly add emoticons to your message (without having to remember all the character equivalents in Table 8-2, earlier in this chapter). Follow these steps:

1. **While you're typing your message, press the menu key.**

2. **On the menu that appears, touch-press Add Smiley.**

   A screen appears displaying all the icons.

3. **Touch-press the emoticon you want.**

   The emoticon is added to your message.

Taking control of your IM app

If you use IM frequently — and you tend to chat with many contacts at the same time — your BlackBerry's physical limitations may cramp your IM style.

It's no doubt slower to type words on the tiny virtual keypad than it is to type on your PC.

Do you just give up on the dream of IMing on the go? Not necessarily. The following sections show how you can power up your BlackBerry IM technique.

When less is more

If you can't keep up with all your buddies, your best bet is to limit your exposure. Take a whack at your contacts list so that only your true friends remain as contacts whom you want to IM from your BlackBerry. Trimming your list is easy. To delete a contact from your IM application, highlight the contact from the main screen of the IM application, press the menu key, and touch-press Delete.

Deleting a contact or buddy from an IM application on your BlackBerry also deletes the person from the desktop or laptop computer version of the app. That's because the list of contacts is maintained at a central location — an IM server, to be precise — and not on your BlackBerry.

Set up two accounts of your favorite IM application: one for your BlackBerry and one for your desktop PC. By using these accounts separately, you can limit the number of contacts you have on your BlackBerry and still maintain a full-blown list of contacts on your desktop.

SMS versus connecting via the Web

SMS messages are short messages designed for cellphones. IM is a step up, evolving from the Internet, where bandwidth is no longer a concern. IM provides a better real-time conversation experience across distances. These two technologies evolved in parallel. As more people use IM, it becomes apparent that this technology has a place in smart phones, in which mobility is an advantage. Some of the IM programs used in the BlackBerry in the past use SMS behind the scenes. And because your BlackBerry can connect to the Internet, other programs use the Internet directly. These differences can affect your monthly bill as well as your messaging experience. Read on.

If you don't have unlimited SMS but have an unlimited data plan, be careful with any third-party IM software. Make sure that it uses the Internet instead of SMS. If it uses SMS, you'll incur charges for every message sent and received. Most network providers charge 20 cents for every SMS message, which can add up quickly and lead to a nasty surprise on your monthly bill.

Chapter 9

Instant Messaging

- -

In This Chapter

▶ Adding contacts

▶ Chatting

▶ Sending files

▶ Broadcasting your message

- -

*I*n Chapter 8, you find a slew of ways to send messages on your BlackBerry Storm. In this chapter, you get the scoop on another way to send messages, using a special application known and loved by BlackBerry.

RIM has entered the IM (instant message) horse race in the form of a spirited filly named (you guessed it) BlackBerry Messenger. This application is based on the PIN-to-PIN messaging technology (refer to Chapter 8), which means that it is mucho fast and quite reliable.

However, with BlackBerry Messenger, you can chat with only those buddies who have a BlackBerry and also have PIN-to-PIN messaging enabled. The application supports IM features common to many other applications, such as group chatting and the capability to monitor the availability of other IM buddies.

Accessing BlackBerry Messenger

You access BlackBerry Messenger in the Applications folder from the Home screen, as shown in Figure 9-1. The first time you run BlackBerry Messenger, a welcome screen asks you to enter your display name. This display name is the one you want other people see in BlackBerry Messenger when you send them a message.

Figure 9-1: Launch BlackBerry Messenger here.

Using BlackBerry Messenger

The next time you open BlackBerry Messenger, you see a contacts list, as shown on the left in Figure 9-2. (Okay, the picture here displays some contacts, but your list should be empty; we'll show you how to populate the list in a minute.)

Consider this a friendly warning rather than a tip. After you have BlackBerry Messenger in your life, it's difficult to live without it. Because it's always connected and you can see when messages have been successfully delivered and read, it's the ultimate form of text-based communication.

 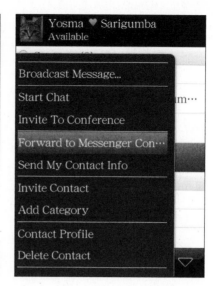

Figure 9-2:
The
BlackBerry
Messenger
contacts list
(left) and
menu (right).

Pressing the menu key lets you do the following, as shown on the right side of Figure 9-2:

- ✔ **Broadcast Message:** Send a message to multiple contacts in your BlackBerry Messenger. The messages appear as conversations in the recipients' BlackBerry Messenger.

- ✔ **Start Chat:** Initiate a conversation with the currently highlighted contact.

- ✔ **Invite To Conference:** Initiate a group conversation. See the later section "Starting a group conversation" for details.

- ✔ **Forward to Messenger Contact:** Send the currently highlighted contact information to your other BlackBerry Messenger contacts.

- ✔ **Invite Contact:** Add a new contact to BlackBerry Messenger. See the next section.

- ✔ **Add Category:** Create custom groupings within your BlackBerry Messenger.

- ✔ **Contact Profile:** Display a screen showing the information of the currently highlighted contact.

  🖛 **Delete Contact:** Delete the currently highlighted contact.

  🖛 **Move Contact:** Delete the currently highlighted contact.

The menu has more items not shown on the right side of Figure 9-2. Finger-scroll down the menu screen to see the following:

  🖛 **My Profile:** Customize your personal information and control how you want others to see you from their BlackBerry Messenger contacts list. You can set the following (see Figure 9-3):

   • Change your picture. Simply tap the default image, navigate to your picture, finger-scroll the picture to center your face in the square, press the menu key, and then touch-press Crop and Save.

   • Change your display name.

   • Allow others to see the title of the song you're currently listening to.

   • Allow others to see that you're currently using the phone.

   • Enter a personal message that others can see.

   • Set your time zone.

   • Allow others to see your location and time-zone information.

   • Display your barcode.

Figure 9-3:
The top
of the My
Profile
screen
(left) and
the rest of
the screen
(right).

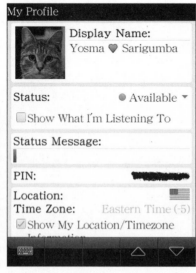

✔ **Options:** Customize the behavior of your BlackBerry Messenger.

✔ **Back Up Contacts List:** Save your list of BlackBerry Messenger contacts to the file system. The location defaults to the media card, but the screen that follows after you touch-press this option allows you to select a different folder and enter a different name for the backup file.

✔ **Restore Contacts List:** Restore your list of BlackBerry Messenger contacts from the file you created from the Back Up Contacts List.

✔ **Delete Backup Files:** Delete a backup file. If you have multiple backups, this option allows you to choose which file to delete.

✔ **Add New Group:** Create custom groupings for your contacts.

This option is helpful if you have a lot of contacts in BlackBerry Messenger. Simply touch-press this menu item, and an Add Group screen appears so you can enter a group name.

✔ **Scan a Group Barcode:** Add members to the open group by scanning your friend's BlackBerry barcode.

Adding a Contact

With no one in your contacts list, BlackBerry Messenger is a pretty useless item. Your first order of business is to add a contact to your list — someone you know who

✔ Has a BlackBerry

✔ Is entered in your contacts list

✔ Has PIN-to-PIN messaging enabled

✔ Has a copy of BlackBerry Messenger installed on his or her device

If you know someone who fits these criteria, you can add that person to your list by doing the following:

1. **In BlackBerry Messenger, press the menu key.**

2. **Touch-press Add a Contact.**

   The screen on the left side of Figure 9-4 appears, listing actions related to adding a contact. The top two options are the ones you use to add a contact to BlackBerry Messenger.

Figure 9-4:
The many
ways to add
a contact
(left) and an
invitation
barcode
(right).

3. **If you want to scan your friend's BlackBerry barcode:**

   a. **On the same screen (Figure 9-4, left) on your friend's BlackBerry, touch-press the third option, which says Show Your Invitation Barcode to Another BlackBerry.**

      A barcode image similar to the right side of Figure 9-4 appears on your friend's BlackBerry.

   b. **On your BlackBerry Storm, touch-press the second option, Scan Invitation Barcode from Another BlackBerry.**

      A Camera application appears for you to capture the barcode. Once captured, the contact information is immediately added to your BlackBerry Messenger contacts list.

   That's it. You're finished. The following steps show how to enter your contact directly from the Add Contact screen.

4. **If instead you want to enter the contact's e-mail address or BlackBerry PIN:**

   a. **Touch-press Enter a Person's Email Address, PIN, or Name.**

      The Invite Contact screen appears.

   b. **Start typing the name of the contact, and when a list of the possible contacts appears, touch-press the name you want to add.**

      BlackBerry sends the request to the potential contact with the message you see in Figure 9-5. You can edit this message.

c. **Type your message.**

d. **Touch-press OK and then touch-press OK again in the screen that follows.**

The application sends your request. As long as the person hasn't responded to your request, his or her name appears as part of the Pending group, as shown in Figure 9-6. When your contact responds positively to your request, the name goes to the official contacts list.

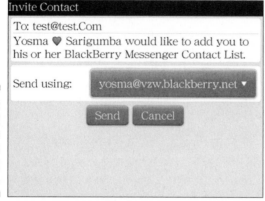

Figure 9-5: Potential contacts are asked before being added.

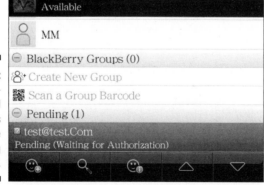

Figure 9-6: To-be-approved contacts are in the Pending group.

Having Conversations

You come to this point because what you really want to do is chat with your friends with BlackBerry Messenger. The short sections here give you a quick rundown on starting individual or group conversations. We also throw in some steps on sharing files and saving your conversation history.

Starting a conversation

You can easily start a conversation with any of your contacts. Follow these steps:

1. **On the BlackBerry Messenger main menu, touch-press the name in your contacts list.**

   A traditional chat interface opens, with a list of old messages at the top and a text box for typing messages at the bottom.

2. **Type your message.**

3. **Touch-press the enter key.**

   Any messages you send (as well as any responses you get) are appended to the history list at the top.

Starting a group conversation

You can also invite others to your BlackBerry Messenger conversation. Follow these steps:

1. **During a conversation, press the menu key.**

   The BlackBerry Messenger main menu appears. This time, an Invite option has been added.

2. **Touch-press Invite to Group Chat.**

   The Select Contacts screen opens, listing your BlackBerry Messenger contacts who are currently available (see Figure 9-7).

3. **Invite people to the chat by touch-pressing the corresponding check boxes.**

   You can choose any number of people.

4. Touch-press OK.

You're back to the preceding conversation screen, but this time the history list shows the contacts you added to the conversation. The newly selected contact(s) can now join the conversation.

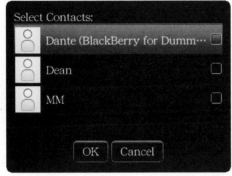

Figure 9-7:
See your
available
contacts
here.

You can set a subject on your message. This is especially useful for group conversations:

1. Press the menu key while you're in the conversation screen and then touch-press Set Subject.

On the screen that follows, the cursor is in the subject line, waiting for you to enter a subject (see Figure 9-8)

2. Enter the subject and then touch-press OK.

The conversation screen is updated with the subject.

Figure 9-8:
Add a
subject
to your
conversation
here.

You can make your name appear snazzy by adding symbols, such as Dante☺ and Yosma✆ (see Figure 9-9):

1. **On the BlackBerry Messenger screen, press the menu key.**

2. **Touch-press Edit My Info.**

3. **Press the menu key and touch-press Add Smiley to choose the symbol you want.**

Figure 9-9:
Add
symbols
to your
name here.

Sending a file

BlackBerry Messenger, like any other instant messaging application, can send files. While on a conversation, just press the menu key, and you'll see several menu items allowing you to share a file:

✔ **Send Picture:** Displays a screen similar to the left side of Figure 9-10, where you can either launch the Camera application to take a picture to send or select the picture file you want to send (you can navigate to a specific folder if necessary). The default location for picture files is the Media Card pictures folder. Just touch-press Camera to launch the Camera application.

✔ **Send Voice Note:** Displays the Voice Note screen (see Figure 9-10, right), where you can record the voice message you want to send. When you're ready to record, follow these steps:

a. **Touch-press Start.**

The Storm is ready to record your voice message. A screen indicating recording appears with a Stop button, as shown on the left side of Figure 9-11.

b. When you have finished speaking your message, touch-press Stop.

A screen similar to the right side of Figure 9-11 appears. You can play the message to review what you said, send the message if you're satisfied, or cancel sending a voice note.

Figure 9-10: Send a picture (left) or start recording a voice message (right).

Figure 9-11: Record and send your voice message here.

    c. Touch-press Send.

    You see a prompt asking you to add a description of your voice message. Touch-pressing No sends the message right away. In this case, you want to describe this message.

    d. Touch-press Yes.

    An Add File Description screen appears.

    e. Enter a description and then touch-press OK.

    A request to transfer the file is sent, and your friend needs to accept it in his or her BlackBerry Messenger for the transmission to begin.

✔ **Send File:** Displays a screen that lists which file types you can send. Aside from giving you a different way of sending pictures and voice messages, the screen lists the following types:

- File: Sends any type of file. When touch-pressed, it shows an Explorer-type screen so you can navigate to the file you want to send. The default folders shown are Media Card and Device Memory.

- BlackBerry Contact: Sends a vCard (see Chapter 4 for details on the vCard). When touch-pressed, it displays Contacts, allowing you to select the contact you want to send.

- Messenger Contact: Lets you choose a name from your list of BlackBerry Messenger contacts and send the info as a file.

Saving the conversation history

While you are in the conversation screen, you can save your chat history in two ways. Both methods are accessible by a simple press of the menu key:

✔ **Copy History:** Copies the existing chat history to the Clipboard. Then you just need to paste it into the application where you want it saved, such as Calendar or MemoPad.

✔ **Email History:** Displays the Compose Message screen, shown in Figure 9-12, with the Subject field prepopulated with `Chat with <Contact>` on `<Date>` and the body of the message prepopulated with the chat history.

Cc:

Subject: Chat with Dante
(BlackBerry for Dummies), MM
on 10/20/2009

Participants:

Yosma ⟨3 Sarigumba, Dante
(BlackBerry for Dummies), MM

Messages:

Dante (BlackBerry for Dummies)
has been invited to join.
MM has been invited to join.
Dante (BlackBerry for Dummies)
has been added to the conference.
MM has been added to the

Figure 9-12:
E-mail your
chat history
here.

Broadcasting a Message

Do you feel the need to start a conversation on the same subject with several
people? You can start with a group chat, but what if you want to get a personal opinion from each individual, something that each person isn't comfortable saying in front of the crowd? The best way to do this is to broadcast
a message to multiple recipients, as follows:

1. **On the BlackBerry Messenger screen, press the menu key.**

2. **Touch-press Broadcast Message.**

   The Broadcast Message screen appears, as shown in Figure 9-13, allowing you to enter your message and select the recipients.

3. **Enter your message.**

4. **Touch-press the recipients.**

5. **Touch-press Send.**

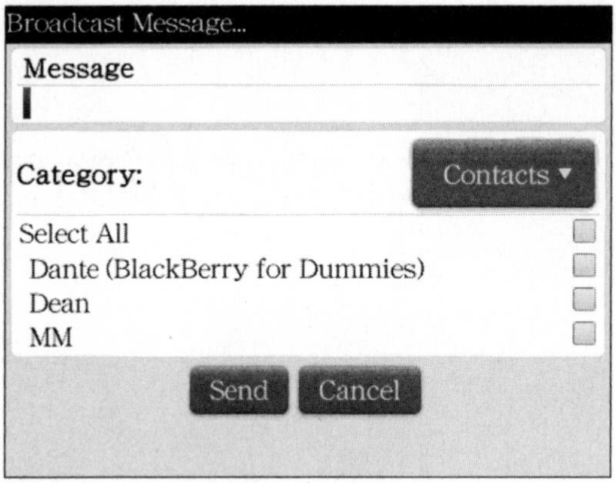

Broadcast Message...

Message

|

Category: Contacts ▼

Select All   ☐
Dante (BlackBerry for Dummies)   ☐
Dean   ☐
MM   ☐

Send   Cancel

Figure 9-13:
Broadcast
a message
here.

Chapter 10

Surfing the Internet Wave

. . . .

In This Chapter

▶ Using the Browser to surf the Web

▶ Creating and organizing bookmarks

▶ Customizing and optimizing Browser

▶ Downloading and installing applications from the Web

▶ Using Browser in businesses

. . . .

*W*eb surfing is becoming a necessity and part of our daily existence. Nearly everyone can surf the Web any time and anywhere from a desktop computer, a netbook, or even a tiny mobile device such as a PDA or a smart phone. And having said that, it should be no surprise that your BlackBerry Storm has a Web browser of its own.

In this chapter, we show you how to use the Browser. We give you shortcuts and timesaving tips, including the coolest ways to make pages load faster, as well as a complete neat-freak's guide to managing your bookmarks.

And because your network service provider may have its own custom browser for you to use, we compare these proprietary browsers with the default Browser so you can decide which best suits your needs.

Kicking Up Browser

The BlackBerry Browser comes loaded on your smart phone and accesses the Web via a cellphone connection. Browser can be named differently, depending on how the service provider customizes it. Sometimes it's named *BlackBerry Browser, Internet Browser,* or (most likely) just *Browser*. We just use *Browser* to make things easier.

Browser has multiple personalities:

- ✔ **One that's connected to your company's BlackBerry Enterprise Server:** BlackBerry Enterprise Server is a software application from RIM (Research In Motion) that companies can use to control and manage BlackBerry devices. The software also allows your device to see your company's network and connects to your company's databases.

  If you're a corporate BlackBerry user, your company administrator may turn off or not install other browsers except for the one that connects through the company's BlackBerry Enterprise Server.

- ✔ **One that goes directly to your service provider's network:** This might be called by the network service provider's brand name.

- ✔ **One that uses a Wi-Fi connection:** This personality applies if you have Storm2.

- ✔ **A WAP browser:** Wireless application protocol, or WAP, was popular in the 1990s, when mobile device displays were very limited and could display only five or six rows of text. WAP lost its appeal with the advent of high-resolution screens.

The following sections get you started using Browser. After you get your feet wet, we promise that you'll be chomping at the bit to find out more!

In today's competitive smart phone game, the Web browsing experience is one of the core functions upon which a platform and device are judged. And by RIM's own admission, this is an area that RIM is working feverishly to improve. RIM's recent acquisition of Torch Mobile, a WebKit-based third-party browser (the iPhone's Safari browser is based on the WebKit browser engine) shows that RIM is serious. In the meantime, be sure to check out Bolt Browser (Boltbrowser.com) and Opera Mini 5 (m.opera.com). Both have loyal followings among CrackBerry readers. SkyFire, another popular third-party Web browser, is currently under a private beta release. *Private beta* means that the app is available to a lucky few individuals, but keep tuning in to our blogs at www.crackberry.com; we'll let you know when SkyFire becomes available for you to download. If you're not satisfied with Browser, give these third-party options a try!

Getting to Browser

Browser is one of the main applications of your device, with its globe icon visible right on the Home screen, as shown in Figure 10-1. Touch-press this icon to open Browser.

Figure 10-1:
You can
open
Browser
from the
Home
screen.

If Browser is your default browser, you can access it from any application that distinguishes a Web address. For example, from Contacts, you can open Browser by opening the link on the Web Page field. If you get an e-mail that contains a Web address, just tap that link, press the menu key, and touch-press Open Link.

When you want to access Browser from another application, you don't have to close that application to jump to Browser. Just press the menu key and touch-press Switch Application, which opens a pop-up screen with application icons. Touch-press the Browser icon to launch Browser.

By default, accessing Browser by touch-pressing a Web link within another application opens the Web page associated with that address. For example, in Figure 10-2, we're opening Browser from the Messages application.

To: Sarigumba, Dante R
Link to smrtcase

Help

Find

Copy

Select

Open Link

Edit

File

Figure 10-2:
Open
Browser
from
Messages.

Opening Browser by touch-pressing its icon on the Home screen gives you a start page similar to Figure 10-3, which list the latest Web sites you've visited. It also shows a Bookmarks link. You find out more about adding bookmarks later in this chapter.

Figure 10-3: Browser with the default empty Bookmarks screen.

Hitting the (air) waves

After you locate Browser, you're ready to surf the Web. Here's how:

1. **Open Browser.**

   Unless the configuration is changed, BlackBerry Storm displays a default start page when you open Browser (refer to Figure 10-3, earlier in this chapter). This page allows you enter a Web address. If you have not changed the start page (see the "Configuring Browser" section to customize the start page), skip to Step 3.

2. **Press the menu key and then touch-press Go To.**

3. **Type a Web address, as shown in Figure 10-4.**

4. **Touch-press Go.**

   The Web page begins to load; the progress is indicated at the bottom of the screen.

Unless you change Browser's configuration (see the "Configuring Browser" section, later in this chapter), BlackBerry displays your bookmarks when you open Browser. And if you already have bookmarks, just press the menu key and then touch-press Go To. For the lowdown on adding bookmarks, see the upcoming section "Bookmarking Your Favorite Sites."

Figure 10-4:
Opening a
Web page is
simple.

When you see a phone number or an e-mail address on a Web page, you can touch-press that information to initiate a phone call or open a new e-mail message, respectively.

Navigating Web pages

Using Browser to navigate to a Web page is easy. Note that hyperlinks are highlighted onscreen. To jump to a particular hyperlink, touch-press the link.

Here are a few shortcuts you can use while navigating a Web page:

- ✔ **Move up and down one full display page at a time.** Press 9 (down arrow) or 3 (up arrow).

- ✔ **Stop loading a page.** Press the escape key (the bottom arrow key).

- ✔ **Go back to the previous page (if there is one).** Press the escape key (the bottom arrow key).

And don't forget the Browser menu (press the menu key). It has some useful shortcuts, as shown in Figure 10-5.

Here are the Browser menu options:

- ✔ **Help:** Displays a quick guide.

- ✔ **Page View:** Appears only if you are in Column view. (See the upcoming bullet.) This view allows you to see the page as you typically would on a PC's Internet browser. The compressed version of the Web page takes up the entire screen first.

✔ **Column View:** Appears only if you are in Page view. With Column view, which is the default view, the Web page is displayed vertically. A wide Web page wraps down, so you must finger-scroll to see more of the page.

✔ **Zoom In/Zoom Out:** Zooms in and out, respectively.

✔ **Find:** Locates and highlights text on the current page. As with any other basic Find tool, choosing this option displays a prompt to enter the text you want to find. After the initial search, a Find Next menu appears for finding the next matching text.

✔ **Select:** Appears only if you tapped text. Use this feature to highlight text onscreen for copying.

✔ **Stop:** Appears only if you're in the middle of requesting a page. Use Stop to cancel such a request. This is the same as pressing the escape key.

✔ **Copy:** Appears if you have highlighted text. Touch-pressing Copy copies the highlighted text into memory so that you can use it later for pasting somewhere else, such as in MemoPad.

✔ **Full Image:** Appears only if you highlight an image and only a portion of the image is displayed onscreen.

✔ **Save Image:** Appears only if you highlight an image, allowing you to save the image in built-in memory or to an microSD card.

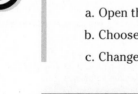

✔ **Home:** Represents the shortcut to your home page. To change the default home page (which can vary from carrier to carrier), follow these steps:

   a. Open the Browser menu.

   b. Choose Options➪Browser Configuration.

   c. Change the Home Page Address field.

Figure 10-5: The Browser menu has lots of good stuff.

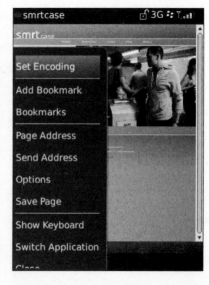

✔ **Get Link:** Appears if you have a highlighted link. Choosing this menu item opens that page of the link.

✔ **Go To:** Opens a Web page when you enter a Web address and touch-press Go. As you enter more addresses, they are listed in the History portion of the screen so you don't have to retype them. To find out how to clear that list, see the "Specifying cache operations" section, later in this chapter.

✔ **Back:** Goes back to the preceding page you viewed. This menu item appears only if you have navigated to more than one Web page.

You can achieve the same function by pressing the escape key (the bottom arrow key).

✔ **Forward:** Progresses one page at a time if you've gone back at least one Web page in your browsing travels; otherwise, it isn't a visible option.

✔ **Recent Pages:** Jumps to any of those Web pages when you highlight the history page and press the enter key twice. Browser can track up to 20 pages of Web addresses you've visited, which you can view on the History screen.

✔ **History:** Displays a list of the Web pages you've visited and allows you to jump back quickly to those pages. The list is grouped by date.

✔ **Refresh:** Updates the current page. This is helpful when you're viewing a page with data that changes frequently (such as stock quotes).

✔ **Set Encoding:** Specifies the encoding used in viewing a Web page. This is useful for viewing foreign languages that use different characters. Most BlackBerry users don't have to deal with this and probably don't know what type of encoding a particular language could display.

When you try to open a Web page, indicators that show the progress of your request appear at the bottom of the screen. The left side of Figure 10-6 shows that Browser is requesting a page; the right side of the figure shows that you've reached the page but the page is still loading.

Figure 10-6:
Requesting a page (left) and then loading it (right).

The icons in the top-right corners of both screens in Figure 10-6 are as follows, from right to left:

- ✔ The **bars** show the strength of the network signals (the same signal indicators for phone and e-mail).

- ✔ Your **connection type** also appears. In Figure 10-6, *3G* means that the connection is using the third-generation network.

- ✔ The **lock icon** indicates whether you're on a secure Web page. Figure 10-6 shows a nonsecure page. Whether a page is secure depends on the Web site you're visiting. If you're accessing your bank, you most likely see the secured icon (a closed lock). On the other hand, most pages don't need to be secure, so you see the unsecured icon (an open lock).

If you lose patience waiting for a page to load and want to browse somewhere else, press the escape key (the arrow key at the bottom of your Storm) to stop the page from loading.

Saving a Web page address

Entering a Web address to view a page can get tedious. Fortunately, you can return to a page without typing the same address. While you're viewing a Web page, simply use the Browser menu (shown in Figure 10-7) to save that page's address.

You can save a Web page address in a couple of ways:

- ✔ **Page Address:** Allows you to view the Web address of the current page through a pop-up screen, which presents you with two options to act on:

  - • Copy Address saves the page's address on your BlackBerry Clipboard and allows you to paste it somewhere else.

  - • Send Address is the same Send Address you see in the Browser menu (as described in the next item).

- ✔ **Send Address:** Presents another screen so that you can choose whether to send the address by

  - • E-mail (Chapter 8)

  - • PIN (Chapter 8)

  - • SMS text (Chapter 8)

  - • MMS (Chapter 8)

  - • Messenger Contact (Chapter 9)

- ✔ **Options:** Displays a screen allowing you to customize the behavior of Browser. See the section "Exercising Options and Optimization Techniques," later in this chapter, for details.

✔ **Save Page:** Saves the Web address of the current page to Messages. A message appears with the Browser globe icon to indicate that the message is a Web link, as shown in Figure 10-8. Touch-press that entry to launch Browser and open the page for your viewing pleasure.

Saving a page to your message list has a different purpose from bookmarking a page. The page initially appears as *unread* in Messages to remind you to check back later.

Note: When you don't have network coverage, and you try to access a Web page, you're prompted to save your request. When you do, your request is automatically saved in the message list. When you do have coverage later, you can open the same Web page from the message list, with the content loaded already!

Figure 10-7:
Use the
Browser
menu to
save a
Web page
address.

Figure 10-8:
Save a
Web-page
link in
Messages.

No place like Home

Changing your Home screen background is a neat trick. You can use an image you have saved in your Pictures list as the background on your Home screen. Here's how:

1. **From the Home screen, touch-press the Media icon and then touch-press Pictures.**

   The Pictures application opens.

2. **Finger-scroll to and touch-press the image you want to set as your background.**

3. **Press the menu key and then touch-press Set As.**

4. **Touch-press Wallpaper.**

Sending an address by e-mail

You can send a Web address to any recipient via an e-mail message by using the Page Address option on the Browser menu. For a more direct way, simply touch-press Send Address on the Browser menu while the Web page is displayed. If you know right away that you'll need to send an address to someone, save a few clicks and use the more-direct method.

Saving Web images

You can save images in JPEG, PNG, GIF, and BMP formats from a Web page. Any saved image is kept in the Pictures application, which enables you to view it later. To save an image, just tap the image, press the menu key, and then touch-press Save Image on the menu that appears.

Bookmarking Your Favorite Sites

You don't have to memorize all the addresses of your favorite sites. Instead, use BlackBerry Browser to keep a list of sites you want to revisit. In other words, make a *bookmark* so that you can come back to a site quickly.

Adding and visiting a bookmark

Add a new bookmark this way:

1. **Open Browser and go to the Web page you want to bookmark.**

2. **Touch-press Add Bookmark from the Browser menu.**

   The menu is always accessible by pressing the menu key.

3. **(Optional) In the Add Bookmark dialog box, change the bookmark name.**

   The name of the bookmark defaults to the Web-site title and, in most cases, is appropriate to use as the name. You always have the option to change this name; refer to the following section, "Modifying a bookmark."

4. **In the Add Bookmark dialog box, navigate to the folder where you want to save the bookmark.**

   The dialog box is shown in Figure 10-9. The default bookmark save folder is BlackBerry Bookmarks, but you can save the bookmark in any folder you create. To see how to create a bookmark folder, skip to the section "Adding a bookmark subfolder," later in this chapter.

5. **Touch-press Add.**

Figure 10-9:
Name the
bookmark
and specify
where to
store it.

Here's how to go to a bookmarked page:

1. **In Browser, touch-press Bookmarks on the Browser menu.**

   You're taken to the Bookmarks screen. From here, you can find all the pages you bookmarked.

2. **Touch-press the bookmark for the page you want to visit.**

Available offline

The Add Bookmark dialog box has an Available Offline check box. When that check box is selected, you not only save a page as a bookmark, but also *cache* it so you can see it even when you're out of range (like when you're stuck deep in a mountain cave). The next time you click the bookmark, that page comes up quickly. This offline feature comes in handy when you're pulling articles on the way to the subway or the street-by-street directions you got from maps.google.com.

Modifying a bookmark

You have the option of changing the attributes of existing bookmarks. Why change them? Say you bookmarked a couple of pages from the same Web site, but the author of the Web pages didn't bother to have a unique title for each page. While happily bookmarking pages, you didn't bother to change the names of the bookmarks that default to the Web-page title. Now you end up with several bookmarks with the same name.

Changing a bookmark is a snap. Follow these steps:

1. **From the Bookmarks screen (touch-press Bookmarks on the Browser menu), tap the name of the bookmark you want to modify, press the menu key, and then touch-press Edit Bookmark.**

2. **On the screen that follows, edit the existing name, the address the bookmark is pointing to, or both.**

3. **Touch-press Save to save your changes.**

Organizing your bookmarks

Over time, the number of your bookmarks will grow, and trying to find a certain site on a tiny screen can be tough. A handy work-around is to organize your bookmarks with folders. For example, you can group related sites in a folder, and each folder can have one or more other folders inside it (subfolders). Having a folder hierarchy narrows your search and allows you to easily find a site.

For example, your sites might fall into these categories:

✔ Reference

   NY Times

   Yahoo!

✔ Fun

        Flickr

        The Onion

✔ Shopping

        Etsy

        Gaiam

Adding a bookmark subfolder

You can add subfolders only to folders that are already listed on the Bookmarks page. That is, you can't create your own root folder. Your choices for adding your first subfolder are under WAP Bookmarks or BlackBerry Bookmarks.

Suppose you want to add a Reference subfolder within your BlackBerry Bookmarks folder. Here are the quick and easy steps:

1. **On the Bookmarks screen, tap BlackBerry Bookmarks.**

   This is the *parent* of the new subfolder. In this case, the BlackBerry Bookmarks folder will contain the Reference subfolder.

2. **Press the menu key and then touch-press Add Subfolder, as shown in Figure 10-10.**

   You see a dialog box where you can enter the name of the folder. (We're using Reference.)

Figure 10-10:
Add a folder
here.

3. **Type the folder name and touch-press OK.**

   The Reference folder now appears on the Bookmarks screen (as shown in Figure 10-11), bearing a folder icon.

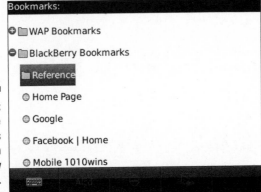

Figure 10-11:
The
Bookmarks
screen with
a new
subfolder.

Renaming a bookmark folder

Although you can't rename the root bookmark folders, such as BlackBerry Bookmarks and WAP Bookmarks, the folders you create under them are fair game. Renaming a bookmark folder that you created is as easy as editing a bookmark. Follow these steps:

1. **On the Bookmarks screen, highlight the name of the folder you want to change.**

2. **Press the menu key and touch-press Rename Folder.**

3. **Type the name of the folder.**

4. **Touch-press OK to save your changes.**

Moving a bookmark

If you keep going astray looking for a bookmark that you think exists in a particular folder but is instead in another, move that bookmark where it belongs. Follow these steps:

1. **Tap the bookmark, press the menu key, and touch-press Move Bookmark.**

2. **Touch-press the folder where you want this bookmark moved.**

   Your bookmark is in its new home.

Cleaning up your bookmarks

Maybe you really like a site but eventually stop visiting it. Or maybe a site disappears, and every time you click the bookmark, you get a 404 Not Found error. Time for a little spring cleaning. From the Bookmarks screen, tap the name of the bookmark you want to delete, press the menu key, and touch-press Delete Bookmark. It's just that easy.

You can — repeat, *can* — clean up bookmarks wholesale by deleting a folder. A word to the wise, though: All the contents of that folder will be deleted, so purge with caution.

Exercising Options and Optimization Techniques

Sure, Browser works out of the box, but folks have their own taste, right? Look to Browser Options for attributes and features you can customize.

Press the menu key and touch-press Options. The Browser Options screen offers four main categories to choose among, as shown in Figure 10-12:

- ✔ **Browser Configuration:** A place to toggle Browser features
- ✔ **General Properties:** Settings for the general look and feel of Browser
- ✔ **Cache Operations:** An area for clearing file caches used by Browser
- ✔ **Gears Settings:** A place to enable certain Web sites that take advantage of Gears

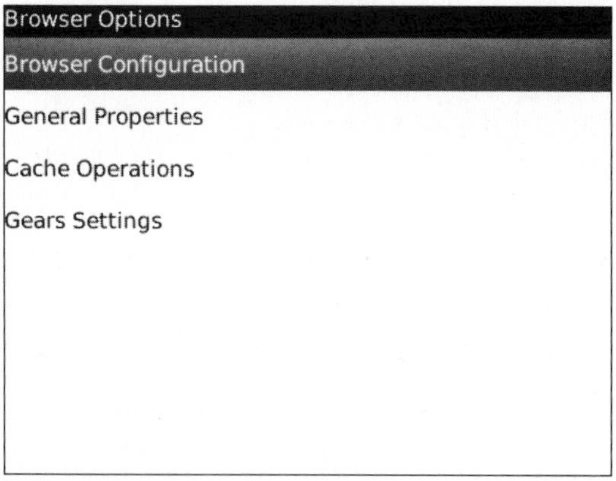

Browser Options

Browser Configuration

General Properties

Cache Operations

Gears Settings

Figure 10-12:
The
Browser
Options
screen.

If you feel speed-greedy after adjusting the options, see the "Speeding up browsing" sidebar, later in this chapter.

Configuring Browser

You can define browser-specific settings from the Browser Configuration screen, which you access from the Browser Options screen. The customization items you can amend (shown in Figure 10-13) are as follows:

- **Support JavaScript:** JavaScript is a scripting language used heavily to make dynamic Web pages. A Web page might not behave normally when this option is turned off. This option is on by default.

- **Allow JavaScript Popups:** Most ad pages are launched as JavaScript pop-ups, so selecting this check box minimizes these ads. Be aware, though, that some important pages are also displayed as JavaScript pop-ups. *Note:* This option appears only if you select the Support JavaScript check box.

- **Prompt to Enable JavaScript Popups:** This option appears and comes into play only if you do not select the Support JavaScript option. The default value for this option is selected (if you browse a page that has JavaScript, Browser will prompt you to either enable JavaScript or not).

- **Terminate Slow Running Scripts:** Sometimes, you find Web pages with scripts that aren't written well. If you select this option, you keep Browser from hanging. This option appears only if you select the Support JavaScript check box.

- **Show Images:** This option controls the display of images depending on the content mode of WML, HTML, or both. Think of WML pages as Web pages made just for mobile devices, such as the BlackBerry. We recommend leaving this option selected for both.

Figure 10-13: The Browser Configuration screen.

Turn on and off the display of image placeholders if you opt to not display images.

✔ **Use Background Images:** A Web-page background image can make the page look pleasing, but if the image is big, it could take time to download it.

✔ **Support Embedded Media:** Touch-press this option to support media such as SVG (scalable vector graphics). Think of SVG as Adobe Flash for mobile devices such as the BlackBerry Storm. SVG can be a still image or an animated one.

✔ **Browser Identification:** This option specifies which browser type your browser emulates. The default is BlackBerry, but Browser can also emulate Microsoft Internet Explorer or Mozilla Firefox.

Keep the default BlackBerry mode. We don't see much difference among the modes.

✔ **Start Page:** Use this option to specify a starting page to load when you open Browser. You can choose Start Page (the default start page); Home Page, which you set with the next option; and Last Page Loaded.

✔ **Default Search Provider:** Allows you to choose Google (the default), Live Search, Wikipedia, or Dictionary.com as the default Web site to use in the search function you see in the Browser initial screen.

✔ **Home Page Address:** Use this option to set your home page. Note that the home page is always available from the Browser menu.

Setting general Browser properties

The General Properties screen is similar to the Browser Configuration screen (see the preceding section) in that you can customize some Browser behaviors. General Properties, however, is geared more toward the features of Browser content, as shown in Figure 10-14. You can configure features and also turn features off or on.

From this screen, use the space key to change the value of a field. You can configure the following features:

✔ **Default Browser:** If you have multiple browsers available, use this to specify which one you want to use when opening a Web link.

✔ **Default Font Family:** When a Web page doesn't specify the text font, Browser will use the one you selected here.

✔ **Default Font Size:** When a Web page doesn't specify the text font size, Browser uses the one you select here. The smaller the size, the more text can fit onscreen.

✔ **Minimum Font Size:** A Web page might specify a font size too small to be legible. Specifying a legible font size will override the Web page.

✔ **Minimum Font Style:** When Browser is using the minimum font size, you can choose what font to use. Some fonts, even in a small size, are more legible than others. If you aren't sure which one to use, leave the default.

✔ **Default View:** You can toggle the default view. Column wraps all Web page elements vertically, so you just finger-scroll up and down the page. Page displays the page like you normally see in your PC's Internet browser. Finger-scroll the pages left, right, up, and down.

✔ **Image Quality:** The higher the quality, the slower the page loads. You have three options: low, medium (the default), and high.

✔ **Repeat Animations:** This option sets the number of times an animation repeats. This pertains to the animated images that most banner ads use. Your choices are Never, Once, 10 Times, 100 Times (the default), and As Many as the Image Specifies.

✔ **Full Screen View:** This option displays the Web page full screen. The default is off, which allows you to finger-scroll.

✔ **Enable JavaScript Location Support:** Web pages that have scripts that take advantage of your BlackBerry's location through GPS will work if you select this option.

✔ **Prompt Before:** You can have BlackBerry Browser give you a second chance before you do the following things:

  • Closing Browser on Escape: You're notified right before you exit BlackBerry Browser.

  • Closing Modified Pages: You're notified right before you exit a modified Web page (for example, some type of online form you fill out).

  • Running WML Scripts: WML is a script that tells a wireless device how to display a page. It was popular years ago, when resolutions of device screens were low, but very few Web sites use it now. We recommend leaving this field deselected.

Specifying cache operations

At any given time, your BlackBerry uses a few cache mechanisms. A *cache* (pronounced *cash*) temporarily stores information used by Browser so that the next time the info is needed, Browser doesn't have to go back to the source Web site. The cache can speed displays when you want to view the Web page again and is also useful when you're suddenly out of network coverage. When you visit a site that uses cookies, Browser caches that cookie. (Think of a *cookie* as a piece of text that a Web site created and placed in your BlackBerry's memory to remember something about you, such as your username.)

Browser also caches pages and content so that you can view them offline, which is handy when you're out of network range.

General Properties

Default Browser: Internet Browser ▼

Default Font Family:
BBAlpha Sans Condensed ▼

Default Font Size: 8 ▼

Minimum Font Size: 6 ▼

Minimum Font Style: Plain ▼

Default View: Page ▼

Image Quality: Medium ▼

Repeat Animations: 100 times ▼

☐ Full Screen View

☐ Enable JavaScript Location support

Prompt Before:

Figure 10-14:
The General
Properties
screen.

Speeding up browsing

On a wireless network, many factors can affect how fast Web pages display. If you find that browsing the Web is extremely slow, you can make your pages load faster, but you lose the ability to take advantage of a few features. Here are some of the speed-enhancing workarounds you can use:

✓ **Don't display images.** You can achieve a big performance improvement by turning off image display. From the Browser menu, touch-press Browser Options, touch-press Browser Configuration, finger-scroll to Show Images, and change the value to No.

✓ **Check your BlackBerry memory.** When your BlackBerry's memory is depleted, its performance degrades. The BlackBerry low-memory manager calls each application every now and then, telling each one to free resources.

Hint: Don't leave many e-mail messages unread. When the low-memory manager kicks in, Messages tries to delete old messages, but it can't delete unread messages.

✓ **Turn off other features.** If you're mostly interested in viewing content, consider turning off features that pertain to how the content is processed, such as Support HTML Tables, Use Background Images, Support JavaScript, Allow JavaScript Popups, and Support Style Sheets. To turn off other Browser features, touch-press Browser from the Home screen, press the menu key, touch-press Options, and then touch-press General Properties.

Warning: We don't advise turning off features while performing an important task such as online banking. If you do, you may not be able to perform some of the actions on the page. For example, the Submit button might not work. Not good.

Some Web sites *push* (send information) Web pages to BlackBerry devices. An icon will appear on the Home screen, allowing you to quickly view the page. After the Web page is delivered to your BlackBerry, the page becomes available even if you go out of the coverage area. If you subscribe to this service, your device will store Web pages in the cache. Also, the addresses of the pages that you visited (or your latest 20 in your history list) make up a cache.

The Cache Operations screen, shown in Figure 10-15, allows you to manually clear your cache. To view the Cache Operations screen, follow these steps:

1. **From the Browser screen, press the menu key.**

2. **Touch-press Options.**

3. **Touch-press Cache Operations.**

The size of each type of cache is displayed on the Cache Operations screen. If the cache has content, you also see the Clear button, which you can use to clear the specified cache type. This is true for all types of caches except history, which has its own Clear History button. You find four types of caches:

- **History:** The list of sites you've visited by using the Go To function. You may want to clear this for the sake of security if you don't want other people knowing which Web sites you're visiting on your BlackBerry.

- **Content Cache:** Any offline content. You may want to clear this whenever you're running out of space on your BlackBerry and need to free some memory. Or maybe you're tired of viewing old content or tired of touch-pressing the Refresh option.

- **Pushed Content:** Any content that was pushed to your BlackBerry from Push Services subscriptions. You may want to clear this to free memory on your BlackBerry.

- **Cookie Cache:** Any cookies stored on your BlackBerry. You may want to clear this for security's sake. Sometimes you don't want a Web site to remember you.

Gears settings

Gears is a mechanism by which Browser sends your geographic location so that sites can provide location-based features catered to where you are. Gears is a relatively new technology initially developed by Google.

Some familiar Web applications such as Gmail, YouTube, and Picasa use Gears, but as of this writing, few Web sites take advantage of it. You will know whether a Web site uses Gears because Browser will prompt you for authorization. After you authorize a Web site, it will be listed on the Gears Settings screen. To get to that screen, from the Browser screen, press the menu key, touch-press Options, and then touch-press Gear Settings.

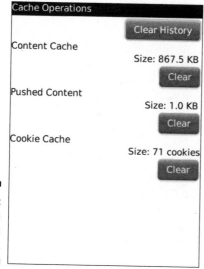

Figure 10-15:
The Cache
Operations
screen.

Installing and Uninstalling Applications from the Web

You can download and install applications on your BlackBerry via Browser — that is, if the application has a link that lets you download and install the files (see Chapter 18 for other installation options). The downloading and installing parts are easy. Follow these steps:

1. **Touch-press the link from Browser.**

   You see a simple prompt that looks like Figure 10-16.

2. **Touch-press the Download button.**

   The download starts.

As long as you stay within network coverage while the download is progressing, your BlackBerry can finish the download *and* install the application for you. If it finishes without any problems, you see a screen similar to Figure 10-17.

As with a desktop computer, the download might or might not work for a variety of reasons. Sometimes the application

  ✔ Requires you to install libraries

  ✔ Works only on a certain version of the BlackBerry OS

Figure 10-16:
A typical page that lets you download an application to your BlackBerry.

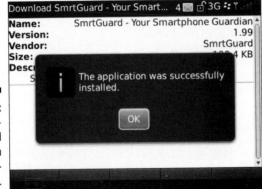

Figure 10-17:
The download and installation are complete.

These issues can be prevented, depending on the sophistication of the site where the link is published. With most reputable sources, these issues are considered, and successful downloading and installation are a snap.

Installing applications from nonreputable sources can cause your BlackBerry to become unstable. Before you download an application from the Web, be sure to read reviews about that particular application. Most of the time, other people who tried the software provide reviews or feedback. Don't be the first to write the bad review! For reviews and feedback on third-party applications, you can visit www.crackberry.com.

Your BlackBerry Enterprise Server administrator can disable the feature in your BlackBerry to download and install an application. This is mostly the case for a company-issued device. If you have problems downloading and installing an application, check your company policy or contact the BlackBerry support person in your company.

If you download an application that turns out to be a dud, you need to uninstall it. See Chapter 18 for more on uninstalling an application from your BlackBerry.

Using Browser in Business

Getting a device from your employer has both a good and an ugly side:

- **Good:** Your company foots the bill.
- **Ugly:** Your company foots the bill.

Because your company pays, the company dictates what you can and cannot do with your BlackBerry Storm. This is especially true with respect to browsing the Web.

Two scenarios come into play when it comes to your browser:

- Your browser might be running under your company's BlackBerry Enterprise Server. With this setup, your BlackBerry Browser is connecting to the Internet by using your company's Internet connection. It's like using your desktop machine at work.
- Your browser is connected through a network service provider. Most of the time, this kind of browser is called by the company's name.

In most cases, your device fits in only one scenario, which is the case where your browser is connected through your company's BlackBerry Enterprise Server server. Some lucky folks may have both. Whatever scenario you're in, the following sections describe the major differences between the two and indicate what you can expect.

Using Browser on your company's BlackBerry Enterprise Server server

In an enterprise setup, your BlackBerry Browser is connected through your company's BlackBerry Enterprise Server server. With this setup, the browser is actually named *BlackBerry Browser.* BlackBerry Enterprise Server is located inside your company's intranet. This setup allows the company to better manage the privileges and the functions you can use on your device.

For the BlackBerry Browser application, this setup allows the company to use the existing Internet infrastructure, including the company's firewall. Because you are within the company's network, the boundaries that your network administrator set up on your account apply to your BlackBerry as well. For example, when browsing the Web, your BlackBerry won't display any Web sites that are blocked by your company's server.

The good thing, though, is that you can browse the company's intranet: That is, all the Web pages you have access to inside your company through your company's PC are available also in your BlackBerry.

Know (and respect) your company's Web-browsing policy. Most companies keep logs of sites you view on your browser and might even have software to monitor usage. Also, your company might not allow downloading from the Web.

Using your network provider's browser

Any new device coming from a network service provider can come with its own branded Web browser. It's the same BlackBerry Browser, but the behavior might differ in the following ways:

- ✔ **The name is different.**
- ✔ **The default home page usually points to the provider's Web site.** This isn't necessarily a bad thing. Most of the time, the network provider's Web site is full of links that you may not find on BlackBerry Browser.
- ✔ **You can browse more sites.** You aren't limited by your company's policy.

Setting the default browser

If you have two Web browsers on your Storm, you have the option to set the *default* browser. This comes into play when you view a Web address by using a link outside the Browser application. For example, when you view an e-mail with a Web link, touch-pressing that link launches the default browser.

To set up the default browser, follow these steps:

1. **Go to the Home screen.**

2. **Touch-press Options and then touch-press Advanced Options.**

3. **Touch-press Browser.**

4. **Touch-press the value of the default browser configuration and then touch-press one of the possible values, as shown in Figure 10-18.**

Figure 10-18: Change the default browser here.

Part III
Going Multimedia with Your Storm

The 5th Wave   By Rich Tennant

DISGUISED RINGTONES FOR NON-CELL PHONE VENUES

BROADWAY PLAY

Cough...cough...

CHURCH SERMON

ZZZZZ...
ZZZZZZ...

LIBRARY   ©RICHTENNANT

SHHHH...
SHHHH...,
SHHHH...

DENTIST'S WAITING ROOM

OW...OW...
OW...OW..
OW...OW..
OW...OW

In this part . . .

Find out how to use your BlackBerry Storm as a still camera and a video camera. You can also get entertained and have fun with the Storm's multimedia capabilities. Get directions from the BlackBerry GPS. And finally, make those all-important phone calls.

Chapter 11

Taking Great Pictures

In This Chapter

▶ Getting ready to take a shot

▶ Saving and organizing your pictures

▶ Sharing your photos with other people

*O*h, shoot, you forgot your camera. Don't worry! Your Storm's there when you need to capture the unbelievable: Grandma's doing a handstand, your Grandpa is doing a cartwheel, or your roommate is doing her laundry.

Before you try taking pictures with your Storm, read this chapter so you know what to expect and how to get the best shot. We also walk you through the easy steps in capturing that funny pose and show you how to store those shots and share them with your buddies.

Saying "Cheese"

Before you ask someone to pose, examine your BlackBerry Storm:

✔ **Is the camera on?** You see the convenience key on the right side of your BlackBerry Storm? It's typically set by the carrier to bring up the Camera app by default. Press it. If the Camera application doesn't come up, you can touch-press the Camera icon from the Home screen.

You can change the applications launched by the right convenience key (or left convenience key, for that matter). From the Home screen, touch-press Options, and touch-press Screen/Keyboard. In the Right Side Convenience Key Opens field, touch-press the value; in the list that follows, touch-press the application you want.

✔ **Is your finger blocking the lens?** The lens is on the back of your device (see Figure 11-1).

✔ **Do you see the image in the screen?** Pressing the camera key again takes the picture. You should hear a funky shutter sound. Neat and easy, isn't it?

Camera lens   Flash

Figure 11-1:
The back of
the Storm.

One of the biggest complaints by owners of the original BlackBerry Storm was that the shutter wasn't fast enough. If you have the Storm2, the shutter speed is improved slightly, but you still can't take pictures in rapid succession. The common mistake most people make when taking a picture is not letting the camera focus first. Press the camera key (convenience key) half down or tap the screen to focus. Pressing the camera key fully or touch-pressing the screen snaps the photo. You'll find that the camera works fastest and captures the best photos if you first focus (tap) and then take the picture (touch-press) instead of touch-pressing once.

Itching to take more pictures? Hold those snapping fingers of yours. If you take a few moments first to familiarize yourself with the camera's features, the effort could go a long way.

Reading the screen indicators

When you open the Camera app, the top portion of the screen shows the image you're about to capture. The bottom part contains icons, as labeled in Figure 11-2.

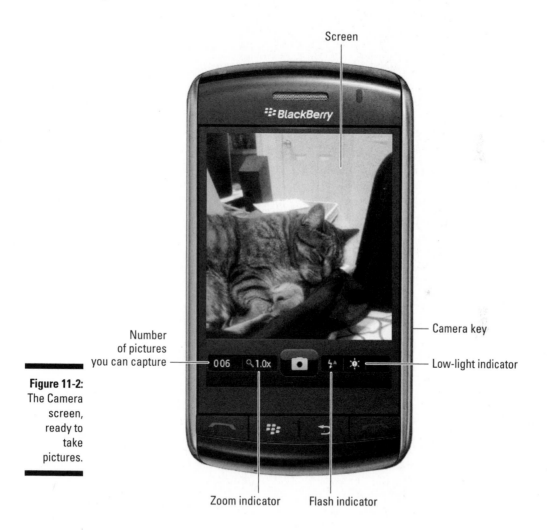

Screen

Number of pictures you can capture

Camera key

Low-light indicator

Figure 11-2: The Camera screen, ready to take pictures.

Zoom indicator

Flash indicator

Choosing the picture quality

BlackBerry Storm can capture up to 3.2 megapixels (mp) of resolution. Saving at this resolution requires a lot of space. You can save at a lower quality and save some space on your BlackBerry.

Get a big microSD card. Nowadays, even a 32GB microSD card is inexpensive, and it holds thousands of pictures.

Here are the three resolutions you can choose:

- ✔ **Normal:** The default setting. Normal picture quality isn't as smooth or fine as the other resolution choices but saves the most pictures.

   If you're just taking pictures of your friends' faces so you can attach them as Caller IDs, Normal is appropriate.

- ✔ **Fine:** A middle setting between Normal and SuperFine. This is a compromise if you're concerned about space and want to capture more pictures. The best use for this setting is for any electronic viewer; this option isn't good for printing.

- ✔ **SuperFine:** The best quality that your camera can capture. Choose this setting if you plan on printing the images.

Changing picture quality is a snap. Follow these steps:

1. **Press the camera key (the right convenience key on your Storm).**

   The Camera application opens.

2. **Press the menu key and touch-press Options.**

   The Camera Options screen appears, as shown in Figure 11-3.

3. **Touch-press Picture Quality.**

4. **Touch-press the picture quality you want.**

   Picture Quality values are Normal, Fine, and SuperFine.

5. **Press the menu key and touch-press Save.**

   The picture quality you've chosen is now active.

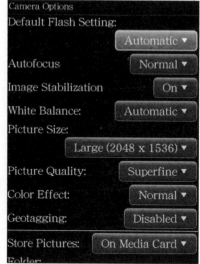

Figure 11-3:
The Camera
Options
screen.

Zooming and focusing

You need to be steady to get a good focus while taking shots. Although it's convenient to use one hand while taking pictures, most of the time, you'll get a blurry image if you try that.

When taking pictures, hold your BlackBerry with both hands, one holding the device steady and the other clicking the button.

Holding the camera with both hands is even more important if you're zooming in. Yes, your camera is capable of providing up to 3x digital zoom. Here's what you need to do for focusing and zooming:

- ✔ **To focus:** Press the camera key halfway.
- ✔ **To zoom in:** Finger-scroll up.
- ✔ **To zoom out:** Finger-scroll down.

While you're zooming, the value in the indicator changes from 1x, 2x, up to 3x, and vice versa, depending on the direction you finger-scroll.

We don't recommend using the zoom. Digital zoom (which is what your camera has) gives poor results because it's accomplished through software and degrades the quality of the picture. The higher the zoom factor, the more pixilated the picture becomes. To get a clearer picture, get closer to the object.

Setting the flash

The lightning icon on the Camera screen (refer to Figure 11-2, earlier in this chapter) is the flash indicator. The default is Automatic, which shows a letter *A* beside the icon. Automatic means that where it's dark, the flash fires; otherwise, it doesn't.

You can turn the flash on or off. When flash is off, the arrow image has a slash, just like you see on a Don't Walk traffic signal. You can toggle the settings in the Camera Options screen. (Press the menu key and touch-press Options to get to the Camera Options screen.)

Setting the white balance

In photography, filters are used to compensate for the dominant light. For instance, a fluorescent versus an incandescent light could affect how warm the picture looks. Instead of using filters, most digital cameras have a feature to correct or compensate for many types of light settings. This feature is *white balance.* And yes, your Storm has it. You can choose Sunny, Cloudy, Night, Incandescent, Fluorescent, or Automatic. *Automatic* means your camera sets what it thinks are the best settings to apply.

You can change the white balance through the Camera Options screen.

The Camera Options screen is accessible by pressing the menu key and touch-pressing Options on the menu that follows.

Setting the picture size

Aside from adjusting picture quality, you can adjust the actual size of the photo:

  ✔ **Large:** 2048 x 1536
  ✔ **Medium:** 1024 x 768
  ✔ **Small:** 640 x 480

Again, camera settings are accessible through the Camera Options screen by pressing the menu key and touch-pressing Options on the menu that appears.

Geotagging

Because your Storm has GPS capability, you can easily determine your location based on longitude and latitude. This information can be added to your media files, including the pictures taken from your camera. Now you don't have to wonder where you took that crazy pose. Adding geographic information is known as *geotagging*.

Geotagging is disabled by default in your Storm. You can enable geotagging from the Camera Options screen. (Press the menu key and touch-press Options to get to the Camera Options screen.)

If you have longitude and latitude information from one of your photos, you can use one of the free sites on the Web to locate that information on the map. One such site is `www.travelgis.com/geocode/Default.aspx`.

Working with Your Pictures

Suppose that you've taken a bunch of pictures, and you want to see them. And maybe delete the unflattering ones. Or perhaps organize them. No problem.

Viewing pictures

If you take a picture, you want to see it, right? *Viewing* a picture is a common function with your camera. You can see the image you just captured right then and there, as shown in Figure 11-4.

All the pictures you take on your camera are filed in a folder whose possible default location is based on whether you opted to save the pictures in

  ✔ **Device memory:** `/Device Memory/home/user/pictures`
  ✔ **Media card:** `/Media Card/BlackBerry/pictures`

Figure 11-4:
The Camera
screen after
taking a
picture.

Let your device file your pictures in the media card (microSD). You can easily move or share your pictures using the microSD card, and device memory is such a limited space that it's better to reserve it for your other applications. The first time you use the Camera application, it asks you whether to save pictures to the media card. If you aren't sure what the current setting is, simply close the Camera application, take out the microSD card, and put it back in. The next time you open the Camera app, it displays the same prompt about letting you save pictures to the media card.

The format of picture filenames, based on the current date and time, is `IMG<counter>-<yyyymmdd>-<hhmm>.jpg`. So if you took the 21st picture at 9:30 a.m. on December 20, 2010, you end up with `IMG00021-20101220-0930.jpg`.

If you're browsing through your picture folders, you can view a picture by simply touch-pressing the picture file.

Creating a slide show

Want to see your pictures in a slide show? Just follow these steps:

1. **Press the camera key (the right convenience key on your Storm).**

2. **Press the menu key and touch-press View Pictures.**

   The Pictures app opens.

3. **Press the menu key and touch-press Slide Show.**

   Voilà! Your BlackBerry Storm displays your pictures one at a time at a regular time interval.

The default interval between each picture is two seconds; you can change it in the Pictures Options screen. (After Step 2, press the menu key and touch-press Options to get to the Pictures Options screen. Touch-press Slide Show Interval and finger-scroll to select the desired interval.)

Trashing pictures

If you don't like the image you captured, you can delete it:

1. **Touch to highlight the picture you want to trash.**
2. **Touch-press the Delete (X) icon.**

    A confirmation screen appears.

3. **Touch-press Delete.**

Listing filenames versus thumbnails

When you open a folder packed with pictures, your BlackBerry automatically lists *thumbnails,* which are small previews of your pictures.

A preview is nice, but what if you're looking for a picture and know the filename? Wouldn't it be nice to see a list of filenames instead of thumbnails? Follow these steps:

1. **Touch-press the Media icon from the Home screen.**
2. **Touch-press Pictures.**
3. **Navigate to the location of your pictures.**
4. **Go to a picture folder.**
5. **Press the menu key and touch-press View List.**

    That's exactly what you get: a list of all the pictures in the folder. The list shows a tiny image, the filename, and the date filed for each of the pictures.

Checking picture properties

Curious about the amount of memory your picture is using? Want to know the time you took the photo and more? Follow these steps:

1. **While in the Camera screen, view the list of your pictures by pressing the menu key and touch-pressing View Pictures.**

2. **Tap the picture in a list.**

3. **Press the menu key and touch-press Properties.**

   You see a screen similar to Figure 11-5.

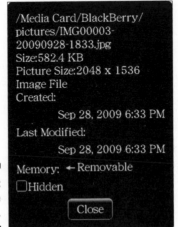

/Media Card/BlackBerry/
pictures/IMG00003-
20090928-1833.jpg
Size:582.4 KB
Picture Size:2048 x 1536
Image File
Created:

Sep 28, 2009 6:33 PM

Last Modified:

Sep 28, 2009 6:33 PM

Memory: ← Removable
☐Hidden

Close

Figure 11-5:
Your picture
properties.

The screen in Figure 11-5 displays the picture's location in your BlackBerry, its size, and its last modification. The arrow with the text *Removable* indicates that the picture is filed in the media card. The Hidden check box allows you to hide the file when navigating through your picture list. Once hidden, the file disappears from the list, and the only way to see the file in your Storm again is to use Explore. Check Chapter 12 for details about Explore.

Organizing your pictures

Organization is all about time and the best use of it. After all, you want to enjoy looking *at* your pictures — not looking *for* them. To accomplish that, you should organize your pictures by changing where they're stored and named. With those capabilities, you should be on your way to organization nirvana.

Renaming a picture file

BlackBerry saves a file when you capture a picture. However, the filename is generic, something like IMG*xxxx*, where *xxxx* is a number.

Make it a habit to rename the file as soon as you've finished capturing the picture. It is easier to recognize `Dean blows out birthday candles` than `IMG00003-20101013-0029`.

Renaming is a snap. Here's how:

1. **Display the picture onscreen or tap it in the list.**

2. **Press the menu key and touch-press Rename.**

   A Rename screen appears.

3. **Type the name you want for this picture.**

4. **Touch-press Save.**

   Your picture is renamed.

Creating a new folder

Being the organized person you are, you must be wondering about folders. Don't fret; it's simple to create one:

1. **In the Camera screen, press the menu key and touch-press View Pictures.**

   The screen displays the list of pictures in the current folder.

2. **Press the menu key and touch-press the Up icon.**

3. **Navigate to the main folder where you want your new folder to be created.**

   You should be *within* the folder where you want your new folder to be created. If not, repeat this step to navigate to that folder.

4. **Press the menu key and touch-press New Folder.**

5. **Enter the name of the folder.**

6. **Touch-press OK.**

   Your folder is created.

Moving pictures

There are many reasons for moving pictures between folders. The most obvious reason is to organize your pictures. Want to try it? Follow these steps:

1. **In the Camera screen, press the menu key and touch-press View Pictures.**

   The screen lists pictures in the current folder. If the picture you want to move isn't in this folder, touch-press the Up icon to navigate up to other folders.

2. **Tap the picture you want to move.**

3. **Press the menu key and touch-press Move.**

   The screen that appears allows you to move the picture to the subfolder of the current folder location of the picture.

4. **If you want to move the picture to the subfolder within the current folder:**

   a. **Touch-press the folder name.**

      Repeat this step until you reach the subfolder you want.

   b. **Press the menu key and touch-press Move Here.**

      Your picture is moved.

5. **If you want to move the picture outside the current folder hierarchy:**

   a. **Press the menu key and touch-press Up.**

      A screen appears, displaying the topmost file folders. You can navigate inside the folder hierarchy from here.

   b. **Touch-press the folder name.**

      Repeat this step until you reach the subfolder you want.

   c. **Press the menu key and touch-press Move Here.**

      Your picture is moved.

You can easily transfer your pictures to your PC or copy pictures from your PC to your Storm as well. See Chapter 12 for more details.

Sharing your pictures

Where's the joy in taking great pictures if you're the only one seeing them? Your BlackBerry has several options for sharing your bundle of joy:

1. **In the Camera screen, press the menu key and touch-press View Pictures.**

2. **Tap a picture you want to share.**

3. **Press the menu key and touch-press Send/Share.**

4. **Touch-press one of the choices on the Send As screen:**

   • **Email:** This goes directly to the Compose EMail screen, with the currently selected picture as an attachment.

- **MMS:** Similar to Email, this opens a Compose MMS screen with the currently selected picture as an attachment. The only difference is that MMS first displays Contacts, letting you select the person's phone number to receive the MMS before going to the compose screen. Another difference is that in MMS, the Storm sends a tiny version of the picture.

- **Send to Messenger Contact:** This option is available if BlackBerry Messenger is installed. This function is similar to MMS but displays only the contacts in BlackBerry Messenger. It uses BlackBerry Messenger to send a tiny version of the picture file.

You might also see other ways to send a picture file if you have other social networking clients installed. For example, if you have Facebook installed, you see the Send to Facebook option.

Setting a picture as Caller ID

Wouldn't it be nice if, when your girlfriend was calling, you also could see her beautiful face? You can do that. If you have a photo of her saved in your BlackBerry, follow these steps to make sure you can:

1. **Touch-press the Media icon from the Home screen.**

2. **Touch-press Pictures and navigate to the locations of your pictures.**

3. **Touch-press to view the photo you want to appear when the person calls.**

4. **Press the menu key, touch-press Set As, and then touch-press Caller ID.**

   The photo is displayed onscreen, with a superimposed portrait-size cropping rectangle. Inside the rectangle is a clear view of the photo; outside the rectangle, the photo is blurry. The clear view represents the portion of the photo that you want to show up as Caller ID.

5. **Finger-scroll the picture to position it inside the rectangle, making sure that the cropped image shows the face.**

6. **Press the menu key and touch-press Crop and Save to crop the image.**

   Contacts appears.

7. **Touch-press the contact for whom you want this picture to appear.**

   A message appears, indicating that a picture is set for that contact.

You can also add a photo to your contacts through the Contacts application (see Chapter 4).

Setting a Home screen image

Suppose that you have a stunning picture that you want to use as the background image for your BlackBerry. Follow these steps:

1. **Touch-press the Media icon from the Home screen.**

2. **Touch-press Pictures.**

3. **Navigate to the location of your pictures and touch-press the picture you want to use.**

4. **Press the menu key, touch-press Set As, and then touch-press Wallpaper.**

Chapter 12

Satisfying Your Senses
with Media Player

. . . .

In This Chapter

▶ Listening to music

▶ Playing and recording videos

▶ Working with your pictures

▶ Choosing a ring tone

▶ Recording voices

▶ Adjusting the volume

▶ Traversing the menus and using Explore

▶ Checking memory use

▶ Customizing the Media app

▶ Importing and downloading media

. . . .

*I*f a word describes today's phone market trends, it's *convergence*. Your BlackBerry Storm is among the participants in this race to bring things together. In addition to sending and receiving e-mail and being a phone, a camera, and a PDA, your BlackBerry Storm is a portable media player. In this small package, you can

✔ Listen to music

✔ Record and watch video clips

✔ Sample ring tones

✔ Snap and view pictures

These capabilities are all bundled into an application with a name you'd recognize even after sipping a couple of pints of strong ale: Media.

Accessing Media

To run Media, simply touch-press the Media icon from the Home screen. The Media icon is easy to distinguish because it has the image of a CD and a musical note.

Media is a collection of media applications:

- ✔ Music
- ✔ Videos
- ✔ Pictures
- ✔ Ring Tones
- ✔ Voice Notes
- ✔ Video Camera
- ✔ Voice Notes Recorder

Each one is represented with an icon that you see upon opening Media, as shown in Figure 12-1. It's not that difficult to figure out what each one of these media icons represents.

Figure 12-1:
Explore
Media here.

As you go through each of these apps, you will soon find out that Videos and Video Camera work together. The videos you capture in the Video Camera app are listed in Videos. You can even launch Video Camera inside the Videos app. This sort of relationship with Videos and Video Camera is replicated for Voice Notes and Voice Notes Recorder, where you can launch Voice Notes Recorder from Voice Notes and play recorded notes within Voice Notes.

Ready to have some fun?

Let the Music Play

You don't need a quarter to play music on your BlackBerry Storm. Just touch-press Music from the Media screen (refer to Figure 12-1). The Music screen appears, listing several potential views of your music collection, as shown in Figure 12-2:

- ✔ **All Songs:** In this view, all your music files are shown in alphabetical order.

- ✔ **Artists:** This view lists your music files by artist, so you can play your John Mayer songs in one go.

- ✔ **Albums:** View your music collection one album at a time.

- ✔ **Genres:** If you prefer not to mingle your country with your cutting-edge techno, navigate through this view.

- ✔ **Playlists:** Organize and play songs as you want — the perfect mixed tape!

- ✔ **Sample Songs:** When you're dying to check out the player but haven't yet put your collection into the BlackBerry Storm, go here. Your Storm comes with a few songs, and this is where you can find them.

- ✔ **Shuffle Songs:** Life is all about variety. When you're tired of the song order in your playlist, touch-press this option.

After you touch-press a view, touch-press one of the songs to start playing it. After Storm starts playing a song, it plays the rest of the music listed in the view you selected. The standard interface is shown in Figure 12-3.

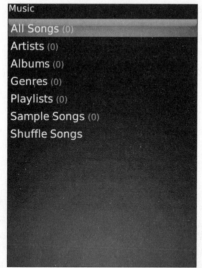

Figure 12-2:
Your music
collection.

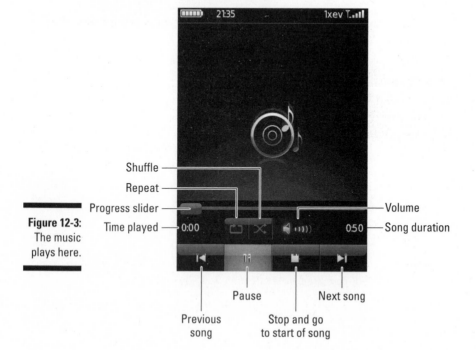

Figure 12-3:
The music
plays here.

Shuffle

Repeat

Progress slider

Time played

Volume

Song duration

Pause

Next song

Previous
song

Stop and go
to start of song

The two small pale icons just above the bottom row of icons indicate repeat and shuffle:

- ✔ If you want just this song to repeat again, touch-press the repeat icon. You can turn repeat off by touching the same icon.

- ✔ If you want the songs to be played again after the last song in the list is played, press the menu key, touch-press the repeat icon, and then touch-press Album.

- ✔ Bored with hearing the same sequence of songs? Touch-press the shuffle icon. Your songs will be played randomly.

You can't fast-forward or rewind the traditional way, but you can position where Storm is playing by finger-scrolling the progress slider.

BlackBerry Storm supports the following music formats (with file extensions):

- ✔ **ACC:** Audio compression formats AAC, AAC+, and EAAC+ (.aac and .m4a)

- ✔ **AMR:** Adaptive Multi Rate-Narrow Band (AMR-NB) speech coder standard (.mmr and .3gp)

- ✔ **MIDI:** Polyphonic MIDI (.mid, .midi, and .smf)

- ✔ **MP3:** MPEG Part 1 and Part 2 audio layer 3 (.mp3 and .mp4)

- ✔ **WMA:** Windows Media Audio 9, Pro, and 10 (.wma and .asf)

The earpiece–mic combo that comes with your BlackBerry Storm is for only one ear, which is an issue when you're on a train. To improve your experience, you can buy a *stereo* (two-ear) headset. A Bluetooth headset is a good option.

Creating a playlist

Sure, you have favorites in your song library. Having a playlist would be nice, right? On your Storm, you can create two types of playlists:

- ✔ **Standard:** A bare-bones playlist in which you manually add the music you want

- ✔ **Automatic:** A playlist in which you specify entries by artist, album, or genre, or any combination thereof

To create a playlist, follow these steps:

1. **Touch-press Music from the Media screen or from the Home screen.**

2. **From the Music screen, touch-press Playlists.**

3. **Touch-press [New Playlist].**

4. **Touch-press Standard Playlist or Automatic Playlist.**

   The screen that follows allows you to enter the name of your playlist and either add songs you select (Standard Playlist) or specify your playlist criteria (Automatic Playlist).

5. **If you selected Standard Playlist, do the following:**

   a. **Press the menu key and touch-press Add Songs.**

   Your music library listing appears.

   b. **Scroll to your music list and touch-press the song you want to add to your playlist.**

   You return to the preceding screen with the selected song added to your playlist.

   c. **Repeat Step 5b for each song you want to add.**

   d. **When you've finished adding songs, press the menu key and touch-press Save.**

   You're finished!

6. **If you selected Automatic Playlist, do the following:**

   a. **Touch-press the + button to the right of the music criteria and select one of the listed combinations.**

   Again, you can choose entries by Artist, Albums, or Genres, or a combination of any of the three options. If you choose by Artist, you'll be presented with a list of artists; the same is true of choosing by Albums and Genres, where a list of albums and genres, respectively, is shown for you to make a selection from.

   b. **Repeat Step 6a if you want to add more values to your criteria.**

   c. **After you add the criteria you want to your automatic playlist, press the menu key and touch-press Save.**

   You're finished!

 From time to time, you may play a song and want to add it to your playlist. No problem. While the song is playing, simply press the menu key and touch-press Add to Playlist. In the screen that follows, select the playlist to which you want to add the song.

Playing from your playlist

Playing your playlist is a no-brainer:

1. **Touch-press Music from the Media screen or from the Home screen.**

2. **From the Music screen, touch-press Playlists.**

3. **Touch the playlist you want to start playing.**

4. **Press the menu key and touch-press Play.**

Now Showing

Playing a video is similar to playing music. Simply follow these steps:

1. **Touch-press Videos from the Media screen.**

   (You can launch Media by touch-pressing the Media icon from the Home screen.) The screen shows Videos and a list of video files at the bottom of the screen.

2. **Touch-press a file to play it onscreen.**

You can record a video either from Videos or through the Video Camera application. To record a video from Video Camera, do the following:

1. **Touch-press Video Camera from the Media screen.**

   (You can launch Media from the Home screen.)

2. **Touch-press the white circle (record button) at the bottom of the screen to start recording.**

   Don't wait for "Cut!" You can pause the camera by touch-pressing the pause button. You see the familiar video and audio controls, which are, from left to right: continue recording, stop, and play. The functions of the other buttons are also obvious: rename (for the filename), delete, and send via email.

3. **Touch-press the stop button when you're ready to wrap up your home video.**

   You wind up at the previous screen with the video clip file listed. We know you're itching to watch it.

To record a video from the Videos app, do the following:

1. **Touch-press Videos from the Media screen.**

2. **Touch-press the white circle (record button) at the bottom of the screen to start recording.**

3. **Touch-press the escape key to wrap up your home video.**

Picture This

If you upgraded from an older BlackBerry, you may know Pictures, which lets you view, zoom into, and rotate pictures:

1. **Touch-press Pictures from the Media screen.**

2. **Touch-press one of the listed views to navigate to your pictures.**

   You can choose among the following views:

   - All Pictures: Displays pictures filed in device memory and on the microSD card.

   - Picture Folders: Displays only pictures filed in the current location of images captured by the Camera app. The default is the picture folder on the microSD card.

   - Sample Folders: Displays sample pictures that come with your smart phone.

3. **Finger-scroll to find the picture.**

4. **Touch-press the file.**

   Easy does it, right?

Check out Sample Pictures. Your BlackBerry comes with nice pictures you can use as the Home screen background. You can assign a cartoon to a contact as a Caller ID until you get a chance to take the person's picture and use that instead. (We describe how to do that in Chapter 11.)

Your Storm supports the following standard picture formats:

- ✔ **BMP:** Bitmap file format (`.bmp`)

- ✔ **JPEG:** Developed by the Joint Photographic Experts Group committee (`.jpg`); typically compresses the image file to a tenth of its size with little perceptible loss of image quality

- ✔ **PNG:** Portable Network Graphics (`.png`), which is a bitmapped image format that employs a lossless data transmission

- ✔ **TIFF:** Tagged Image File Format (`.tif`), which is mostly used in scanners and is under the control of Adobe Systems

- ✔ **WBMP:** Wireless Bitmap (`.wbmp`) file format, which is optimized for mobile devices

Viewing in Pictures

When you're in Pictures and navigating a folder, the default view always shows thumbnails. This allows you to quickly view many pictures at the same time before deciding which one to open.

Want to view them all? Run a slide show. When you've navigated to the folders where your pictures are listed, press the menu key and touch-press View Slide Show.

A convenient way to view pictures is to finger-scroll sideways. Scrolling right transitions the view to the next picture; you'll see a smooth sideways movement of the picture in the screen. Scrolling left transitions in the opposite direction until the preceding picture is displayed.

Zoom to see details

To zoom in a photo, do the following. Open the photo, press the menu key, and touch-press Zoom In. You can repeat this step to increase the degree of the zoom. After you are zoomed, you can finger-scroll to slide the picture around the screen. To zoom out, press the menu key and touch-press Zoom Out.

An image is normally defaulted to fit the screen, but you can toggle it by pressing the menu key and touch-pressing Fit to Screen or View Actual Size.

Lord of the Ring Tones

Ah, the proliferation of ring tones; that's history. Nothing beats hearing a loud, funky ring tone while you're sleeping on a bus or a train. You can wake other passengers, too, whether you want to use the top 40, old-fashioned digital beats, or something you recorded yourself.

To hear the ring tones that come with your BlackBerry Storm, do the following:

1. **Touch-press Ring Tones from the Media screen.**

   You see two views, All Ring Tones and My Ring Tones.

2. **Touch-press All Ring Tones.**

   All ring tones, including the preloaded ones, are displayed.

3. **Touch-press any one of them and enjoy.**

   While playing a ring tone, touch-press the right arrow to go to the next tone; touch-press the left arrow to go the previous one.

4. **Stumble on a ring tone you like.**

5. **Press the menu key and touch-press Set as Ring Tone.**

   You see a screen allowing you to choose the profile to which this ring tone applies (check out Chapter 3 for a quick refresher on profiles). You can choose All Profiles, Normal Profile Only, or Cancel.

6. **Touch-press either All Profiles or Normal Profile Only.**

   That ring tone plays when your phone rings on the profile you selected.

A ring tone is similar to a music file and includes the same music formats:

✓ ACC: Advanced Auto Coding format, used by iTunes

✓ AMR: Adaptive Multi-Rate, a popular audio format for mobile transmission and mobile applications

✓ M4A: A subset of ACC for audio only

✓ MIDI: Musical Instrument Digital Interface, a popular audio format for musical instruments

✓ MP3: MPEG Audio Layer 3, the most popular music format

✓ WMA: Windows Media Audio, a Microsoft audio file format

If you're familiar with audio-editing software, you can make your own ring tone. Save the tone as one of the formats just listed and copy it to your Storm (see the "Working with Media Files" section, later in this chapter, to see how to copy files from your PC to your Storm). The Internet has a plethora of ring tones, and many are free. The only possible harm you get from downloading one is being annoyed with how it sounds. The default Home page on Browser (mobile.blackberry.com) has links to sources of ring tones; touch-press the Fun and Pages link on the Home page.

Recording Your Voice

A feature-packed smart phone like your Storm *should* come with a voice recorder, and it does. Within Media is Voice Notes Recorder, a neat recording application. Now you can record your billion-dollar ideas without having to type every detail:

1. **Touch-press Voice Notes Recorder.**

   The Voice Notes Recorder application launches, sporting the simple and clean screen shown in Figure 12-4.

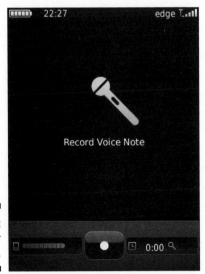

22:27   edge

Record Voice Note

0:00

Figure 12-4:
Record your
voice here.

2. **When you're ready, touch-press the record button (the white circle).**

   The app starts recording and the record button changes to the pause
   button.

   Your BlackBerry's microphone is designed to be close to your mouth,
   like any mobile phone should be.

3. **Press the pause button.**

   Familiar audio and video controls appear, from left to right: continue
   recording, stop, and play. Other buttons are rename (for renaming the
   file), delete, and send via email.

4. **Press the stop button to wrap it up.**

   You return to the Record Voice Notes screen, which now ready to
   record again.

Playing Your Voice Notes

After you recorded your billion-dollar idea, recalling or playing it back is a
snap:

1. **From Media, touch-press Voice Notes.**

   The Voice Notes app launches, with your voice notes listed.

You can launch Voice Notes Recorder from Voice Notes. To record, simply touch-press Voice Notes Recorder on the Voice Notes screen. Voice Notes Recorder is listed near the top of the screen. Then you can follow the procedure in the "Recording Your Voice" section, earlier in this chapter, starting with Step 2.

2. **Touch-press your voice recording when you need to hear your brilliant idea.**

Turning It Up (or Down)

Whether you're listening to music, watching a video, or listening to your voice recording, adjusting the volume is easy.

Your Storm comes with dedicated volume buttons on the top-right side of the device. The top button (with the plus sign) turns the volume up, and the bottom button (with the minus sign) turns the volume down. The onscreen volume slider reflects anything you did to the volume buttons.

Navigating the Menu

All Media applications except Pictures have a common menu. The menu items are mostly self-explanatory, but this section quickly highlights what you'll see. Because Pictures is the odd man out, we'll start with it.

Navigating the menu in Pictures

In the Pictures menu, press the menu key while you're viewing an image. On the menu that appears, you see the following items:

- **Next:** Jumps to the next item in the list. This option appears only if an item is after this image file in the current folder.
- **Previous:** Jumps to the previous item. This option appears only if a previous item is in the current folder.
- **Delete:** Deletes the image file.
- **Move:** Moves the file to a different folder.
- **Rename:** Renames the image file.
- **Properties:** Displays the image file's location, size, and time of last modification.

Navigating the menu in Music, Videos, Ring Tones, and Voice Notes

Whether you are watching a video or playing music, a ring tone, or a voice note, you see the following items after pressing the menu key:

- ✔ **Replay:** Plays the media file again from the start.
- ✔ **Repeat:** Plays the same media file after it reaches the end.
- ✔ **Show Playlist:** Displays the list of media files in the current folder or playlist.
- ✔ **Activate Handset:** Mutes the device's speaker. Use this if you want to use the earpiece. This menu item appears only if you have activated the speakerphone.
- ✔ **Activate Speakerphone:** Uses the device's speaker and mutes the earpiece. This menu item appears only if the handset is activated.

Using Explore

You can navigate to a media file in many ways, but Explore is the quickest way to find a file. It has similarities to Windows Explorer and a search facility similar to Find in BlackBerry applications such as Contacts, MemoPad, and Tasks.

To launch Explore, touch-press Media from the Home screen, press the menu key, and touch-press Explore. The Explore screen displays the device's topmost folders, which are Media Card and Device Memory.

Folders are in a tree hierarchy. You get into the *child* folders, or subfolders, by touch-pressing from the *parent* folder, or top folder.

If you've turned on a picture's Hidden property, using Explore is the only method in your Storm through which you'll be able to locate the file again:

1. **Navigate to the folder where your picture file is located.**

   If you don't know exactly where the picture file is located, you may have to touch-press different folders until you find the file.

2. **Press the menu key and touch-press Show Hidden.**

The default location for pictures taken by the Camera application is `/Device Memory/home/user/pictures` or `/Media Card/BlackBerry/pictures`.

Memory Use

Don't leave home for vacation without extra space for photos. Wonder how much space is left on your media card? Do the following:

1. **Touch-press Media from the Home screen.**

2. **Press the menu key and touch-press Memory Use.**

   A Memory Use screen similar to the left side of Figure 12-5 appears; giving you a rundown of how much space is used and remaining on the media card and in device memory. Touch-press the Details button if you want a breakdown, as shown on the right side of Figure 12-5.

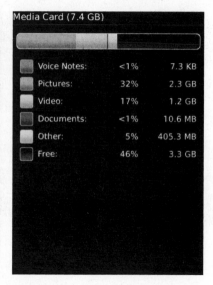

Figure 12-5: Memory use on the media card.

Changing the Media Flavor

As with the rest of your Storm applications, you can customize some parts of the media applications. You do so through the Options screen in Media:

1. **Press the menu key while in the Media app.**

   You can press the menu key while you're in any application inside Media too.

2. **Touch-press Options.**

   The Media Options screen appears, as shown in Figure 12-6. Each option is described in the following sections.

Figure 12-6:
Top of the
Media
Options
screen (left)
and the bot-
tom (right).

Customizing Media

Starting at the top of the Media Options screen and below the General section, you can finesse the following options:

- ✓ **Close Media Player When Inactive:** The default is Off, but you can set
  this option to 5, 10, 20, 30, or 45 minutes. This option can save battery
  life if you get distracted and leave your Storm on a table playing your
  favorite video.

- ✓ **Set Convenience Keys:** Change the settings for the right and left convenience keys, which are shortcut keys to an application. The right
  convenience key defaults to launching the Camera app, and the left convenience key defaults to launching Voice Dialing.

Going down the Media Options screen, under the Playback section, you can
customize the following options:

- ✓ **Headset Equalizer:** The default is Off, but if you want a different audio
  setting, you have several options: Bass Boost, Bass Lower, Dance, Hip
  Hop, Jazz, Lounge, Loud, R&B, Rock, Treble Boost, Treble Lower, and
  Vocal Boost.

- ✓ **Audio Boost:** You can set this option On or Off.

- ✓ **Turn Off Auto Backlighting:** Your Storm includes a backlight feature,
  which provides additional screen lighting. The backlight turns on when
  you move the Storm from shade to direct sunlight. When backlighting
  keeps bothering you when you're watching a movie, this is the place to
  toggle it off.

Turn off backlighting when you badly need battery juice.

- **Display Closed Captions:** This option applies only to videos that support closed captions. The options are Yes (the default) and No.

- **Appearance:** This option changes the appearance of Media. Choose Style 1 or Style 2 (the default).

- **Position:** This option refers to the location of the playback controls. You can choose Top Left, Top, Top Right, Bottom Right, Bottom (the default), or Bottom Left.

- **Font Scale:** Choose the size of the font you can use in Media during playback: Largest, Larger, Large, Normal (the default), Small, Smaller, or Smallest.

The box with a line that displays `For your viewing pleasure` works with Display Closed Captions. If you opt to display closed caption, this box shows up as a way to illustrates where the closed caption is going to appear during playback.

Customizing Pictures

Toward the bottom of the Media Options screen and below the Pictures section, you can change the Pictures app in the following ways:

- **Sort By:** This option toggles file sorting based on recent updates or the filenames of your pictures.

- **Slide Show Interval:** When viewing your files in a slide show, a picture appears for this many seconds before moving to the next picture.

- **Exclude Folders:** Navigate to a picture folder and exclude the display of pictures inside it. The fewer pictures you have or the fewer pictures that are displayed, the faster Pictures loads the list. So this option isn't really intended for your secret folders, but hey, you can use it for hiding something too.

Working with Media Files

To acquire media files for your BlackBerry Storm, you have as many choices as there are ice cream flavors. This section describes the most common ways to get media files: using the Storm as a flash drive, using Media Manager, synchronizing with iTunes, and downloading sounds.

Because the Storm does not have a physical keyboard, you lose the speed inherent in keyboard shortcuts. App developer NikkiSoft introduced QuickLaunch for the original BlackBerry Storm, and it remains a must-have app. QuickLaunch enables you to set shortcuts for common tasks, such as calling your significant other, e-mailing your boss, or visiting a specific Web site. Setting a convenience key to open QuickLaunch allows you to access these shortcut commands immediately, saving time and touch-screen presses.

Using your Storm as a flash drive

If you are a Windows user, the most common way to manipulate media files into and out of your Storm is to attach it to a PC and use Windows Explorer:

1. **Connect your BlackBerry to your PC, using the USB cable that came with your Storm.**

   Only folders and files stored on the microSD card will be visible to your PC. Make sure that the microSD card is in your BlackBerry Storm before you connect your Storm to the PC.

   When connected, the Storm screen displays a prompt for enabling mass storage mode.

2. **On the Storm screen, touch-press Yes.**

   A screen appears on your Storm, asking for your password.

3. **On the Storm screen, type your BlackBerry password.**

   The device is now ready to behave like an ordinary flash drive. On your PC, the Removable Disk dialog box opens.

4. **On your PC, in the Removable Disk dialog box, click Open Folder to View Files and then click OK.**

   The familiar Windows Explorer screen appears.

5. **Manipulate your media files as you want.**

   You can do anything you typically do with a normal Windows folder, such as drag and drop, copy, and delete files.

6. **Close Windows Explorer when you're finished.**

If you are a Mac user, you can easily manipulate media files by connecting your Storm to your Mac:

1. **Connect your BlackBerry to your Mac, using the USB cable that came with your Storm.**

Only folders and files stored on the microSD card are visible to your Mac. Make sure the microSD card is in your BlackBerry Storm before you connect the Storm to the Mac.

When connected, the Storm screen displays a prompt for enabling mass storage mode.

2. **On the Storm screen, touch-press Yes.**

   A screen appears on the Storm, asking for your password.

3. **On the Storm screen, type your BlackBerry password.**

   The device is now ready to behave like an ordinary flash drive, and a disk drive icon titled BLACKBERRY appears on the Mac desktop.

4. **On your Mac, click the BLACKBERRY disk drive icon.**

   The familiar Finder screen appears.

5. **Manipulate your media files as you want.**

   You can do anything you typically do with a normal Mac folder, such as drag and drop, copy, and delete files.

6. **Close Finder when you're finished.**

Meet and greet Media Manager

Roxio is known for its CD-ripping software. (*Ripping* converts music files in CD format to other popular compressed formats.) RIM licensed a portion of Roxio and packaged it with the Windows version of BlackBerry Desktop Software. Even though this version doesn't offer the entire Roxio software suite, you can still take advantage of fantastic features, such as

- ✔ Ripping CDs
- ✔ Converting files to get the best playback on your Storm
- ✔ Managing music files
- ✔ Syncing media files to your device

If you have an old version of Media Manager, just point your desktop Internet browser to http://na.blackberry.com/eng/services/desktop for directions on downloading the latest version for free and installing it on your PC.

In the following sections, we show you the Media Manager interface and how to copy a video file onto your Storm.

Accessing Media Manager

You can access Media Manager through BlackBerry Desktop Manager, which Chapter 15 describes in detail. Get to Desktop Manager this way:

1. **On your PC, click the Windows Start button.**

2. **Choose All Programs⇨BlackBerry⇨Desktop Manager.**

   BlackBerry Desktop Manager appears, as shown in Figure 12-7.

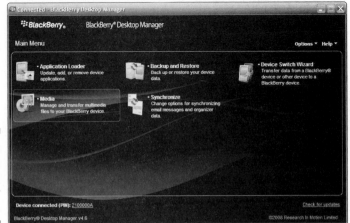

Figure 12-7: Access Media Manager here.

3. **Click the Media icon.**

   A screen appears, showing Media Manager and BlackBerry Media Sync sections. Each section has a Start button.

4. **In the Media Manager section, click the Start button.**

   The initial Media Manager screen is well organized and gives you the following options: Manage Pictures, Manage Music, Manage Videos, and View Connected Devices.

5. **Click one of the options.**

The Media Manager screen (shown in Figure 12-8) is easy to use and has the same interface as Windows Explorer:

✔ The left side is where you navigate to your folders and files.

✔ The right side displays the files in the folder you selected on the left side.

Other features of Media Manager

Spend some time exploring Media Manager. It has interesting features you may find useful. Here's a quick rundown of what you can do with Media Manager:

✔ Import media files

✔ E-mail media files

✔ Enhance photos and apply special effects to photos by using PhotoSuite

✔ Set song info (such as the title, the artist, the album, the genre, the year, or an image) to show as track art when playing a song

✔ Record audio

✔ Customize photo printing

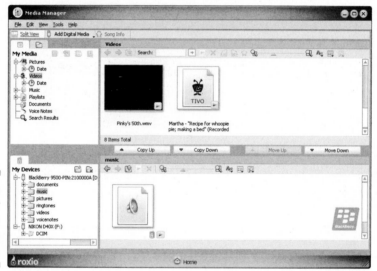

Figure 12-8: View your media files in this screen.

The top-left section — My Media — represents your desktop; the bottom-left section — My Devices — represents your Storm. You can move or copy files easily. When you're copying, for example, one section can be the source, and the other section can be the destination. By simply dragging the files between the two sections, you can copy on the same screen. Neat.

Importing media files to Media Manager

Here's a quick and easy way to import media files:

1. In Windows Explorer, navigate to find the media files you want.

2. Drag and drop the files into Media Manager.

You can drag and drop files to the folder in the left part of the screen (where the folder tree appears) or to the right part (where the files are listed). Just make sure that when you're doing the latter, the current folder in the tree view is the folder where you want the media files to be imported.

You can also use Media Manager to locate the files you want without going through Windows Explorer. The trick is to change the view to Folders. Check out the two tabs in the top-left corner. The first tab, My Media, is the default view. The Folders tab, just to the right of My Media, bears an icon of (go figure) a folder.

Click the Folders tab. You see a tree view, but this time it looks exactly like you see it in Windows Explorer, as shown in Figure 12-9. The files can be on your local hard drive or in a network folder accessible by your desktop computer.

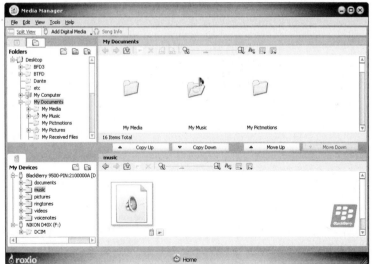

Figure 12-9: Navigate to your desktop media files here.

Not all media file types are directly compatible with your Storm. This is especially true for video files. But Media Manager can convert most media files to a usable Storm format.

Adding a media file to your Storm

Time to copy files to your Storm. Here's the rundown:

1. Connect your Storm to your PC, using the USB cable that came with your BlackBerry.

2. **On the Media Manager screen, drag and drop your media files from the My Media view to any folder in My Devices.**

   You can drag and drop an entire album. After dropping a media file, you're prompted to convert the file to a format that's usable by your Storm, as shown in Figure 12-10.

Figure 12-10:
Choose to
convert your
media files
for optimum
playback.

3. **Select a conversion option:**

   • **Convert for Optimal Playback:** This is the safest bet and is the default. This option is applicable to video files where the converter makes sure that the video fits perfectly with the Storm's screen resolution.

   • **Copy with No Conversion:** Copies the file faster. The file is copied to your Storm as is, but the file might not play on your Storm.

   • **Advanced Conversion Options:** From here, another screen lets you downgrade the quality to minimize the file size. The option also allows you to crop the video so that the entire screen is filled instead of showing dark margins.

4. **Click OK to begin the transfer.**

Synchronizing with iTunes using BlackBerry Media Sync

If you have an iPod, you're probably using iTunes and maintaining a playlist and perhaps a subscription to podcasts or videocasts. Podcast files are downloaded to iTunes via RSS. *RSS* — Really Simple Syndication — is a kind of digital file publish-subscribe mechanism. RSS is the mechanism iTunes uses to receive audio and video recordings, which most people refer to as *podcasts* and *videocasts,* respectively.

To sync your Storm with iTunes, follow these quick and easy steps:

1. **Connect your Storm to your desktop PC, using the USB cable that came with your BlackBerry.**

2. **Click the Windows Start button.**

3. **Choose All Programs➪BlackBerry➪Desktop Manager.**

4. **When BlackBerry Desktop Manager appears (refer to Figure 12-7, earlier in this chapter), click the Media icon.**

   A screen appears, showing Media Manager and BlackBerry Media Sync sections. Each section has a Start button.

5. **In the BlackBerry Media Sync section, click the Start button.**

   A new screen appears, such as the one shown in Figure 12-11.

Figure 12-11:
The
BlackBerry
Media Sync
screen.

6. **Click the Show iTunes Playlist icon (in the bottom-left corner).**

   A list of what you have in iTunes appears, as shown in Figure 12-12. This is the part of the screen where you choose iTunes media file types.

Downloading sounds

RIM offer a Web site from which you can sample and download new ring tones, alarms, notifiers, and tunes. On your Storm, simply go to `http://mobile.blackberry.com`. Finger-scroll down to the Personalize section and touch-press the Ringtones link. A list of available ring tones is displayed. And did we mention that they're free?

Touch-pressing the ring tone link gives you an option to play the tone or download it to your Storm. Downloaded ring tones are filed in the My Ring Tones section of the Ring Tones screen when you open the Ring Tones app inside the Media application.

RIM isn't the only site where you can find ring tones. The Web is a treasure trove, and ring tones and other media files are safe to download, so go hunting.

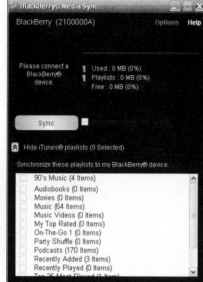

Figure 12-12:
Choose
iTunes
playlists,
videos, and
podcasts
here.

The best place to find BlackBerry-related software, including ring tones, is to visit the ever-growing BlackBerry community on the Web. Check out `http://crackberry.com`, `http://blackberrycool.com`, and `http://blackberryreview.com`, to name a few.

Chapter 13

Getting Around with BlackBerry GPS

· ·

In This Chapter

▶ Using GPS safely

▶ Preparing to use GPS on your BlackBerry

▶ Choosing a GPS application

· ·

A few years back, when some Northern American network carriers introduced *global positioning system (GPS)* on their versions of the BlackBerry, we were quite impressed . . . until we tried it. The response time was slow, and it wasn't accurate. On top of that, the network carriers charged an arm and a leg for this inferior service. As it turns out, those GPS functions weren't actually embedded in the BlackBerry. How low-tech!

Today, many BlackBerry models, including your BlackBerry Storm2, come with built-in GPS.

Depending on your network carrier, your BlackBerry Storm2 GPS might be disabled. For example, Verizon Wireless has a history of disabling GPS capabilities and steers users toward Verizon's own GPS application, VZ Navigator. However, an application such as Google Maps uses both GPS and the network to find your location. So if GPS is disabled, Google Maps can still approximate where you are on the map.

Putting Safety First

Some GPS features are useful not only while you're walking on the street, but also while you're driving a car. Although you'll be tempted to use BlackBerry GPS while driving, we *strongly* suggest that you not adjust it while you're driving.

Before you start using BlackBerry GPS in your car, you need to get a car holder (preferably a car kit with a car charger) and to resolve the BlackBerry backlight idle timeout issue. Your BlackBerry Storm's screen automatically dims when idle to conserve battery power, but this presents a problem when you are driving.

You can buy a car kit online by searching for *BlackBerry car kit.* Or go to one of the following links:

✔ www.shopblackberry.com

✔ www.shop.crackberry.com

Now that you have all you need to keep you safe, keep on reading.

Getting What You Need

GPS requires *navigation maps,* which are usually downloaded in little pieces as needed.

While you are using the map, the more you move about and use your GPS, the more map pieces you'll download, which means you might have to pay when your data quota is used up. If you didn't subscribe to an *unlimited* data plan from your network carrier, be aware that going over your monthly data quota might result in extra charges from your carrier.

In general, for BlackBerry GPS to work, you need

✔ A BlackBerry with a built-in GPS *or* a BlackBerry with an external GPS and a Bluetooth connection (which the BlackBerry Storm has)

✔ A data plan from your network carrier (an unlimited data plan is recommended)

✔ To be in an area with a radio signal (so you can download the maps)

Choosing GPS Application Options

We've identified three GPS applications that you can use on your BlackBerry:

✔ BlackBerry Maps

✔ Google Maps

✔ TeleNav GPS Navigator

Both BlackBerry Maps and Google Maps are free.

BlackBerry Maps

Out of the box, your BlackBerry comes with the BlackBerry Maps application. See Figure 13-1.

Figure 13-1: BlackBerry Maps on the BlackBerry Storm.

You can use BlackBerry Maps to do the following:

✔ Find a location by typing an address or by using Contacts

✔ Get point-to-point directions (from an airport to a hotel, for instance)

✔ E-mail or SMS a location to colleagues and friends

✔ Turn GPS on or off

✔ Zoom into and out of the map

You can turn GPS on or off. You can still perform these functions with it turned off, but you won't see your location.

You can tweak the light setting in BlackBerry Maps as follows:

1. **Press the menu key and touch-press Maps.**

2. **Press the menu key and touch-press Options.**

3. **In the Backlight Timeout When field, touch-press < 50% Battery.**

   You can set this to whatever you like, but we recommend <50% or <25%.

4. **Press the menu key and touch-press Save.**

Google Maps

Google Maps is the mobile version of `maps.google.com`. It has most of the online features, including satellite imaging and traffic information. Best of all, it's free. Like BlackBerry Maps, Google Maps can be used even without GPS.

You can search for businesses and landmarks. It's like having the ultimate 411 (with a map) at the tip of your fingers.

Because Google Maps doesn't come with your BlackBerry, you need to download it. Follow these steps:

1. **Open your BlackBerry Storm Browser.**

2. **Go to www.google.com/gmm.**

   The Web page loads, and its icon appears on your Home screen.

3. **After Google Maps is loaded, press the menu key.**

   From here, you can do the following:

   - Find businesses and landmarks, including phone numbers, street addresses, and Web addresses

   - Find and map exact addresses

   - Get step-by-step directions from point A to point B

   - View satellite images of the current map

   - Get traffic information for major highways

   With GPS on, your current location is a blue blinking dot; see Figure 13-2.

Figure 13-2: Google Maps showing a street view (left) and a satellite view (right) of the current location.

You need to have a radio signal to download maps to your BlackBerry Storm. In addition, we recommend having an unlimited data plan if you use GPS a lot.

TeleNav GPS Navigator

TeleNav GPS Navigator is a full-featured GPS solution; it's a GPS *device replacement,* which means that the folks at TeleNav want you to use your BlackBerry in the car. Unlike the other products listed earlier, TeleNav has turn-by-turn voice instructions to get you to your destination.

If you are going on a road trip, we highly recommend that you first purchase a car kit mount so your Storm2 is easily visible while you are driving; see Chapter 19 for information on car mount kits.

TeleNav's feature list is extensive and includes these features:

- ✔ 3D maps
- ✔ Real-time compass
- ✔ Wi-Fi hotspot finder

The feature we like the most is the human-voice step-by-step driving directions. Depending on your network carrier, TeleNav costs about $10 a month and offers a 60-day free trial. Visit www.telenav.com for more information. After the product is downloaded, an icon appears on your screen.

Chapter 14

Calling Your Favorite Person

In This Chapter

▶ Using the Phone application

▶ Making and receiving calls

▶ Customizing your BlackBerry phone

▶ Conferencing with more than one person

▶ Talking hands free on your BlackBerry phone

▶ Multitasking with your BlackBerry phone

T he BlackBerry phone operates no differently from any other phone you've used. Why bother with this chapter? Your BlackBerry phone can do things your run-of-the-mill cellphone can't. For example, when was the last time your phone was connected to your to-do list? Have you ever received an e-mail and placed a call directly from that e-mail? We didn't think so. But with your BlackBerry, you can do all these things and more.

Using the BlackBerry Phone Application

The folks at RIM have created an intuitive user interface to all the essential Phone features, including making and receiving calls.

Making a call

To make a call, follow these steps:

1. **Press the green send key.**

2. **Touch-press the phone number of the person you want to call.**

3. **Press the green send key again to call.**

Calling from Contacts

Because you can't possibly remember all your friends' and colleagues' phone numbers, calling from Contacts is convenient and useful. To call from Contacts, follow these steps:

1. **Press the green send key.**

   The Phone application opens.

2. **Press the Contacts tab (top-right tab).**

   Contacts opens. From here, you can search as usual for the contact you'd like to call.

3. **From Contacts, touch-press your call recipient.**

4. **Press the green send key.**

   This makes the call.

Using a calling card or dialing an extension

Have you ever dialed a long-distance number using a calling card? First you call the calling-card access number, then you enter the code, and then you dial the long-distance number. Major pain in the behind. Although not as bad, dialing someone's extension isn't fun either.

In Contacts, under the Contact Phone Number field, you type x and the extension number. The next time you call that contact, a screen asks if you want the extension dialed for you (see Figure 14-1). You can do the same with a calling-card access number, but add the access number and x in front of the phone number.

Figure 14-1: Using a calling card to call internationally with ease.

For example, if you're in the United States and using a calling card for a United Kingdom number, the phone number field in Contacts would look like this: 800-555-1314x011-44-775-555-1212. The phone number is 011-44-775-555-1212; the calling-card access number is 800-555-1314.

Getting a call

Receiving a call on your BlackBerry is even easier than making a call. You can receive calls in a couple of ways:

- ✔ **Use your automated answering feature.** Automated answering is triggered when you take your BlackBerry out of your holster; in other words, just taking out the BlackBerry forces it to automatically pick up any call, so you can start talking right away. The disadvantage of this is that you don't have time to see who is calling you (on your Caller ID).

- ✔ **Answer manually.** When you get a call, your screen will look something like Figure 14-2. Just touch-press Answer to pick up the phone.

Figure 14-2: There's an incoming call for you!

To disable autoanswering, make sure the Auto Answer Call option is set to Never. You can get to the Auto Answer Call option by pressing the menu key from the Phone application, touch-pressing Options from the Phone menu, and then touch-pressing General Options.

What's the advantage of disabling autoanswering? Manual answering allows you to answer or ignore a call, as shown in Figure 14-3. This way, you can see on your Caller ID who's calling and then pick up or ignore.

Figure 14-3:
The
BlackBerry
Storm
screen
while you're
on a call.

Muting your call

Muting lets you hear but not be heard. This option is useful when you're on a conference call (see the upcoming section "Arranging Conference Calls"). Maybe you're on the bus or have kids in the background.

To mute or unmute your call, toggle the Mute icon.

Turning down the volume

You can adjust the call volume, a simple yet important action on your BlackBerry phone, by pressing the volume up or volume down key on the right side of your BlackBerry Storm during a call.

Customizing Your Phone

For your BlackBerry phone to work the way you like, you first have to set it up the way you want. This section offers some settings that can make you the master of your BlackBerry phone.

Setting up your voice mail number

This section shows you how to set up your voice mail access number. Unfortunately, the instructions for setting up your voice mailbox vary, depending on your service provider. But usually, you can access the voice mail by pressing the menu key in the Phone application and touch-pressing the Call Voice Mail option.

Most service providers are more than happy to walk you through the steps to get your mailbox set up in a jiffy.

To set up your voice mail access number:

1. **Press the green send key.**

   The Phone application opens.

2. **Press the menu key and touch-press the options item.**

   A list of phone options appears.

3. **Touch-press Voice Mail.**

   This opens the Voice Mail Configuration screen.

4. **In the Access the Number field, type your voice mail access number.**

   If this field is empty and you don't know this number, contact your service provider and ask for your voice mail access number. Typically, it's your mobile number.

5. **Touch-press the menu key and then touch-press Save.**

Using call forwarding

The BlackBerry has two types of call forwarding:

- **Forward All Calls:** Any calls to your BlackBerry are forwarded to the number you designate. Another name for this feature is *unconditional forwarding.*

- **Forward Unanswered Calls:** Calls that meet different types of conditions are forwarded to different numbers as follows:

  - If Busy: You don't have call waiting turned on, and you're on the phone.

  - If No Answer: You don't hear your phone ring or can't pick up your phone. (Perhaps you're in a meeting.)

  - If Unreachable: You're out of network coverage and can't get a signal.

Out of the box, your BlackBerry forwards any unanswered calls, regardless of conditions, to your voice mail number by default. However, you can add new numbers to forward a call to.

You need to be within network coverage before you can change your call forwarding option. After you're within network coverage, you can change your call forwarding settings by doing the following:

1. **Press the green send key.**

   The Phone application opens.

2. **Press the menu key and touch-press Options.**

   A list of phone options appears.

3. **Touch-press Call Forwarding.**

   Your BlackBerry attempts to connect to the server. If successful, you see the Call Forwarding screen.

   If you don't see the Call Forwarding screen, wait until you have network coverage and try again.

4. **Press the menu key and touch-press Edit Numbers.**

   A list of numbers appears. If this is the first time you're setting call forwarding, mostly likely your voice mail number is the only one in the list.

5. **To add a new forwarding number, press the menu key and touch-press New Number.**

   A pop-up menu prompts you to type the number.

6. **Type the number.**

   The new number you entered now appears in the call-forwarding list. You can add this new number to any call-forwarding types or conditions.

7. **Press the escape key.**

   You return to the Call Forwarding screen.

8. **Touch-press the If Unreachable field.**

   A drop-down menu lists numbers from the call-forwarding list, including the one you just added.

9. **Touch-press the number you want to forward to and then touch-press to confirm.**

   The selected number appears in the If Unreachable field. You can see this on the Call Forwarding screen.

10. **Press the menu key and touch-press Save.**

    Your changes are confirmed.

Arranging Conference Calls

To have two (or more) people on the phone with you — the infamous *conference call* — do the following:

1. **Use the Phone application to call the first person.**

2. **While the first participant is on the phone with you, touch-press the Add Participant button on the screen (refer to Figure 14-3, earlier in this chapter).**

   This automatically places the first call on hold and brings up a New Call screen.

3. **Type the phone number of the second person.**

   You can dial the number by using the onscreen number pad, by selecting a number from your call log, or by accessing it from your Contacts.

4. **Press the green send key.**

   The call to the second meeting participant is just like any other phone call (except that the first participant is still on hold on the other line).

5. **While the second person is on the phone with you, press the menu key and touch-press Join Conference, as shown in Figure 14-4.**

   This connects the first and second participants. Now you can talk with both participants at the same time.

Figure 14-4: Join two people in a conference call.

Having two people on the phone with you is also known as *three-way calling*. If you want to chat with four people — or even ten people — at the same time, you certainly can. Simply repeat Steps 2–5 until all the participants are on the phone.

Talking privately to a conference participant

During a conference call, you might want to talk to one person privately. This is called *splitting* your conference call. Here's how you do it:

1. **While on a conference call, press the menu key and touch-press Split Call.**

   A pop-up screen lists all the conference-call participants.

2. **Touch-press the person you want to speak with privately.**

   This puts all other participants on hold and connects you to the participant you selected. On the display screen, you can see who you're connected to; this confirms that you chose the right person to chat with privately.

3. **To talk to all participants again, press the menu key and touch-press Join Conference.**

Alternating between phone conversations

Whether you're in a private conversation during a conference call or you're talking to someone while you have someone else on hold, you can switch between the two conversations by *swapping* them. Follow these steps:

1. **While talking to someone, press the menu key and touch-press Hold.**

   That person is put on hold.

2. **Press the menu key and touch-press Swap.**

   You switch from the person with whom you're currently talking to the person who was on hold.

3. **Repeat Step 2 to go back to the original conversation.**

Communicating Hands Free

More and more places prohibit the use of mobile phones without a hands-free headset. Luckily for you, BlackBerry offers hands-free options.

Using the speaker phone

The speaker phone function is useful under certain situations, such as when you're in a room full of people who want to join in the conversation. Or you might be all by your lonesome in your office but are stuck rooting through your files — hard to do with a BlackBerry scrunched up against your ear. (We call such moments *multitasking* — a concept so important that we devote an entire upcoming section to it.)

To switch to the speaker phone while you're on a phone call, press the Speaker button onscreen (refer to Figure 14-3, earlier in this chapter).

Pairing your BlackBerry with a Bluetooth headset

Your Storm comes with a wired hands-free headset, so you can start using yours by plugging it into the headset jack on the right side of the Storm. You can adjust the headset's volume by pressing the volume up or volume down keys.

Using the wired hands-free headset can help, but the wired headset can get in the way if you're multitasking on your BlackBerry. The whole Bluetooth wireless thing comes in here. You can buy a Bluetooth headset to go with your Bluetooth-enabled BlackBerry.

After you purchase a Bluetooth headset, you can pair it with your BlackBerry Storm. Think of *pairing* a Bluetooth headset with your Storm as registering the headset with your Storm so that it recognizes the headset.

First things first: You need to prep your headset for pairing. Now, each headset manufacturer has a different take on this process, so consult your headset documentation for details.

With that out of the way, continue with the pairing as follows:

1. **From the Home screen, press the menu key and touch-press Connection Manager.**

   A pop-up screen appears.

2. **Touch-press the Enable check box next to Bluetooth and then touch-press Set Up Bluetooth.**

   If this is the first time you're using Bluetooth, you're asked to set a name for your device so that others can see your Storm when trying to connect to you via Bluetooth.

   If this isn't the first time, you see an Add Device pop-up screen with the following options:

   - Search: If you want to reach out to other devices
   - Listen: If you want other devices to find you.
   - Cancel: If you want to cancel this operation

3. **Touch-press Search.**

   You see the Searching for Devices progress bar . . . um, progressing. When your BlackBerry discovers the headset, a Select Device dialog box appears with the name of the headset.

4. **Touch-press the Bluetooth headset.**

   A dialog box prompts you for a passkey code to the headset.

5. **Type the passkey and touch-press Okay.**

   Normally, the Bluetooth passkey is 0000, but refer to your headset documentation.

   After you successfully enter the passkey, your headset is listed in the Bluetooth setting.

6. **Press the menu key and touch-press Connect.**

   Your BlackBerry attempts to connect to the Bluetooth headset.

Using your voice to dial

With your headset and the Voice Dialing application, you can truly be hands free. You may be wondering how to activate the Voice Dialing application without touching your BlackBerry. Good question. The majority of hands-free headsets (Bluetooth or not) come with a multipurpose button.

Usually, a multipurpose button on a hands-free headset can mute, end, and initiate a call. Refer to your hands-free headset's manual for more info.

To use hands-free dialing:

1. **Activate your headset.**

2. **Press its multipurpose button.**

   The Voice Dialing application is activated, and a voice states, "Say a command."

3. **Say "Call *name of person/number.*"**

 The Voice Dialing application is good at recognizing the name of the person and the numbers you dictate. However, we strongly suggest that you try the voice dialing feature before you need it.

Taking Notes While on the Phone

You're not stuck just talking to someone on the phone. When you're on your BlackBerry, you can use it for other tasks at the same time. Why not

- ✔ Take meeting notes while you're in a conference call?
- ✔ Look up (in BlackBerry Contacts) a phone number that your caller is asking you for?
- ✔ Make a to-do list while you're planning a party?
- ✔ Compose an e-mail thanking the caller for his time?

It makes sense to multitask while you're using a hands-free headset or a speaker phone. Otherwise, your face would be stuck to your BlackBerry.

After you don your hands-free headset or turn on a speaker phone, you can start multitasking:

1. **While in a conversation, from the Phone application, press the icon that looks like a house.**

   This gets you to the Home screen.

2. **Start multitasking.**

   While on the phone and multitasking, you can access the Phone menu from other applications. For example, you can end a call or put a call on hold from your to-do list.

Do this to take notes on your call:

1. **During a phone conversation, press the menu key.**

   Or you can press the notepad icon (see the bottom of Figure 14-3, earlier in this chapter); if you do, then go to Step 3.

2. **Touch-press Notes.**

   The Notes screen appears.

3. **Type notes for the conversation, as shown in Figure 14-5.**

   When the call ends, the notes are automatically saved for you.

Figure 14-5: Take notes while on a phone call.

Accessing phone notes

From the Call History list, you can access notes you've made during a call. In addition, you can edit and add new notes. Follow these steps:

1. **Press the green send key.**

   The Phone application opens.

2. **Touch-press the call log tab and highlight a call log (see Figure 14-6).**

3. **Press the menu key and touch-press View History.**

   The View Call Log opens for the highlighted call (see Figure 14-7).

4. **Press the menu key and choose one of the following:**

   • Add Notes: If the call has no notes

   • Edit Notes: If the call already has notes

6:13 PM
1x
My Number: 908 930 3621
9085551212
09/27
6:12p
7328881212
09/27
6:12p

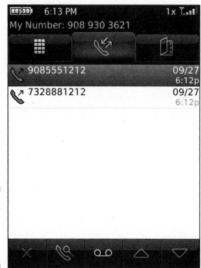

Figure 14-6: A screen showing call logs.

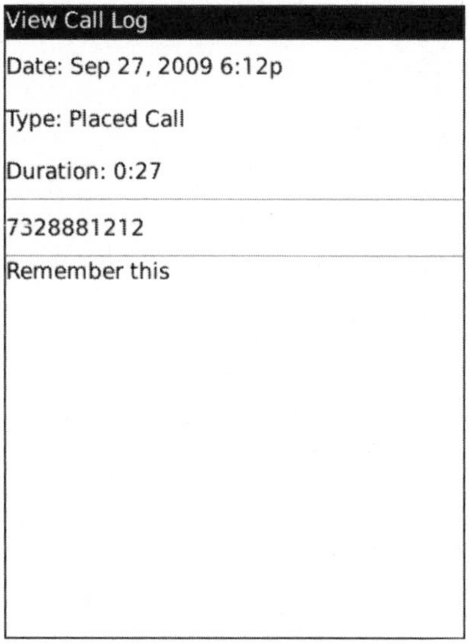
View Call Log
Date: Sep 27, 2009 6:12p
Type: Placed Call
Duration: 0:27
7328881212
Remember this

Figure 14-7: You can see conversation notes.

Forwarding phone notes

You can forward your phone notes just like an e-mail:

1. **While in the View Call Log screen (refer to Figure 14-7, in the preceding section), press the menu key.**

2. **Touch-press Forward.**

   A new e-mail opens, with the body of the e-mail filled with call details and notes. You can forward call notes via e-mail (no SMS or PIN messages). You can send the e-mail as you would any other e-mail. See Chapter 7 for more information on e-mail.

3. **Send the e-mail as you would send any other e-mail.**

   See Chapter 7 for details on sending an e-mail.

Part IV
Working with BlackBerry Desktop Manager

"Most of our product line is doing well, but the expanding touch pad on our PDA keeps opening unexpectedly."

In this part . . .

Here you discover essential information about some behind-the-scenes-yet-integral processes. Read all about BlackBerry Desktop Manager, which you direct to monitor and control database synchronization, and how to leverage Device Switch Wizard to migrate your existing data to your new BlackBerry. You also find out how to back up your data and the many ways of installing applications to your BlackBerry Storm.

Chapter 15

Syncing the Synchronize Way

In This Chapter

▶ Introducing BlackBerry Desktop Manager (PC and Mac)

▶ Preparing your desktop for PIM synchronization

▶ Using manual and automatic synchronization

*W*hat better way to keep your BlackBerry Storm updated than to synchronize it with your desktop application's data? Arguably, most of the data you need to synchronize is from your personal information manager (PIM) applications: notes, appointments, contacts, and tasks. The crucial piece for data synchronization to and from your device and desktop computer is Synchronize. This software within BlackBerry Desktop Manager allows you to synchronize your PIM data as well as to upload and download media files between your PC and your smart phone.

In this chapter, you explore Synchronize and see how to manually and automatically synchronize your Storm with your desktop computer. You find tips about which options you may want to use. Before delving into all that, however, we have a section on BlackBerry Desktop Manager.

If you're a Mac user, good news! The folks at Research In Motion have finally rolled out a Mac version of BlackBerry Desktop Manager. You are no longer left to use PocketMac, which is way behind on features and capabilities compared to its Windows cousin BlackBerry Desktop Manager. In this book, we show you how to use BlackBerry Desktop Manager on both Windows PC and Mac.

If you're using a corporate BlackBerry Storm that's running under BlackBerry Enterprise Server, you can skip this chapter. BlackBerry smart phones running under BlackBerry Enterprise Server synchronize over the air (OTA), via serial bypass, or wirelessly.

Data Synchronization on a Windows PC

BlackBerry Desktop Manager is the centerpiece of desktop activities, such as data synchronization, switching smart phones, and data backup on the BlackBerry.

BlackBerry Desktop Manager under Windows is a suite of programs that includes the following:

- ✔ **Application Loader:** Installs BlackBerry applications and updates the BlackBerry OS.

- ✔ **Backup and Restore:** Backs up your Storm data and settings. Check out Chapter 17 for details.

- ✔ **Synchronize:** Synchronizes Storm data with your PC (um, the topic of this chapter).

- ✔ **Media Manager:** Uploads media files to your Storm from your PC and vice versa (another topic in this chapter).

- ✔ **Device Switch Wizard:** Helps you transfer data from your existing mobile device to your Storm. See Chapter 16 for details.

BlackBerry Desktop Manager is software loaded on the CD that comes with your Storm. Your Storm's packaging provides instructions on how to install BlackBerry Desktop Manager on your desktop computer. For corporate users, check with your BlackBerry system administrator for details.

Installing BlackBerry Desktop Manager and Desktop Redirector

As we mention in the preceding section, use the CD that comes with your Storm to install BlackBerry Desktop Manager on your PC. At the same time, you can install Desktop Redirector. Desktop Redirector allows you to redirect e-mail that you receive in Outlook. This means that even if you get e-mails through Outlook (such as work e-mails), you can have those e-mails redirected to your Storm. (Read more about configuring e-mails in Chapter 7.)

Only e-mails from mailboxes connected to your Outlook mailbox are redirected. Your PC and the redirector must run all the time to keep redirection active.

When you insert the CD, the installation wizard runs automatically. Follow the onscreen instructions. On one of the wizard screens, you choose whether this installation is for personal e-mail or work e-mail. Choosing the option for work e-mail enables you to use Desktop Redirector for both personal and work e-mail.

If you aren't using a corporate BlackBerry Enterprise Server and want to redirect your Outlook e-mail to your Storm, when you're installing BlackBerry Desktop Manager, make sure that you select the Redirect Messages Using the BlackBerry Desktop Redirector option on the installation screen, as shown in Figure 15-1.

Figure 15-1:
Configure
the
BlackBerry
Desktop
Manager
installation
to include
Desktop
Redirector.

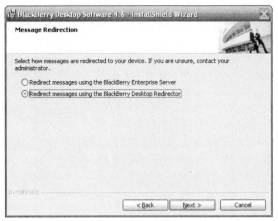

If your Storm is running under a corporate BlackBerry Enterprise Server, your e-mail is already redirected to your smart phone wirelessly, and choosing the BlackBerry Desktop Redirector could really mess things up. So don't do it! Most companies are protective of corporate data, including your work e-mails. Make sure you aren't violating your company's policy before you decide to redirect your work e-mails to your personal BlackBerry.

Launching BlackBerry Desktop Manager

In most Windows installations, you find the shortcut to launch BlackBerry Desktop Manager through your computer's Start menu. Follow these steps to launch BlackBerry Desktop Manager:

1. **Choose Start➪All Programs➪BlackBerry➪Desktop Manager.**

2. **Connect your Storm to your computer using the USB cable that came with your device.**

With the microSD card in your Storm, upon connecting to your PC, your Storm displays a prompt for enabling mass storage mode. It also asks for your Storm's password when you answer Yes to the prompt. Answer Yes and enter your password, and your Storm will behave like a flash drive. A drive letter will be added to My Computer (or just plain Computer in Microsoft Vista) in Windows Explorer, allowing you to treat the microSD card as a normal flash drive.

3. Launch BlackBerry Desktop Manager.

The BlackBerry Desktop Manager opening screen appears, as shown in Figure 15-2.

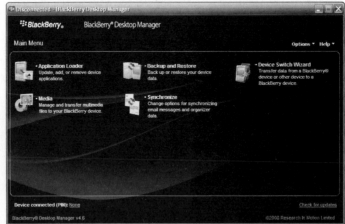

Figure 15-2:
BlackBerry
Desktop
Manager
under
Windows.

BlackBerry Desktop Manager installation can vary from phone provider to provider. You should see at least the following four icons, or applications:

- ✔ Application Loader (see Chapter 18)
- ✔ Backup and Restore (see Chapter 17)
- ✔ Media (see Chapter 12)
- ✔ Synchronize

Connecting BlackBerry Desktop Manager to your Storm

You establish a connection between your Storm and BlackBerry Desktop Manager through the USB cable. After BlackBerry Desktop Manager is running, it tries to find a BlackBerry (your Storm) on the type of connection specified. The default connection is USB, so you shouldn't need to configure anything.

Follow these steps to connect your Storm to BlackBerry Desktop Manager:

1. Plug your device into your desktop computer.

Keep your device on.

2. **Launch BlackBerry Desktop Manager.**

   BlackBerry Desktop Manager tries to find a BlackBerry (your Storm) on a USB connection.

3. **If your device has a password, BlackBerry Desktop Manager prompts you for the password.**

4. **Enter the password.**

   You see `Connected` as the screen heading. If, for some reason, you see `Disconnected` and no password prompt, one of the following is happening:

   • BlackBerry Desktop Manager can't find the device being connected via the USB cable. Make sure that the USB cable is properly attached at both ends.

   • The connection setting isn't set to use USB. To check this connectivity setting, go to Step 5.

5. **Choose Options⇨Connection Options on the right side of the BlackBerry Desktop Manager screen.**

   The screen shown in Figure 15-3 appears. Make sure that the connection setting uses USB.

6. **From the Connection Type drop-down list, select the USB connection with your Storm's PIN.**

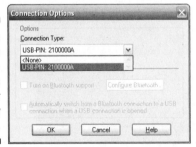

Figure 15-3: Possible connection types for your BlackBerry Storm.

Running BlackBerry Desktop Manager for the first time

If you're running BlackBerry Desktop Manager for the first time, the program does the following:

✔ Tries to make the initial configuration on your machine, which includes security encryption setup. It may ask you to randomly move your mouse to generate security encryption keys.

✔ Checks which applications are on your device and which required applications need to be installed. If it can't find a required application on your device, it prompts you to install it. You have the option to cancel and install later.

✔ Looks at the settings you have for your Synchronize software. If auto-synchronization is turned on, BlackBerry Desktop Manager attempts to run synchronization for your PIM. This is discussed in the section "Synchronizing automatically," later in this chapter.

Setting Up Synchronize on a Windows PC

Synchronize is the part of BlackBerry Desktop Manager that allows you to synchronize your data between your desktop computer and the Storm. (If the Storm is running on BlackBerry Enterprise Server, your data is already synced wirelessly, so you don't need your desktop for synchronization.) The Synchronize icon on the BlackBerry Desktop Manager screen appears with two opposing arrows on top of two paper images. To launch Synchronize, simply double-click its icon. A screen like the one shown in Figure 15-4 appears.

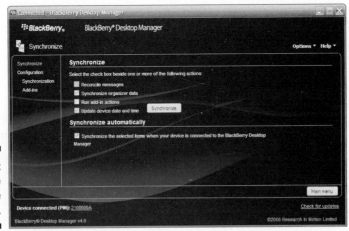

Figure 15-4:
The
Synchronize
screen.

The Synchronize screen is divided into two sections. You can navigate through the links on the left side:

✔ **Synchronize** (the default view) allows you to manually trigger synchronization. (Refer to Figure 15-4.) See the "Using on-demand synchronization" and "Synchronizing automatically" sections, later in this chapter, for more details and for when you use this screen.

✔ **Configuration** is where you can set up configuration and rules for reconciling data. Under the Configuration link are two subsections, Synchronization and Add-ins. These further help you organize the interface. Most of the configuration options you want to set are accessible through the Synchronization Configuration screen, which is shown in Figure 15-5. The following section helps you do that.

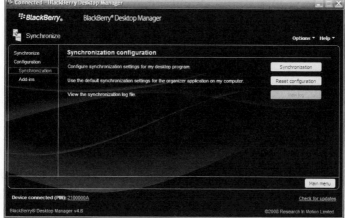

Figure 15-5: The Synchronization Configuration screen.

Configuring PIM synchronization

The important item in the Synchronization Configuration subsection, as shown in Figure 15-5, is the Synchronization button. You use that button to configure PIM synchronization.

Click the Synchronization button to display the screen shown in Figure 15-6. You can see that the names correspond to BlackBerry Storm applications, except for Contacts, which goes by the name Address Book. This screen is the entry point for the entire synchronization configuration for PIM applications. Selecting an application on this screen allows you to pair the PIM handheld application with a desktop application (most likely Outlook).

From the PIM configuration screen, select which application data you want to sync with your Storm. The following popular PIM applications can be synced to your Storm: ACT!, ASCII Text File Converter, Lotus Notes, Lotus Organizer, Microsoft Outlook, Microsoft Outlook Express, and Microsoft Schedule.

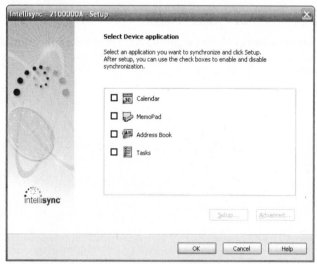

Figure 15-6:
The PIM
configura-
tion screen.

The types of application data that can be synchronized to your Storm are

- **Calendar:** Synchronize the appointments and events stored in your favorite PIM application.
- **MemoPad:** Synchronize any notes or text that you have been storing in your PIM application.
- **Address Book:** Synchronize any contact information with your Storm.
- **Tasks:** Synchronize your to-do list.

Follow these steps to set up your device's synchronization:

1. **Connect your Storm to BlackBerry Desktop Manager.**

2. **Click the Synchronize icon and then click the Synchronization link.**

    (The Synchronization link is below the Configuration link on the left side of the screen; refer to Figure 15-5, earlier in this chapter.)

3. **Click the Synchronization button.**

4. **Select the check box next to the application data type (Calendar, MemoPad, Address Book, or Tasks) that you want to synchronize.**

    For this example, select the Calendar application data type.

5. **Click the Setup button.**

    This opens the screen for the application — in this case, the Calendar Setup screen.

6. Select a PIM application from which to retrieve application data by clicking your desired application.

BlackBerry Desktop Manager pulls your selected application data from the application selected on this screen. In Figure 15-7, we selected Microsoft Outlook. This means that when we synchronize the Storm, BlackBerry Desktop Manager retrieves Calendar data from Microsoft Outlook.

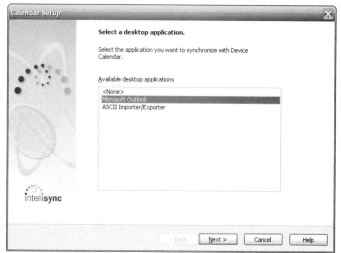

Figure 15-7:
Choose the desktop application here.

7. Click Next.

8. On the Synchronization Options screen that opens, select which direction the synchronization will follow (see Figure 15-8).

Here are the three available synchronization options:

- Two Way Sync allows you to synchronize changes in both your Storm and in your desktop application.

- One Way Sync from Device synchronizes only the changes made to your Storm. Changes to your desktop application aren't reflected in your Storm.

- One Way Sync to Device synchronizes changes made in your desktop application with your Storm. Any changes made in your Storm aren't reflected in your desktop application.

9. Click Next.

The Options screen opens for the PIM application you selected in Step 6. Figure 15-9 shows the Microsoft Outlook Options screen.

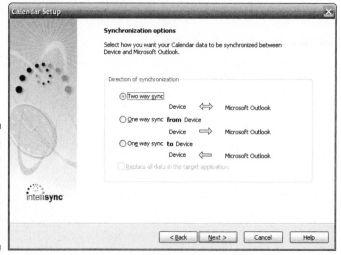

Figure 15-8:
Decide
which
direction
synchro-
nization
follows.

Figure 15-9:
Select
specific
application
settings
here.

For synchronization to Microsoft Outlook, make sure that you choose the correct user profile from the Outlook User Profile drop-down list. This is particularly pertinent in cases in which you have multiple user profiles in your computer. Choosing the wrong one may put the wrong data into your Storm.

You can also control the amount of data that is reconciled or synchro-nized in a given application. For example, in Figure 15-9, the center por-tion of the configuration allows you to specify whether to transfer all Calendar items, a set of appointments in the future, or items within a range of dates you enter.

Select the Remove Alarm for Past Items check box if you don't want to keep the alarm setting for events that have already occurred.

10. **Click Next and then click Finish.**

    Clicking the Next button brings you to the Calendar Setup Finish screen, and clicking the Finish button completes the configuration of the Calendar synchronization you selected.

Mapping fields for synchronization

For all four PIM applications, Synchronize is intelligent enough to know what information — such as names, phone numbers, and addresses in Contacts — corresponds to information in Outlook. A specific bit of information, or attribute, is a *field*. For instance, the value of a home-phone-number field in Contacts needs to be mapped to the corresponding field in Outlook so that information is transferred correctly.

But not all fields on the desktop side exist on the smart phone (and vice versa). For example, a Nick Name field doesn't exist in Storm Contacts but is available in Exchange (Outlook) Address Book. In some instances, Synchronize provides an alternative field and lets you decide whether to map it.

If you ever need to change the default mapping, you can. The interface is the same for all PIM applications. We use Contacts as our example in the following steps as we illustrate how to map and unmap fields:

1. **From BlackBerry Desktop Manager, click the Synchronize link.**

   The Synchronize screen appears.

2. **Click the Synchronization link.**

3. **Click the Synchronize button.**

   The PIM configuration screen appears (refer to Figure 15-6, earlier in this chapter).

4. **Select the Address Book check box.**

   The Advanced button is enabled.

5. **Click the Advanced button.**

   The Advanced screen opens, as shown in Figure 15-10.

6. **Click the Map Fields button.**

   The Map Fields screen for the Address Book/Contacts application appears; see Figure 15-11. To map or unmap, click the arrow icons.

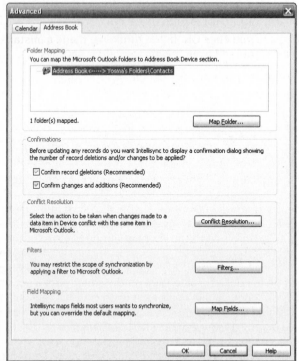

Figure 15-10:
The
Advanced
screen for
Address
Book.

Figure 15-11:
The Map
Fields
screen for
Address
Book.

If you aren't careful, you can inadvertently unclick a mapping (such as Job Title), and suddenly your titles aren't in sync. Double-check your mapping before you click OK. If you think you made a mistake, click Cancel to save yourself from having to restore settings.

7. **Click OK to save your changes.**

Confirming record changes

Face facts: Doing a desktop synchronization isn't a very interesting task, and few people perform it on a regular basis.

You can tell Synchronize to prompt you for any changes it's trying to make (or perhaps undo) on either side of the fence. The Advanced screen comes into the picture here. To get to this view, follow these steps:

1. **From BlackBerry Desktop Manager, click the Synchronize link.**

   The Synchronize screen appears.

2. **Click the Synchronization link.**

3. **Click the Synchronize button.**

   The PIM configuration screen appears (refer to Figure 15-6, earlier in this chapter).

4. **Select the Address Book check box.**

   If you want a PIM application other than Address Book, select that application from the list.

5. **Click the Advanced button.**

   The Advanced screen for Address Book appears (refer to Figure 15-10, in the preceding section). This screen has a Confirmations section and gives you two options:

   - Confirm Record Deletions (Recommended)
   - Confirm Changes and Additions (Recommended)

   Regardless of whether you select the first option, Synchronize displays a prompt if it detects that it's about to delete *all* records.

Resolving update conflicts

Synchronize needs to know how you want to handle any conflicts between your Storm and your desktop application. A conflict normally happens when the same record is updated on your Storm and also in Outlook. Suppose that you change Jane Doe's mobile number on both the Storm and Outlook on the PC. Where you resolve these conflicts is the same for all PIM applications. Again, for illustration, we use Address Book as an example:

1. **From BlackBerry Desktop Manager, click the Synchronize link.**

   The Synchronize screen appears.

2. **Click the Synchronization link.**

3. **Click the Synchronize button.**

   The PIM configuration screen appears (refer to Figure 15-6, earlier in this chapter).

4. **Select the Address Book check box.**

   If you want a PIM application other than Address Book, select that application from the list.

5. **Click the Advanced button.**

   The Advanced screen for Address Book appears (refer to Figure 15-10, earlier in this chapter). This screen has five sections, and the third section is Conflict Resolution.

6. **Click the Conflict Resolution button.**

   The Conflict Resolution screen is shown in Figure 15-12. From the Conflict Resolution screen, you can tell Synchronize to handle conflicts in a few ways. Here are the options:

Figure 15-12: Manage conflicts here.

Conflict Resolution - Address Book
Select the action to be taken when changes made to a data item in Device conflict with changes made to the same item in Microsoft Outlook.
○ Add all conflicting items
○ Ignore all conflicting items
⊙ Notify me when conflict occur
○ Device wins
○ Microsoft Outlook wins
OK   Cancel   Help

- Add All Conflicting Items: When a conflict happens, add a new record to the Storm for the changes on the desktop and add a new record to the desktop for the changes on the Storm.

- Ignore All Conflicting Items: Ignores the change and keeps the data the same on both sides.

- Notify Me When Conflicts Occur: This option is the safest. Synchronize displays the details of the conflict and lets you resolve it.

- Device Wins: This option tells Synchronize to disregard the changes in the desktop and use handheld changes every time it encounters a conflict. Unless you are sure that this is the case, you should not choose this option.

- Microsoft Outlook Wins: If you aren't using MS Outlook, this option is based on your application. This option tells Synchronize to always discard changes on the smart phone and use the desktop application change when it encounters a conflict. We don't recommend this option because there's no telling on which side you made the good update.

7. **Select the option you want.**

8. **Click OK to save the settings.**

Ready, set, synchronize!

Are you ready to synchronize? Previously in this chapter, we show you ways to define synchronization filters and rules for your e-mail and PIM data. Now it's time to be brave and click the button. You can synchronize in one of two ways:

- ✔ **Manually:** Click the Synchronize Now icon.
- ✔ **Automatically:** Choose How Often on the calendar.

Using on-demand synchronization

On-demand synchronization is a feature in Synchronize that lets you run synchronization manually. Remember that even if you set up automatic synchronization, actual synchronization doesn't happen right away. So if you make updates to your appointments in Outlook while your Storm is connected to your PC, this feature allows you to be sure that your updates make it to your Storm before heading out the door.

Without delay, here are the steps:

1. **From BlackBerry Desktop Manager, click the Synchronize link.**

   The Synchronize screen appears (refer to Figure 15-4, earlier in this chapter). The following four check boxes let you be selective:

   - Reconcile Messages: You want to synchronize your e-mails between Outlook and your Storm.

   - Synchronize Organizer Data: You want to include notes, appointments, addresses, and tasks.

   - Run Add-In Actions: You have third-party applications that require data synchronization between your PC and your Storm.

- Update Device Date and Time: You want both the PC and Storm to have the same time. This ensures that you're reminded of your appointments at the same time for both Outlook and your Storm.

2. **Select the check boxes for the data you want to synchronize.**

3. **Click the Synchronize button.**

   Synchronize starts running the synchronization, and you see a progress screen. If you set up prompts for conflicts, and Synchronize encounters one, a screen appears so that you can resolve that conflict. When finished, the progress screen disappears and the Synchronize screen reappears.

   If you turned on automatic synchronization (see the next section), the items you select in Step 2 automatically sync every time you connect your Storm to your PC.

4. **Click the Close button.**

Synchronizing automatically

How many times do you think you reconfigure your Synchronize setup? Rarely, right? After you have it configured, that's it. And if you're like us, the reason you open BlackBerry Desktop Manager is to run Synchronize. So opening Synchronize and clicking the Synchronize button are annoying.

To make Synchronize run automatically every time you connect your Storm to your PC, simply make sure that you select the last check box on the Synchronize screen (refer to Figure 15-4, earlier in this chapter) — Synchronize the Selected Items When Your Device Is Connected to the BlackBerry Desktop Manager.

You may be asking, "What items will autosynchronization sync?" Good question. Synchronize automatically syncs the items you selected in the top portion of the Synchronize screen. Note that if you make a change, selecting or deselecting an item on the Synchronize screen, only the selected items will be synced automatically the next time you connect your Storm to your PC.

Data Synchronization on the Mac

The focus of your Mac activities — such as data synchronization and data backup on the BlackBerry — is *BlackBerry Desktop Manager*.

BlackBerry Desktop Manager for Mac has been a highly anticipated software program for a good reason: Folks in the Mac world have been waiting for a replacement of PocketMac, which is limited in functionality. BlackBerry Desktop Manager for Mac is fairly new, and if it doesn't come with your Storm packaging, no worries; you can download an installation program from RIM's Web site.

Installing BlackBerry Desktop Manager

We're assuming that you're not holding a CD of BlackBerry Desktop Manager for Mac, so in this section, we include the download steps. Here is a quick rundown on how to go about installing the application:

1. **Download the BlackBerry Desktop Manager installation file from** `http://na.blackberry.com/eng/services/desktop/desktop_mac.jsp.`

2. **On the download page, fill in the form and click Download.**

   After the file is downloaded, the screen showing two icons (BlackBerry Desktop Manager.mpkg and BlackBerry Desktop Manager Uninstaller) appears.

3. **Double-click BlackBerry Desktop Manager.mpkg.**

   A standard Mac warning message appears, telling you that you're about to run an installation of a program.

4. **Click Continue on the warning screen.**

   Another warning message appears. This time, the message tells you that PocketMac or the Missing Sync software will no longer be able to connect to your BlackBerry. Hey, you're probably installing the BlackBerry Desktop Manager because you're itching to replace PocketMac or the Missing Sync, so no worries there.

5. **Click Install Anyway.**

   An installation welcome screen appears.

6. **Click Continue.**

   Another prompt appears, this time asking you to agree to the license agreement.

7. **Click Agree.**

   A screen appears, allowing you to choose the location of the install. The default is your Mac's hard drive.

8. **Click Continue.**

   You're prompted for your Mac password.

9. **Enter your Mac password and click OK.**

   Before the installation starts, a screen appears, telling you that when the installation finishes, you need to restart your Mac.

10. **Click Continue Installation.**

    At this point, the installation kicks in. This may take a minute or two. When the installation is complete, you see a message to restart the Mac.

11. **Click Restart.**

Opening BlackBerry Desktop Manager for the first time

BlackBerry Desktop Manager will not be on your Mac's Dock (the bottom bar with application icons on Mac OS 10.5 or later) or on your Mac's desktop after your installation. You need to use the Finder app to locate it:

1. **If you have Mac OS 10.5 or later:**

   a. **Click the Finder application (the leftmost icon) on your Mac's Dock.**

      The Finder is launched with a screen displaying your Mac file system.

   b. **In the search text box (topmost-right corner) of the Finder screen, type** BlackBerry Desktop.

      The listing on the screen is the result of your search, and BlackBerry Desktop Manager is at the top of the list.

2. **If you have Mac OS prior to 10.5:**

   a. **Press Command+F to launch the Find utility.**

      The Find utility of the Finder application opens.

   b. **In the Find text box of the Find screen, type** BlackBerry Desktop.

      The listing on the screen is the result of your search, and BlackBerry Desktop Manager is at the top of the list.

3. **Connect your BlackBerry Storm to your Mac.**

4. **Click BlackBerry Desktop Manager in the Finder screen.**

   The screen in Figure 15-13 appears, displaying the BlackBerry connected to your Mac. In your case, it displays your Storm's PIN.

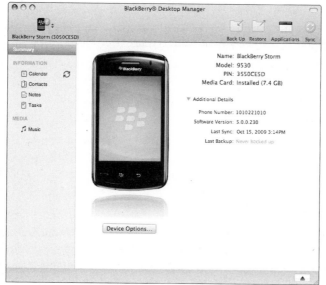

Figure 15-13:
BlackBerry
Desktop
Manager for
Mac main
screen.

Synchronizing, Mac Style

Synchronizing PIM data and music files is what most of us look for when talking about BlackBerry Desktop Manager. Just follow the succeeding short sections as we delve into the details on configuring the sync, doing a manual sync, and doing an automatic sync.

Setting synchronization options

You need to set synchronization options probably only once, but let's make sure you get them right. After all, the data between the Mac and the BlackBerry Storm should be synced the way you want it.

Device Options

At the bottom center of the BlackBerry Desktop Manager screen (refer to Figure 15-13, in the preceding section) is a Device Options button. Click this button, and you get the screen shown in Figure 15-14.

An important option you need to set is This Device Is Synchronized. If you sync your Storm with other machines or even if you have Google Sync for Calendars and Contacts, we advice that you choose With Other Computers. This ensures that the automatic sync option is disabled. One side effect of automatic sync is creating duplicate contacts on your Storm and your other desktop machines. However, if you sync Storm only with this Mac, select With This Computer Only.

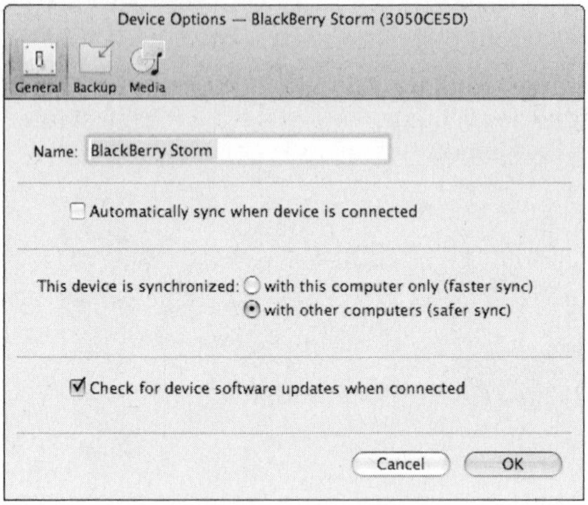

Device Options — BlackBerry Storm (3050CE5D)

General   Backup   Media

Name: BlackBerry Storm

☐ Automatically sync when device is connected

This device is synchronized: ◯ with this computer only (faster sync)
◉ with other computers (safer sync)

☑ Check for device software updates when connected

Cancel   OK

Figure 15-14:
Decide
whether you
want your
Storm to
sync only on
this Mac.

The listing on the left (under the Summary heading) contains links for navigating to the option screens. We describe each option in the following sections.

Calendar

Clicking the Calendar link on the BlackBerry Desktop Manager screen displays the screen shown in Figure 15-15. You can configure how your appointments are synced as follows:

- ✔ **Sync Calendar:** Include Calendar in the sync by selecting Two Way, or skip it by choosing Do Not Sync.

  A quick way to know that you set Calendar for Two Way sync is seeing two circular arrow icons next to the Calendar link on the left side of the BlackBerry Desktop Manager screen. This is true for Contacts, Notes, Tasks, and Music as well.

- ✔ **Sync:** This section applies only if you have multiple calendar applications on your Mac. You can include all calendars or choose one from the list. Your Storm handles the display of multiple calendar applications. The Storm Calendar app uses different colors to indicate which calendar an appointment belongs to.

- ✔ **Add Events Created on BlackBerry Device To:** The default Calendar on your Storm does not tie directly to any Mac applications. Appointments you create in your BlackBerry will not be synced to any Mac applications. Setting this option tells BlackBerry Desktop Manager to sync those appointments or events to a particular Mac application.

- ✔ **(Advanced Settings) Sync:** This setting allows you to limit the amount of appointments or events to sync on your Storm. After all, past events just occupy valuable space on your smart phone with no purpose but a record. Here, you can control which ones your Storm carries. Choose All Events (the default), Only Future Events, or Only Events *n* Days Prior and *n* Days

After. The last option allows you to have a range of dates relative to the current day. The default is 14 days in the past and 90 days after.

🖊 **(Advanced Settings) Replace All Calendar Events on This BlackBerry Device:** Keep this deselected unless you want a fresh start and want to copy to your Storm appointments or events from your Mac.

Figure 15-15:
Configure
Calendar
sync here.

Contacts

The Contacts link on the BlackBerry Desktop Manager screen displays the screen shown in Figure 15-16. Here, you can do the following:

🖊 **Sync Contacts:** Choose to include Contacts in the sync by selecting Two Way. Otherwise, select Do Not Sync.

🖊 **Sync:** Choose here to include all contacts and groups on syncing or click Selected Groups to sync only the groups you want.

🖊 **(Advanced Settings) Replace All Contacts on This BlackBerry Device:** Keep this deselected unless you want a fresh start and want to copy all contacts from your Mac to your smart phone.

Notes

The Notes link on the BlackBerry Desktop Manager screen displays the screen shown in Figure 15-17. This screen is where you configure how you want Notes or MemoPad items on your Storm synced:

✓ **Sync Notes:** Lets you configure whether or not you want Notes included in the sync. Choose Two Way or Do Not Sync (the default).

✓ **Sync Account:** If you have multiple note-keeping programs in your Mac, this setting allows you to choose which one you want to tie the sync into. The default is Apple Mail Notes.

✓ **(Advanced Settings) Replace All Notes on This BlackBerry Device:** If you select this option, the Mac side becomes your master. Keep this deselected unless you want a fresh start and want to copy to your Storm all notes from your Mac.

Tasks

Clicking the Tasks link on the BlackBerry Desktop Manager screen displays the screen shown in Figure 15-18. Note that the screen is similar to Calendar because most of the Tasks items have associated dates and are essentially tied to your Calendar. You can configure how your tasks are synced as follows:

✓ **Sync Tasks:** Choose to include Tasks in the sync (Two Way) or not (Do Not Sync).

✓ **Sync:** This section applies only if you have multiple calendar applications on your Mac. You can include all calendars or choose one of those listed. Your Storm handles the display of multiple calendar applications. The Storm Calendar app uses different colors to indicate which calendar an appointment belongs to.

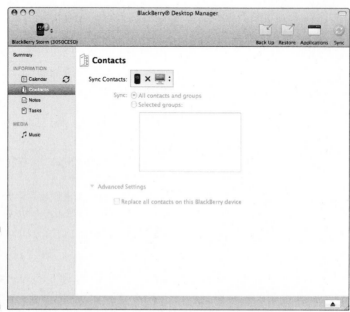

Figure 15-16:
Configure
Contacts
sync here.

Figure 15-17:
Configure
Notes sync
here.

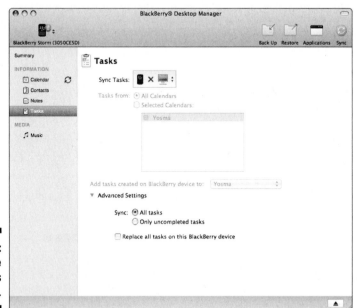

Figure 15-18:
Configure
the Tasks
sync here.

✔ **Add Tasks Created on BlackBerry Device To:** The default Calendar on your Storm does not tie into any Mac application. Tasks you created in your BlackBerry will not be synced to any of your Mac applications. Setting this option tells BlackBerry Desktop Manager to sync those tasks to a particular Mac application.

✔ **(Advanced Settings) Sync:** This setting allows you to limit the tasks to sync on your Storm so that the tasks that are completed don't simply occupy valuable space on your smart phone with no real purpose. Choose either All Tasks (the default) or Only Uncompleted Tasks.

✔ **(Advanced Settings) Replace All Tasks on This BlackBerry Device:** Keep this deselected unless you want a fresh start, deleting current calendar items in your smart phone and copying all appointments or events from your Mac.

Music

You can easily sync your iTunes playlists to the BlackBerry by using the Music link on the BlackBerry Desktop Manager screen. And this is the place to configure how you want it synced, as you can see in Figure 15-19.

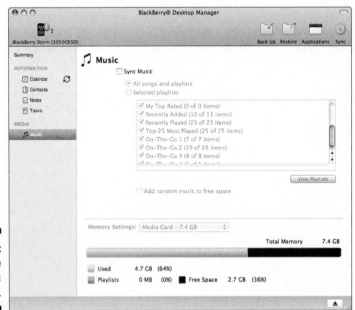

Figure 15-19:
Configure
Music sync
here.

Here, you can choose the following:

✔ **Sync Music:** Choose to include Music in the sync or not. Just below this check box, you have options to sync All Songs and Playlists (the default) or Selected Playlists. If you have a big music library in iTunes, we recommend that you choose Selected Playlists and choose only the music you want to carry with you, up to the capacity of your media card.

✔ **Add Random Music to Free Space:** If you want BlackBerry Desktop Manager to sync random songs from iTunes that are not included in your playlist, select this check box. You can find the songs in the Random Music playlist in the Music application of your Storm.

✔ **Memory Settings:** Choose where you want your music stored in your Storm. Values are Device Memory and Media Card (the default). We recommend the default setting because music files can take up a lot of space, and the device memory is fairly limited and something you want reserved for the use of other BlackBerry applications.

Some useful information on this screen is related to the memory space of your smart phone so you have some idea how much memory your playlist is occupying and how much free space is left on your device.

Deleting all music files on your Storm

You might be wondering why we bother to include a section on deleting music files. What does deleting music files have to do with data synchronization? This is the first time you installed and ran BlackBerry Desktop Manager on your Mac. With BlackBerry Desktop Manager, you have the option to sync your Storm with iTunes playlists, including album art. It makes sense to start fresh and clear your Storm of whatever music files it has.

To do a one-time delete of all music files on your Storm:

1. **Connect your Storm to your Mac.**

2. **On your Mac, click BlackBerry Desktop Manager on the Dock or on the desktop.**

   If you have Mac OS 10.5 or later and can't find BlackBerry Desktop Manager on the Dock:

   a. **Click the Finder application (the leftmost icon) on your Mac's Dock.**

   b. **In the search text box (topmost-right corner) of the Finder screen, type** BlackBerry Desktop.

   c. **Connect your BlackBerry Storm to your Mac.**

   d. **Click BlackBerry Desktop Manager in the Finder screen.**

If you have Mac OS prior to 10.5 and can't find BlackBerry Desktop Manager on your desktop:

    a. Press Command+F to launch the Find utility.

    b. In the Find text box of the Find screen, type BlackBerry Desktop.

    c. Connect your BlackBerry Storm to your Mac.

    d. Click BlackBerry Desktop Manager in the Find screen.

 3. Click the Device Options button.

 4. Click the Media icon.

 5. Click Delete.

A confirmation prompt asks whether you really want to delete your music files on the device.

 6. Click OK.

Doing a manual sync

Ready to sync? You've chosen the sync configuration you want. If you haven't, make sure to read the sections preceding this one.

To do a manual sync, click the Sync button, which is located in the top-right corner of the BlackBerry Desktop Manager screen. If this is your first attempt running the sync, you'll see the prompt shown in Figure 15-20. BlackBerry Desktop Manager needs to establish the latest copy of your data, and to do that, it needs to know how you want to proceed:

- ✔ **Merge Data:** Click this button if you want BlackBerry Desktop Manager to merge your Mac to your Storm data. Merging is basically combining two sets of data with no duplicate checking. If you have synced your Mac before, using a different type of software such as PocketMac, you will end up with duplicates.

- ✔ **Replace Device Data:** Click this button if you want to have a fresh copy of Mac data on your smart phone. After the sync, your Storm data will be the same as what you have on your Mac.

Figure 15-20:
The options you get doing a manual sync for the first time.

You are about to synchronize your Notes data for the first time.

Replacing your device data with your computer data is recommended, especially if you have synchronized with this computer before. Merging your data will duplicate most entries. What do you want to do?

Cancel   Merge data   Replace device data

Configuring an automatic sync

It's annoying to click the Sync button every time you want to sync. Simply follow these steps, and every time you connect the Storm to the Mac, the sync will occur automatically:

1. **Connect the Storm to the Mac.**
2. **On the Mac, click BlackBerry Desktop Manager on the Dock.**
3. **Click the Device Options button.**
4. **Select Automatically Sync When Device Is Connected.**
5. **Click OK.**

Chapter 16

Switching Devices

· ·

In This Chapter

▶ Switching from an old BlackBerry to a BlackBerry Storm

▶ Switching from a PDA to a BlackBerry Storm

· ·

*W*ouldn't it be nice if you could just make one device's data available to another? That's the future. But right now, RIM (Research In Motion) wants to make switching devices as painless as possible. That's why Device Switch Wizard is part of the suite of applications in BlackBerry Desktop Manager.

Device Switch exists only in the Windows version of BlackBerry Desktop Manager. If you are a Mac user, you may skip this chapter.

Switching to a New BlackBerry

Switching from an older BlackBerry to your new Storm is no big deal. When you want to transfer application data (e-mails and contacts, for example) to your new Storm, Device Switch Wizard backs up your old BlackBerry and loads that backup to your new device.

On your PC, the following steps help you transition from your old device to your new BlackBerry Storm:

1. **On your PC, choose Start⇨All Programs⇨BlackBerry⇨Desktop Manager.**

   The Desktop Manager screen opens, displaying Device Switch Wizard, as shown in Figure 16-1.

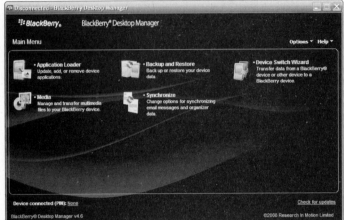

Figure 16-1:
Launch
Device
Switch
Wizard
here.

2. **Click the Device Switch Wizard icon.**

   The Device Switch Wizard screen lets you choose whether to switch
   from BlackBerry to BlackBerry Storm or from non-BlackBerry to
   BlackBerry Storm. The BlackBerry-to-BlackBerry section tells you to
   connect your current (old) BlackBerry to your PC.

3. **Connect your old BlackBerry to your PC with the USB cable.**

   Keep your BlackBerry on when connecting.

4. **Click the Start button below Switch BlackBerry Devices.**

   The next screen lets you verify the PINs for both devices — the old
   BlackBerry on the left and your new Storm on the right, as shown in
   Figure 16-2. Because you connected only your old BlackBerry, its PIN
   should be preselected.

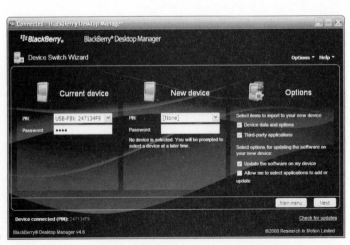

Figure 16-2:
Verify that
your old
BlackBerry
is con-
nected to
the PC and
decide
what data
to include
here.

Your BlackBerry PIN isn't a password; it's your BlackBerry smart phone identifier. You can find the PIN by choosing Options⇨Status on your BlackBerry.

5. Decide whether to include user data and third-party applications and then click Next.

If you want all the data, leave the screen untouched; this backs up everything. *Third-party applications* are all the programs you installed — the ones that didn't come with the device originally.

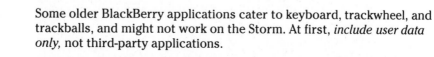

Some older BlackBerry applications cater to keyboard, trackwheel, and trackballs, and might not work on the Storm. At first, *include user data only,* not third-party applications.

A status screen appears, showing the progress of the backup operation. When the backup is finished, the next screen prompts you to connect your new BlackBerry Storm.

6. Connect your BlackBerry Storm to your PC with the USB cable.

The next screen, shown in Figure 16-3, lets you verify that your Storm is connected properly, with your Storm's PIN preselected in the drop-down list. It also asks for the password. Because data is already backed up from the old BlackBerry, it doesn't matter whether you keep the old device connected in succeeding steps.

Figure 16-3: Type your device password here.

Device connection

Select your new device:

PIN: USB-PIN: 2100000A

Password:

OK   Cancel

7. Enter the password of your Storm and then click OK.

A screen similar to Figure 16-4 tells you what will be restored to the new device. Nothing has been done to your new BlackBerry Storm yet, and this is your last chance to cancel the process.

8. Click Finish.

A progress screen displays the loading process.

9. When the Success screen appears, click the Close button.

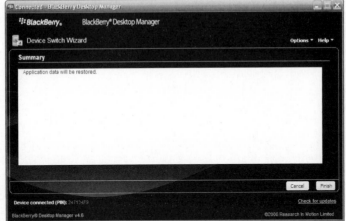

Figure 16-4:
Confirming
the loading
of data onto
your new
BlackBerry
Storm.

Switching from a Non-BlackBerry Device

This section is applicable only to Windows. BlackBerry Desktop Manager on the Mac shows support only for BlackBerry devices.

Device Switch Wizard supports two types of non-BlackBerry devices:

- Palm
- Microsoft Windows Mobile

This doesn't mean you can't import your old data if you have another device; Device Switch Wizard just makes it simpler for these two types of devices. Check Chapter 15 for synchronization options for your desktop PIM application if your old device is neither a Palm nor a Microsoft Windows Mobile.

Palm device requirements

Your PC and Palm have to meet three prerequisites for Device Switch Wizard to import data from Palm to your BlackBerry Storm:

- Your PC must be running Windows 2000 or later.
- One of the following Palm Desktop Software versions must be installed on your desktop: 4.0.1, 4.1, 4.1.4, or 6.0.1.
- The installed Palm Desktop software is synchronizing properly with the Palm device.

You can check your Palm user guide for more details about your Palm device and synchronizing it to your PC. You can also download the user guide from www.palm.com/us/support/index.hml. Navigate to this page by selecting the Palm model you have and the wireless network provider on which it runs.

Windows Mobile device requirements

You need the following for Device Switch Wizard to work properly with a Windows Mobile device:

- ✔ Your PC must be running Windows 2000 or later.
- ✔ Microsoft ActiveSync versions must be installed on your PC.
- ✔ The mobile device must run one of the following operating systems: Microsoft Windows Mobile 2000, 2002, 2003, 2003SE, or 2005/5.0 for Pocket PC; or Microsoft Windows Mobile SmartPhone software 2002, 2003, or 2003 SE.

Run the wizard

Before you run the wizard, make sure that all the requirements for your device are in place.

We recommend hot-syncing or synchronizing your Palm or Windows Mobile device; this ensures that the data you're sending to your Storm is current. Palm Desktop Software, as well as Microsoft ActiveSync, should come with help information on how to hot-sync.

Although the following steps migrate Windows Mobile data to the Storm, the steps are similar for Palm as well. We indicate at what point the steps vary. Do the following to get your other device's data migrated to your new Storm:

1. **Connect both the Windows Mobile device and BlackBerry Storm to your desktop computer.**

2. **On your PC, choose Start⇨All Programs⇨BlackBerry⇨Desktop Manager.**

   The Desktop Manager screen appears (refer to Figure 16-1, earlier in this chapter).

3. **Click the Device Switch Wizard icon.**

4. **When Device Switch Wizard appears, click the image next to Switch from Another Device to BlackBerry Device.**

The Welcome screen, shown in Figure 16-5, describes what the tool can do.

Figure 16-5:
Migrating
data from
a non-
BlackBerry
device.

5. **Click Next.**

A screen prompts you to decide whether you're migrating from Palm or Windows Mobile, as shown in Figure 16-6. The wizard is intelligent enough to enable the option associated with the connected device, which in this figure is a Windows Mobile device.

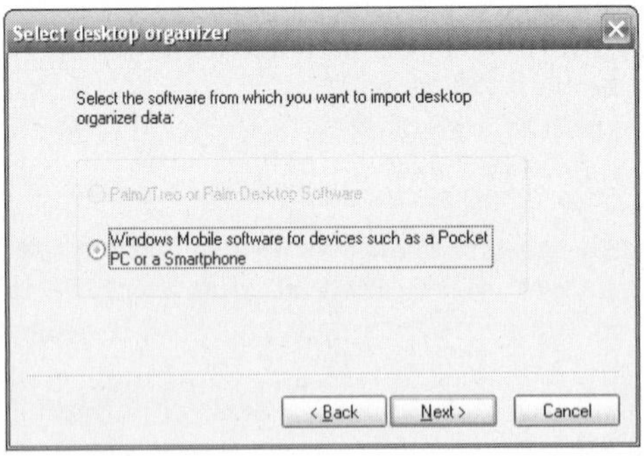

Figure 16-6:
The wizard
has already
selected
which
device to
port.

6. **Click Next.**

Hot-syncing the Windows Mobile device kicks in at this point. You see a series of screens for each application's data, such as Calendar, Contacts, and MemoPad. A sample of Calendar data is shown in Figure 16-7. The screen indicates what to sync and will be empty if you performed a hot-sync before running the wizard. Otherwise, syncing will take some time, depending on how much data there is to sync between the device and the desktop software.

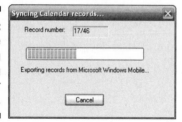

Figure 16-7:
A message
showing
hot-syncing
on your
device.

7. Click OK.

A progress screen appears. Before the data is applied to your Storm, the wizard prompts you about the change, as shown in Figure 16-8. Click the following buttons in this screen to either confirm or reject the change:

- Details: You want to know the records the wizard is trying to apply.

- Accept: You just want the data migrated.

- Reject: Ignore this data and continue.

- Cancel: Change your mind and cancel the whole operation.

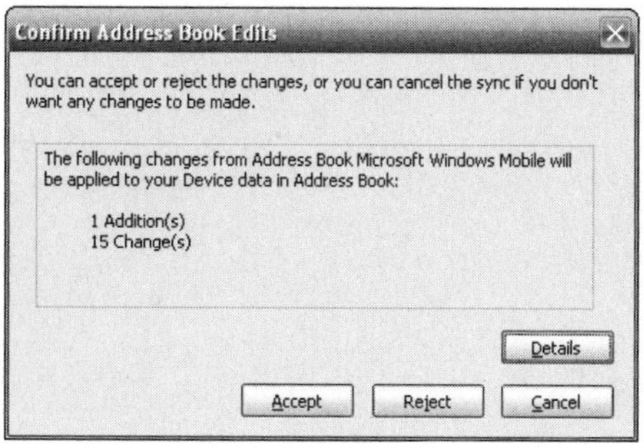

Figure 16-8:
Confirm the
importing of
data here.

8. Click the Accept or the Reject button in any confirmation screens that appear.

The wizard migrates all the data you accepted. Obviously, the wizard skips everything you rejected. When the migration process is finished, a success screen appears.

9. Click Finish.

Chapter 17

Protecting Your Information

In This Chapter

▶ Getting into backup and restore

▶ Performing a full backup of your BlackBerry Storm data

▶ Restoring from backups

▶ Backing up, restoring, and clearing in your own way

▶ Backing up and restoring your Storm wirelessly

*I*magine that you left your beautiful BlackBerry Storm in the back of a cab. You've lost your Storm for good. Okay, not good. What happens to all your information? How are you going to replace all those contacts? What about security?

One thing that you don't need to worry about is information security — *if* you set up a security password on your BlackBerry. With security password protection on your Storm, anyone who finds it has only ten chances to enter the correct password; after those ten chances are up, it's self-destruction time. Although it isn't as smoky as *Mission Impossible,* your BlackBerry Storm does erase all its information, thwarting your would-be data thief.

Set up a password for your Storm *now!* For information on how to do so, see Chapter 3.

Now, how to get back all the information that was on your BlackBerry Storm? If you're like us and store important information on your BlackBerry, this chapter is for you. Vital information, such as clients' and friends' contact information, notes from phone calls with clients — and, of course, those precious e-mail messages — shouldn't be taken lightly. Backing up this information is a reliable way to protect it from being lost forever.

If you work for a large corporation, your BlackBerry is typically in a BlackBerry Enterprise Server. If that's not the case for you, usually BlackBerry Desktop Manager is the only way to back up and restore information to and from your desktop PC. But in recent months, a software package called SmrtGuard has come up with a wireless backup and restore service for those who aren't in the habit of plugging their BlackBerry into their PC. If that's you, go to the end of this chapter, where we introduce SmrtGuard's backup and restore solution, which will give you peace of mind when it comes to protecting your data.

Accessing Backup and Restore

Backup and Restore is a BlackBerry Desktop Manager application. It allows you to back up all the sensitive data on your BlackBerry, including contacts, e-mails, memos, to-dos, all personal preferences, and options.

Note: For most of you, e-mails are already stored in accounts such as Gmail or Yahoo! Mail. But some people still like to back up e-mails, just in case.

To get started with BlackBerry Desktop Manager:

1. **Install BlackBerry Desktop Manager on your PC.**

   For instructions on installing BlackBerry Desktop Manager, see Chapter 15.

2. **Connect your Storm to your PC with the USB cable that came with your BlackBerry.**

   If everything is set up right, a window appears on your PC, asking you to type your BlackBerry security password.

3. **Type your password.**

   The BlackBerry connects to the PC.

4. **Double-click the Backup and Restore icon on the BlackBerry Desktop Manager screen.**

   The Backup and Restore screen opens; see Figure 17-1. You're ready to back up data from or restore information to your BlackBerry.

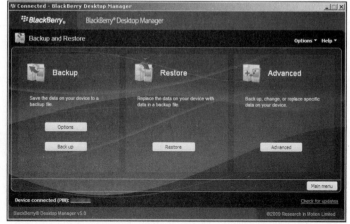

Backing Up BlackBerry Style

We all know that backing up your data provides tremendous peace of mind.
So do the folks at RIM, which is why backing up your information is easy. You
can back up your BlackBerry Storm manually or by autopilot.

Backing up your Storm manually

To back up your BlackBerry Storm on demand, follow these steps:

1. **Connect your Storm to your PC with the USB cable.**

2. **From the BlackBerry Desktop Manager screen, double-click the
   Backup and Restore icon.**

   The Backup and Restore screen appears (refer to Figure 17-1, in the
   preceding section).

3. **Click the Backup button.**

   The dialog box shown in Figure 17-2 appears, so you can name the
   backup file and figure out where on your PC you want to save it.

4. **Name your backup file and choose a place to save it.**

5. Click Save.

BlackBerry Desktop Manager starts backing up your BlackBerry information onto your PC. Figure 17-3 shows the backup progress in the Transfer in Progress window.

Don't unplug your BlackBerry Storm from the PC until the backup is finished! The folks at RIM have made the USB transfer fast, so you don't have to wait that long!

6. When the Transfer in Progress window disappears, you can unplug the BlackBerry from the PC.

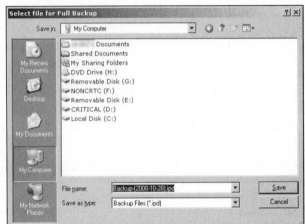

Figure 17-2:
Decide where to save your backup file.

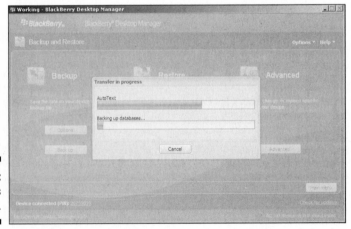

Figure 17-3:
A backup is in progress.

Setting up automatic backups

What's better than backing up your information once? Remembering to back up regularly! What's better than backing up regularly? You guessed it — running backups automatically. After you schedule automated BlackBerry backups, you can really have peace of mind when it comes to preventing information loss.

Follow these steps to set up an autobackup:

1. **From BlackBerry Desktop Manager, double-click the Backup and Restore icon.**

   The Backup and Restore screen appears.

2. **Click the Options button.**

   The Backup Options screen, where you can schedule automatic backups, appears. See Figure 17-4.

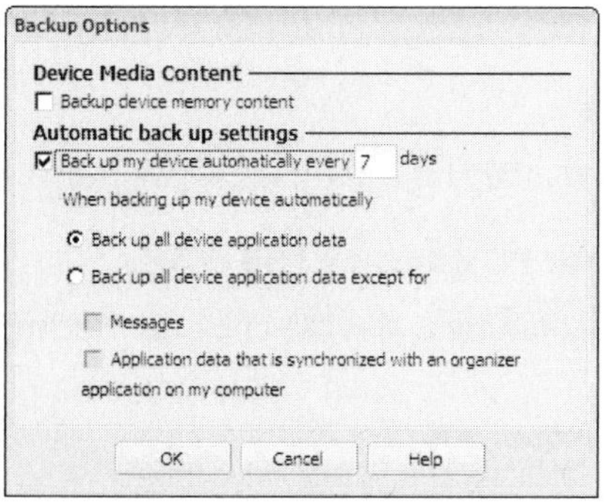

Figure 17-4: Set autobackups here.

3. **Select the Back Up My Device Automatically Every option.**

   This lets you make more decisions (check boxes and options become active), such as how often you want BlackBerry Desktop Manager to back up your BlackBerry.

4. **In the Days field, enter a number of days between 1 and 99.**

   This interval sets how often your BlackBerry Storm is backed up. For example, if you enter **14**, your Storm is backed up every 14 days.

5. **Select the Back Up All Device Application Data option.**

   This option backs up all the data on your BlackBerry Storm each time autobackup runs.

Although you can exclude e-mail messages and information such as Contacts, to-do's, and memos, we recommend that you back up *everything* each time.

6. **Click OK.**

Now you can get on with your life without worrying when to back up your Storm.

To run a backup, you must connect your BlackBerry Storm to your PC. Make sure that you plug your Storm into your PC once in a while so autobackup has a chance to back up your information.

Restoring Your Data from Backup Information

We hope that you never have to read this section more than once. A *full restore* brings back all your information from a backup. It probably means you've lost information that you had hoped to find from the backup you created on your PC.

The steps to fully restore your backup information are simple:

1. **Connect your Storm to your PC using the USB cable.**

2. **From BlackBerry Desktop Manager, double-click the Backup and Restore icon.**

   The Backup and Restore screen appears.

3. **Click the Restore button.**

   An Open File dialog box asks where the backup file is on your PC.

4. **Choose a backup file and click Open.**

   A warning window appears when you're about to do a full restore (see Figure 17-5), alerting you that you're about to overwrite existing information.

5. **Click Yes to go ahead with the full restore.**

   A progress bar appears.

   It might take a while for the full restore to finish. Don't unplug your BlackBerry Storm from your PC during this time!

6. **When the progress bar disappears, unplug the device from the PC.**

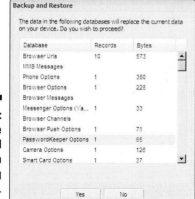

Backup and Restore

The data in the following databases will replace the current data on your device. Do you wish to proceed?

Database	Records	Bytes
Browser Urls	10	573
MMS Messages		
Phone Options	1	380
Browser Options	1	228
Browser Messages		
Messenger Options (Ya...	1	33
Browser Channels		
Browser Push Options	1	71
PasswordKeeper Options	1	65
Camera Options	1	126
Smart Card Options	1	37

Yes   No

Figure 17-5:
Be careful when overwriting existing info.

Protecting Your Data Your Way

A certain burger joint and BlackBerry have in common that you can have it *your way* with their products. Just like you can get your burger with or without all the extras (such as pickles and onions), you can choose to not back up and restore things that you know you won't need.

Say you've accidentally deleted your Internet bookmarks, and now you want them back. *Don't* restore all the information from your last backup. That could be more than 90 days ago (depending on how often your autobackup runs, if at all). You might unintentionally overwrite other information, such as e-mail or new contacts. You want to restore bookmarks only.

If you lose something in particular or want something specific back on your BlackBerry, use the selective backup and restore function in BlackBerry Desktop Manager and restore only what you need. The same goes with backing up. If you're a big e-mail user, back up *just* your e-mails and nothing else.

In this section, we use the term *databases*. Don't worry; this isn't as technical as you think. Think of a database as an information category on the BlackBerry. For example, saying "backing up your Browser bookmarks database" is just a fancy way of saying "backing up all your Browser bookmarks on your BlackBerry."

We start with a selective backup and then describe a selective restore.

Backing up your way

To back up specific information, follow these steps:

1. **Connect your Storm to your PC using the USB cable.**

2. **From BlackBerry Desktop Manager, double-click the Backup and Restore icon.**

   The Backup and Restore screen appears.

3. **Click the Advanced button.**

   The advanced Backup and Restore screen appears, as shown in Figure 17-6. The right side of the screen shows different information categories, or databases.

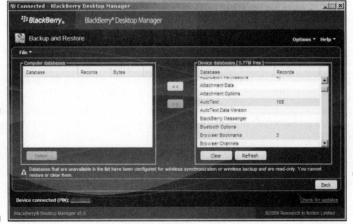

Figure 17-6: The advanced Backup and Restore screen.

4. **In the right column, Ctrl+click the databases you want to back up.**

5. **Click the left-pointing (backup) arrow.**

   A progress bar moves while your BlackBerry Storm is backed up. This step merely transfers the databases onto your PC; it doesn't save them. When the backup transfer is finished, you can see the two databases on the left side of the window.

6. **Choose File⇨Save As.**

   A file chooser appears.

7. **Name your file and specify where you want to save it on your PC.**

   This saves your selective backup on your PC. Make sure to name it something specific so you know what exactly is in the backup.

Looking at backup BlackBerry files

Whether you use the one-button-push backup method or manually back up your file, the file is saved on your PC as an `.ipd` file. Those curious readers out there might be asking, "Can I read these backup files without a BlackBerry?" The answer is yes! With a third-party product called ABC Amber BlackBerry Converter, you can view any `.ipd` file. What's the point? Suppose you lost your BlackBerry Storm but need to read an old e-mail or to get contacts from your backup files. This tool allows you to

convert anything in your backup file (e-mails, SMS messages, PIM messages, and contacts) to PDF or Microsoft Word documents. For more information and to try ABC Amber BlackBerry Converter for free, go to `www.processtext.com/abcblackberry.html`.

Because anyone with Amber BlackBerry Converter can look into your backups, make sure that you secure your backup files so only you can get to them.

You need to manually save the backup file on your PC even after you choose a location for the file in Step 4. A selective backup doesn't automatically save your backup on your PC.

Restoring your way

When restoring selectively, you must already have a backup file to restore from. Although this might sound obvious, the point we're making is that you can selectively restore from any backup — auto or manual.

Say you have autobackup running every other day, and you want to restore only your e-mail messages from two days ago. You don't need to do a full restore; that would overwrite the new contact you put in your Contacts yesterday. Rather, you can use the selective restore method and get back only your e-mail messages.

To restore your way, follow these steps:

1. **Connect your Storm to your PC using the USB cable.**

2. **From BlackBerry Desktop Manager, double-click the Backup and Restore icon.**

   The Backup and Restore screen appears.

3. **Click the Advanced button.**

   The advanced Backup and Restore screen appears (refer to Figure 17-6, earlier in this chapter). The right side of the screen shows your different information categories, or databases.

4. **Choose File⇨Open.**

   A window opens so you can choose which backup file you want to restore from.

   A BlackBerry backup file has an `.ipd` extension.

5. **Select a backup file.**

6. **Click the Open button.**

   The different information categories, or databases, appear on the left side of the screen. You're ready for a selective restore.

7. **Select categories (or databases).**

   You can select multiple databases by Ctrl+clicking the databases you want.

8. **Click the right-facing (Restore) arrow.**

   You'll likely see a warning window asking whether you want to replace all the information with the data you're restoring (refer to Figure 17-5, earlier in this chapter).

   If your BlackBerry Storm has the same categories as the ones you're restoring (which is likely), you'll overwrite *any* information you have on your BlackBerry.

   You can confidently move on to Step 9 if you know that the database you're restoring has the information you're looking for.

9. **Click OK.**

   A progress bar appears during the selective restore. When the progress bar window disappears, the information categories that you've selected are restored on your BlackBerry.

Clearing BlackBerry information your way

You can also delete information on your BlackBerry Storm from BlackBerry Desktop Manager. When would you use selective deletion?

Suppose that you want to clear only your phone logs from your BlackBerry. One way is to tediously select one phone log at a time and press Delete, repeating until all phone logs are gone. However, you could delete a database from the advanced Backup and Restore screen by using the Backup and Restore function.

To selectively delete databases on your BlackBerry, follow these steps:

1. **Connect your Storm to your PC using the USB cable.**

2. **From BlackBerry Desktop Manager on your PC, double-click the Backup and Restore icon.**

   The Backup and Restore screen appears.

3. **Click the Advanced button.**

   The advanced Backup and Restore screen appears (refer to Figure 17-6, earlier in this chapter). The right side of the screen shows your BlackBerry's different databases.

4. **Ctrl+click the database you want to delete.**

   The database is highlighted.

5. **Click the Clear button on the right side of the screen.**

   A warning window asks you to confirm your deletion.

6. **Click OK.**

   A progress bar shows the deletion. When the progress bar disappears, the database (information category) you selected is cleared from your BlackBerry.

Backing Up and Restoring Wirelessly

Your BlackBerry Storm can back up and restore without being on BlackBerry Enterprise Server. To do so, you use a piece of software called SmrtGuard for BlackBerry (www.SmrtGuard.com) that sits in your Storm and can wirelessly back up your data. Currently, SmrtGuard supports address book contacts, memos, calendar, phone log, and to-dos, e-mail, and SMS messages; it plans to support pictures soon. SmrtGuard also supports the Android platform, so you can migrate your data from the Android phone to your BlackBerry Storm.

In addition to its backup and restore capabilities, SmrtGuard has features to help you locate, recover, or destroy device-side data. Its tracking, or Find My BlackBerry, feature helps you determine whether you misplaced the device or whether it was stolen. If the device was stolen, you can send a signal to have your data destroyed via the SmrtGuard Dashboard on www.SmrtGuard.com.

Chapter 18

Installing and Managing Third-Party Applications

In This Chapter

▶ Installing app-store applications

▶ Getting started with Application Loader

▶ Installing a BlackBerry Storm application

▶ Uninstalling applications

▶ Upgrading your Storm's operating system

---

*T*hink of your Storm as a minilaptop where you can run preinstalled applications as well as install new applications. You can even upgrade the operating system. (Yup, that's right — your Storm has an OS.)

This chapter starts by introducing BlackBerry App World, which you use to load applications (who'd have guessed?) onto your Storm. Next, we describe the Application Loader application on PC and the BlackBerry Desktop Manager on Mac, which you use to install and uninstall apps to and from your Storm. Then we explore how you can upgrade the OS of your smart phone.

In the Part of Tens, you'll find a few great games that make your BlackBerry that much more fun.

Using BlackBerry App World

Your Storm comes with BlackBerry App World, an application store (or app store) that provides an organized listing of apps, both free and for purchase.

Navigating App World

What better way to describe BlackBerry App World than opening the app and navigating to the screen? To launch the store, simply touch-press BlackBerry App World from the Home screen. BlackBerry App World sports an icon similar to the one on the menu key but enclosed in a circle. After you launch App World, you see a progress screen momentarily, followed by a Featured Items screen similar to Figure 18-1.

Figure 18-1:
BlackBerry
App World,
showcasing
featured
applications.

If you don't have App World on your Storm, you can download it from the RIM Web site at `http://na.blackberry.com/eng/services/appworld`.

The bottom part of the screen in Figure 18-1 shows a few icons that you can use to quickly navigate the store. From left to right, they are as follows:

- ✔ **Categories:** Apps are organized and showcased in a series of categories. It's easy to explore a certain type of app by going to this link.

- ✔ **Top Free:** Find it here first. If you're lucky, the type of app you are looking for is offered free of charge. This is the place to find the most popular free apps.

- ✔ **Top Paid:** Best-selling apps are listed here.

- ✔ **Search:** If you know the app you're looking for, go here. The link allows you to enter the name and search for it from the store.

- ✔ **My World:** This lists the apps you've downloaded from the store.

If you are sitting at a desktop computer, you'll be glad to know that RIM created a Web version of App World. Using your desktop Internet browser, you can visit the site at `http://appworld.blackberry.com/`. The site allows you to send an e-mail to your device with a download link for the app you are interested in.

Installing an application using App World

Found a free-time killer game from the store? Installing the app is easy, and you probably see all the links on the screen. But here's a quick rundown on how to do an installation anyway:

1. **Touch-press BlackBerry App World on the Home screen.**

2. **Navigate to the application you want to install.**

3. **Touch-press the application's icon.**

   You see a screen similar to Figure 18-2, which in this example shows a Download button for Google Talk.

4. **Touch-press the Download button.**

   The My World screen appears. At the top are the app you're downloading and a progress bar, as shown in Figure 18-3. When the download has finished, the installation kicks in and is indicated with a progress screen, as shown in Figure 18-4. You'll surely get a prompt after the app is installed.

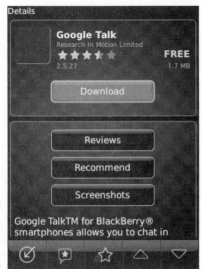

Figure 18-2: Download an app.

Figure 18-3:
The
progress
of the
download.

Figure 18-4:
App
installation
in progress.

Any app you download is located in the Downloads folder on the Home screen.

Finding and Installing Applications from Other App Stores

BlackBerry App World is not the only app store out there in BlackBerry Land. You can also check out the following pioneers. Why do you need additional app stores? BlackBerry App World has a minimum price of $2.99 to be listed as a non-free app, so this limits app developers who want to sell their apps for less.

- ✔ **Handango (www.handango.com):** Handango is one of the oldest store-fronts that sell applications for mobile devices. They started selling apps through their Web site but eventually created an app store. Handango's app store can be downloaded from their Web site.

- ✔ **CrackBerry On-Device App Store (http://crackberryappstore. com):** Partnering with MobiHand, CrackBerry also provides an app store where you can find great applications to download.

- ✔ **BlackBerry Application Center:** This is software built by RIM, but the carrier has control over what shows up in Application Center. The app is typically already installed on your Storm, possibly under the brand name of your wireless carrier.

This might sound like a shameless plug, but it's not. We're just looking out for your best interests and your pocketbook! Although RIM's BlackBerry App World launched in April 2009, CrackBerry has been offering apps via its app store since the site launched in February 2007. Following are some of the compelling reasons why thousands of BlackBerry users visit CrackBerry.com's App Store regularly in addition to App World:

- ✔ **Web version available:** Although on-device app stores are all the rage these days, CrackBerry also offers a computer-optimized version of their app store. This makes it easy to browse apps, view feature-rich info (video demos), and purchase multiple applications in one transaction versus just one at a time, as is the case with on-device clients.

- ✔ **99-cent minimum pricing:** Developers have the option to price their apps as low as 99 cents. Due to App World's pricing restrictions, you can often find the same app that sells in App World for $2.99 for $1.99 or even 99 cents in the CrackBerry App Store.

- ✔ **Deal of the Day and promotions:** CrackBerry App Store offers a Deal of the Day, in which every day, one application for your device is on sale at a deep discount (often 50 percent off!). The CrackBerry App Store also gives developers the ability to promote their apps, via sales and coupon codes.

- ✔ **Payment options:** CrackBerry App Store accepts both credit cards and PayPal for payments.

- ✔ **Support:** In addition to technical support from developers, CrackBerry's App Store features a dedicated support team if you run into order issues.

- ✔ **Refunds:** Unlike App World, the CrackBerry App Store offers refunds.

The list goes on! You can find out more and download the CrackBerry App Store client by visiting http://crackberry.com/appstore.

Accessing Application Loader

In this chapter, you work closely with your Windows PC and your Storm. On your PC, you use BlackBerry Desktop Manager, which comes on a CD along with your Storm. You can find Application Loader in BlackBerry Desktop Manager.

For an introduction to BlackBerry Desktop Manager, see Chapter 15.

After installing BlackBerry Desktop Manager on your PC, do the following to access Application Loader:

1. **On your PC, choose Start⇨All Programs⇨BlackBerry⇨Desktop Manager.**

2. **Connect your Storm to your PC via USB cable.**

   If the connection is successful, you see the password dialog box, as shown in Figure 18-5.

Figure 18-5: The password dialog box on your PC.

Device Password Required
Device: USB-PIN: 247134F9
Please enter your device password (1/10).
Password:
OK   Cancel

If the connection isn't successful, see whether the USB cable is connected properly to both your PC and your Storm and then try again. If all else fails, contact the technical support department of your service provider.

3. **Enter your password.**

   Your Storm-to-PC connection is complete.

4. **On your PC, double-click the Application Loader icon in BlackBerry Desktop Manager.**

   The Application Loader screen opens, as shown in Figure 18-6. At this point, you're ready to use Application Loader.

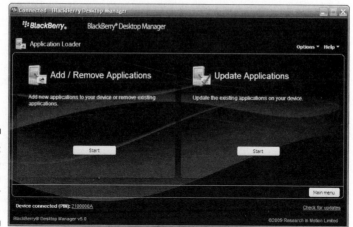

Figure 18-6:
The
Application
Loader
screen.

Installing an Application

In this chapter, we show you how to install iSkoot for Skype for BlackBerry. iSkoot is a free application that connects to the Web directly and allows you to use Skype. You can download this application at

```
www.download.com/iSkoot-for-Skype-BlackBerry-/3000-7242_4-10797721.html
```

Installing, Windows Style

No matter what application you're installing from your PC to your Storm, the steps are the same. Use the following steps as a guide to installing the application of your choice:

1. **Download the application installation files to your PC.**

   Refer to the app publisher's instructions on how to download the installation files. This is the only part of the installation process that varies from vendor to vendor. Some vendors allow you to download a ZIP file, and some vendors do the extra effort of giving you a self-extracting file. After following their instructions, you should end up with a set of files, and one of those files should have an .alx extension.

2. **Locate the application's ALX file.**

   You can usually find a file with the .alx extension in the folder where you installed the application on your PC.

The ALX file doesn't get installed on your Storm. It tells Application Loader where the actual application file is located on your PC.

3. **Double-click the Application Loader icon in BlackBerry Desktop Manager.**

The Application Loader screen appears (refer to Figure 18-6, in the preceding section).

4. **Use the USB cable to connect your Storm to your PC.**

A screen appears, prompting you to enter your Storm password.

5. **Enter your password (refer to Figure 18-5, in the preceding section).**

After you enter your password, the Application Loader screen indicates that your device is connected.

6. **Click the Start button, below Add/Remove Applications.**

The screen lists the applications you can install.

7. **Click the Browse button, and locate and select the ALX file you want to install.**

You return to the Application Loader screen, where iSkoot is one of the applications in the list, as shown in Figure 18-7.

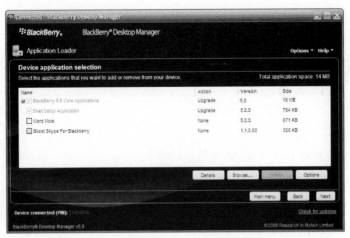

Figure 18-7: Your application is added to the list of installed applications and can be installed on your Storm.

8. **Select the application you want to install (for this example, select iSkoot Skype for BlackBerry) and then click Next.**

A summary screen appears, listing only the applications that will be installed or upgraded.

9. **Click Finish.**

   The installation process starts, and a progress window appears. When the progress window disappears — and if all went well — the application is in the Applications folder of your Storm.

If you get an invalid signature error after clicking the Finish button, the solution depends on how you received your Storm:

   ✔ **If you didn't get your Storm from your employer,** something is probably wrong with the application. You need to contact the software vendor.

   ✔ **If you got your Storm from your employer,** you don't have permission to install applications on your Storm. The IT department rules the school.

You don't have to use Application Loader to get the goods onto your Storm, though. You can install applications in other ways as well:

   ✔ **Wirelessly, through an *over-the-air* (OTA) download:** See the section on installing and uninstalling applications from the Web in Chapter 10 for more on wireless installations.

   ✔ **BlackBerry Enterprise Server wireless install (if your Storm was provided by your employer):** In this case, you have no control over the installation process. Your company's BlackBerry system administrator controls which applications are on your Storm.

   ✔ **Through the PC using Microsoft Installer:** Some application installations automate the preceding steps. All you need to do is connect your Storm to the PC and then double-click the installation file. The application installation's file using Microsoft Installer bears the `.msi` file extension.

Installing, Mac Style

For Mac users, a newly minted BlackBerry Desktop Manager allows you to add applications to and remove applications from your Storm.

To install an app, follow these steps

1. **Connect the Storm to your Mac.**

2. **On your Mac, click BlackBerry Desktop Manager on the Dock.**

   Can't find the BlackBerry Desktop Manager icon? Use the Finder, which is located at the left end of the Dock.

If you haven't installed BlackBerry Desktop Manager, Google *BlackBerry Mac.* The first entry on the search results page should take you to the download page.

3. In the BlackBerry Desktop Manager screen, click the Applications icon.

The next screen (see Figure 18-8) lists applications installed on your Storm as well as those available for installation. Your next step is to add the ALX file for the application you want to install.

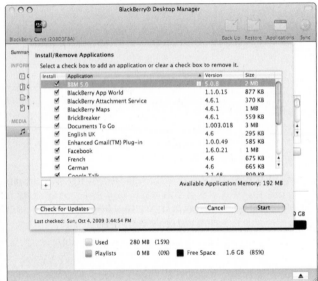

Figure 18-8:
Install or uninstall applications here.

4. Click the + button (on the bottom left), and locate and select the ALX file you want to install.

You return to the Install/Remove Applications screen (refer to Figure 18-8), where iSkoot is one of the applications in the list.

5. In the Install column, select the application(s) you want to install.

For an installed app, deselecting it from the list will uninstall the app. Keep it selected if you want to keep the app on your Storm.

6. Click the Start button.

BlackBerry Desktop Manager starts installing your selected apps. This may take time, depending on the sizes of these apps.

Uninstalling an Application

You can uninstall an application in three ways:

- Using Application Loader under Windows PC
- Using BlackBerry Desktop Manager on the Mac
- Using your Storm

We use iSkoot as an example here and assume that you've already installed the iSkoot application. You can follow the same steps for uninstalling other applications.

Uninstalling with Application Loader under Windows PC

To uninstall a BlackBerry application using Application Loader on your PC, follow these steps:

1. **On your PC, double-click the Application Loader icon in BlackBerry Desktop Manager.**

2. **Use the USB cable to connect the Storm to the PC.**

   A screen prompts you to enter your Storm password.

3. **Enter your password.**

   If your handheld isn't connected properly, the PIN of your device won't appear in the Application Loader screen. Connect your Storm to the USB cable and then connect the USB cable to the PC.

   After you enter your password, the Application Loader screen indicates that your device is connected.

4. **Click the Start button, below Add/Remove Applications.**

   A screen appears listing applications (similar to Figure 18-7, earlier in this chapter).

5. **Scroll to the application you want to delete and then deselect its check box.**

   For example, when we deselect the iSkoot Skype for BlackBerry check box, the Action column for iSkoot indicates Remove.

6. **Click Next.**

   You see a summary screen that lists the action of Application Loader. It indicates that iSkoot is to be removed from your Storm.

7. **Click Finish.**

   The uninstall process starts, and a progress window appears. When the progress window disappears, you have uninstalled the application from your Storm.

Uninstalling with BlackBerry Desktop Manager on the Mac

The steps for uninstalling an app using the BlackBerry Desktop Manager on the Mac should be familiar to you because they use the same screen as the one for installing an app. Follow these steps:

1. **Connect the Storm to the Mac.**

2. **On the Mac, click BlackBerry Desktop Manager on the Dock.**

3. **In the BlackBerry Desktop Manager screen, click the Applications icon.**

4. **Deselect the application(s) in the list that you want to uninstall.**

5. **Click the Start button.**

   BlackBerry Desktop Manager starts uninstalling the selected apps.

Uninstalling with the Storm

When you don't have access to your PC, you can uninstall an application directly from your Storm. Follow these steps:

1. **Locate the application icon on the BlackBerry Home screen.**

   By default, any applications you installed on your Storm are filed in the Downloads folder on the Home screen. However, you always have the option to move the application to other folders or to the Home screen.

2. **Tap the application icon, press the menu key, and touch-press Delete.**

3. **In the confirmation dialog box that appears, touch-press Delete to confirm the deletion.**

   You're given a choice to restart now or at a later time. After the restart, the deleted application is uninstalled.

Upgrading the BlackBerry Storm OS

The OS used by Storm has gone through a few revisions. The BlackBerry OS update comes from BlackBerry Handheld Software, which is available from three sources:

- ✔ Your network service provider
- ✔ The Research In Motion Web site
- ✔ Your BlackBerry system administrator

Because the handheld software might differ from provider to provider, we recommend getting it from the service provider's Web site. RIM has a download site for different service providers at

```
http://na.blackberry.com/eng/support/downloads/download_sites.jsp
```

In this section, we assume that the latest BlackBerry Handheld Software for Storm is already installed on your PC. For help with installing BlackBerry Handheld Software, refer to the instructions that come with it.

If you plan to upgrade your BlackBerry OS, and you've installed many third-party applications, check whether those applications support the new OS revision. Third-party applications work as is most of the time, but there is always a possibility of losing third-party application data.

You may think that the latest operating system, or firmware, for your device is what is approved by your carrier and available via the `blackberry.com` Web site. However, often a newer version is "unofficially" available. Research In Motion continuously works on the operating system for each device model they sell, turning out a new build each week. Occasionally, these internal builds — which are stepping stones along the way to the next official release and may not see carrier approval — leak onto the Internet. Typically, the newer the firmware version, the better, and a cult following of BlackBerry owners feverishly anticipate the next leaked build. To stay on top of the latest official and unofficial BlackBerry OS releases, visit `crackberry.com` and click the BlackBerry OS category under Articles, or visit the OS and OS Beta forums in the CrackBerry forums.

Upgrading the Storm OS, Windows Style

If you are a Windows user, you can start the upgrade process by doing the following:

1. **Enter your Storm password (if you have set one) into BlackBerry Desktop Manager on your PC.**

2. **Double-click the Application Loader icon on the Desktop Manager screen.**

   The Application Loader screen appears (refer to Figure 18-6, earlier in this chapter).

3. **Click the Start button below Add/Remove Applications.**

   A list of software appears, as shown in Figure 18-9.

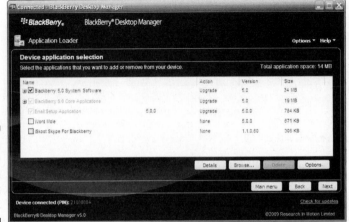

Figure 18-9: Application updates that are available.

4. **With your mouse, you can opt out of the upgrade by deselecting the OS portion.**

   The OS appears as BlackBerry 5.0 System Software in Figure 18-9.

   The OS is listed only if you need an upgrade — meaning that your BlackBerry OS is out of date. If the OS doesn't appear in the list, the handheld software you installed on the desktop machine is the same as the one installed on your device or a previous version compared with the one installed on your device.

   You also need to back up your device in case something goes wrong with the upgrade. Backup options can be accessed through the Options button.

5. Click Options.

The Options screen appears, as shown in Figure 18-10. This is where you decide whether you want to back up your Storm content before upgrading your OS. We suggest that you do so.

Figure 18-10:
Choose
whether
to back
up before
upgrading.

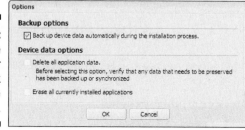

Figure 18-10: Choose whether to back up before upgrading.

6. Select the Back Up Device Data Automatically During the Installation Process check box and then click OK.

You return to the screen shown in Figure 18-8, earlier in this chapter.

7. Click Next.

A summary page confirms your actions — a final chance for you to proceed with the OS upgrade or not.

8. Click Finish.

The BlackBerry OS upgrade starts, complete with a progress window that shows a series of steps and a progress bar. The entire process takes about ten minutes, depending on your PC model and the OS version you're upgrading to.

At times during the BlackBerry OS upgrade, your Storm's display goes on and off. Don't worry; this is normal.

When the progress window disappears, the OS upgrade is complete.

Upgrading the Storm OS, Mac Style

Upgrading your Storm OS from your Mac is no different from installing an app. Here's how:

 1. Connect the Storm to your Mac.

 2. On your Mac, click BlackBerry Desktop Manager on the Dock.

 3. In the BlackBerry Desktop Manager screen, click the Applications icon.

 4. Click the Check for Updates button (bottom left in Figure 18-8, earlier in this chapter).

    BlackBerry Desktop Manager checks online for any new versions of the OS for your Storm. If it finds one, it downloads that update and lists it on the Applications screen (refer to Figure 18-8).

 5. Click to select the check box next to the OS in the list (BBM 5.0 in Figure 18-8).

 6. Click the Start button to start the upgrade.

Part V
The Part of Tens

The 5th Wave   By Rich Tennant

In this part . . .

If the previous parts of this book are the cake and frosting, this part is the cherry on the top. Delve into these three short but sweet chapters to find BlackBerry accessories, games to enjoy, and Web sites to visit.

Chapter 19

Ten Great Storm Accessories

In This Chapter

▶ Unify AV Solution

▶ microSD card

▶ Full keyboards

▶ Stereo headphones

▶ Case and belt clip

▶ Screen protector and skins

▶ Extra battery, charger, and power station

▶ External speaker

▶ Bluetooth Music Gateway

▶ Car mount

*T*he BlackBerry retail box contains a few essentials: a battery, a charger, a micro USB cable, a belt clip, and a microSD card. If you're like most of us, though, you're not satisfied with what is included in the box. In this chapter, you find accessories that supplement your Storm2 — and where to get them.

Check out our companion Web site, www.blackberryfordummies.com, for an updated accessories list.

If you like to accessorize your Storm2, check out site promotions. Every now and then, a site such as www.crackberry.com runs a promotion and gives a big discount. Also look at RIM's Web site at www.shopblackberry.com. They usually offer accessory bundles.

Unify AV Solution

Unify AV Solution is an innovative product of Unify4Life that makes smart phones (including your BlackBerry) a universal remote control. You can find a suite of features on the Unify4Life Web site, but a sample includes complete TV listings in your BlackBerry for informative channel switching. You can purchase it directly from http://unify4life.com/products.html.

microSD Card

Your new BlackBerry normally comes with external memory: a *microSD card*. But if you're not satisfied with its capacity, go hunt for a much bigger one. After all, you want to carry with you a boatload of music and video files, right? Many electronic gadgets use microSD cards, so they're easy to find.

A normal price range at this writing is $45 for 16GB capacity and $85 for 32GB capacity. Special promotions come and go, but you can always find a good deal somewhere on the Internet. For any Internet purchase, take into consideration the shipping and handling costs plus the vendor's return policy (or lack thereof).

Any brand will do, as long as you make sure that you're buying a microSD card.

Full Keyboards

As netbooks become more popular, people forget that the BlackBerry they already carry is a mininetbook. Internet? Check! E-mail? Check! Microsoft Word docs and Microsoft Excel spreadsheets? Check! Sure, the screen is a bit smaller and the keyboard is small, but with a little help from a Bluetooth keyboard, your BlackBerry will save you the cost of a netbook and still do the things a netbook can do.

You have the choice of Bluetooth and non-Bluetooth connection options. We recommend Bluetooth to minimize the clutter. A Bluetooth keyboard is the most convenient option for the obvious reasons: You don't have to carry cables, and you can position your BlackBerry any way you want.

For less than $100, you can own the cool iGo Stowaway Ultra-Slim Bluetooth keyboard, available at www.amazon.com. Or you can buy the ThinkOutside Stowaway Shasta Bluetooth keyboard for BlackBerry, available at http://yahooshopping.com for $45. We also recommend the Freedom Universal Bluetooth keyboard, which you can find under Bluetooth keyboards at http://shop.crackberry.com or Amazon.com.

Stereo Headsets

Although your new BlackBerry is a stereo music player, it doesn't come with stereo headphones. You will definitely yearn for stereo sound the moment you listen to music or watch video clips. A quick search on the Internet for *BlackBerry + stereo headphones* yields many results. But you want to be able to talk, too.

You could spend $30 to $200. Several good headsets follow:

- ✔ BlackBerry stereo headset with noise-isolating ear gels
- ✔ V-MODA Vibe duo in-ear headphones with mic
- ✔ Motorola S9 stereo Bluetooth headset

The best place to get stereo headphones for your BlackBerry is good ol' Amazon: www.amazon.com.

Case and Belt Clip

You have plenty of cases to choose among, with looks ranging from sporty to professional. These cases can set you back anywhere from $20 to $40, which isn't too bad for looking hip. Here's where you can buy a new case or belt clip:

- ✔ http://shop.crackberry.com
- ✔ www.amazon.com
- ✔ www.bberry.com
- ✔ www.blackberryden.com
- ✔ www.blackberrysource.com

When you buy a new belt case or clip, buy one made specifically for your BlackBerry Storm2. Also, it's important that the case or clip come with a small magnet. BlackBerry is holster-aware and conserves battery juice, and this magnet is the key for the BlackBerry to know that it is inside a holster.

Screen Protector and Skins

If the protector case described in the preceding section is a bit stressful for your wallet, try the Blackberry Pro high-definition screen protector with mirror effect. That's a mouthful, but for about $10, it protects your screen from scratches. Go to www.accessorygeeks.com.

Other popular best sellers are skin cases. They come in many colors and keep your BlackBerry looking new. The price is usually between $9 and $12. Go to http://shop.crackberry.com or www.accessorygeeks.com.

Extra Battery, Charger, and Charging Pod

An extra battery for your BlackBerry will come in handy if you're a daily user. You'll spend around $50 for the extra battery.

Buy your battery only from Research In Motion, at www.shopblackberry. com, or an authorized RIM reseller, not from some unknown vendor. A faulty battery can damage your BlackBerry beyond repair.

Make sure that the battery you buy is for your BlackBerry model.

If you watch video on your BlackBerry, you know that the battery needs to be charged every few hours. And if you're always on the go, you'd better have a portable charger on hand. The charger included with your BlackBerry is great to carry around town (and the world) because it has multiple adapters for different countries' electric plugs.

If you're a road warrior, get the BlackBerry car charger. It will set you back around $30. To top it off, you can also get a power station or charging pod, which connects to a power supply for charging and at the same time holds your BlackBerry firmly in place on your desk or nightstand. On your nightstand, you can take advantage of sleep mode, which sets the device to not disturb you by doing things such as dimming the light and turning off the LED. The charging pod costs $12 to $30, depending on how fancy it is.

Make sure that the charger and the charging pod you buy are for the Storm.

You can get a BlackBerry car charger and charging pod from the following sites:

- ✔ http://shop.crackberry.com
- ✔ www.amazon.com
- ✔ www.blackberrysource.com
- ✔ www.shopblackberry.com (RIM's official store)

External Speaker

BlackBerry comes with a speaker, but if the sound quality just isn't good enough for your listening taste, an external Bluetooth speaker can bring your outdoor listening to the next level. We recommend the following:

- ✔ Blueant M1 Bluetooth stereo speakers
- ✔ Motorola EQ5 wireless travel stereo speaker

For about $110, you can get either of them from `http://shop.crack berry.com`.

Bluetooth Music Gateway

If you already have a great set of speakers or an audio entertainment system, using a RIM Bluetooth Music Gateway is the perfect way to stream music to your existing system. Simply pair your BlackBerry with the Bluetooth Music Gateway via Bluetooth (hence the name), and you are ready to go. What is even better is that this hockey puck–like Music Gateway can be paired with your PC or Mac, so you get more use out of it. Find it at `http://shop.crackberry.com`.

Car Mount

To complete your BlackBerry car experience, mount your BlackBerry in your car. The market offers many products, ranging from $15 to $30. You can search the Web. You can also get a car mount from these BlackBerry sites:

- `http://shop.crackberry.com`
- `www.amazon.com`
- `www.blackberrysource.com`

Make sure that the product you're choosing supports your BlackBerry model.

The latest wireless speakerphone from RIM is BlackBerry Visor Mount SpeakerPhone VM-605. It's a Bluetooth speakerphone that you attach to your car's visor, just like you attach your garage door opener. You can get one for $99 at `www.shopblackberry.com`.

Chapter 20

Ten Fun Games for Your Storm

In This Chapter

▶ Top-rated free games

▶ Nintaii

▶ Bookworm

▶ Crash Bandicoot Mutant Island

▶ Air Traffic Control

▶ World Poker 2—Texas Hold 'Em

▶ Bubble Army

▶ Aces Mahjong

▶ Next Dual Pack

▶ Chuzzle

Who says BlackBerry is all work and no play? True, you can get tons accomplished on your Storm, but what you do doesn't necessarily have to be related to work. A few games come with your Storm, but you can beat those games only so many times before you get bored.

BlackBerry is a popular smart phone, and numerous BlackBerry game companies are making more and more fun titles. For example, you can play a few holes on the Pebble Beach golf course or a game of online Texas Hold 'Em with other BlackBerry users. You can find a huge selection of games. What's even better is that some great games are free.

After this chapter, you might play so many games on your Storm that you'll have to watch your productivity level. Please check our companion Web site — www. blackberryfordummies.com — for an updated list.

The games we list here are available at BlackBerry App World and CrackBerry App Store. If you need to download and install them, just point Browser to the following links:

✔ **BlackBerry App World:** www.blackberry.com/appworld

✔ **CrackBerry App Store:** http://crackberry.com/crackberryapp store

Top-Rated Free Games

Hundreds of free games are available. The following is a sample of some top-rated ones. All are available at BlackBerry App World:

- **Ka-Glom:** A high-pressure game of falling blocks, similar to the classic Tetris.

- **GT Blackjack:** More than half a million players are in on this game. You can be one of them.

- **Beach Party:** Go to the beach in this community game. Build sand castles and gain some friends.

- **Pixelated:** You'll never mind waiting in your doctor's office. Have fun wasting time on this puzzle game, changing the color of the squares in the least amount of time. Of course, you'll gain tricks by playing the game.

- **GT Slots:** Sometimes you just need a game that doesn't require a lot of thinking. That's what a slot machine is all about. See if you can win a jackpot.

- **Vegas Pool Shark Lite:** Do you want a nice little game of pool? Enjoy this game, but beware — sharks surround you, ready to make a hole in your pocket (game money, of course). See how long you last before you mortgage your house.

- **Sudoku Lite:** This is the Sudoku game that people are crazy about.

Nintaii

Nintaii is a puzzle game of rolling blocks and switches with more than 100 levels to challenge your brain. This game won the best game award of the 2008 BlackBerry Developer Challenge. A lot of brainpower has been put into this mind-twisting game. For $4.99, you can download Nintaii. Just look for it in BlackBerry App World or CrackBerry App Store.

Bookworm

A warning: The Bookworm word game is addictive. It is part crossword puzzle, part word jumble, and part arcade puzzler. Your job is to make Lex, the hungry bookworm, well fed with words. If you are up to the challenge, you can buy it for $6.99 or download a free trial version. Look for Bookworm in BlackBerry App World or CrackBerry App Store.

Crash Bandicoot Mutant Island

Ever play Crash Bandicoot on PlayStation? This game on the Storm can be as addictive as the bigger version. Be a crazy Bandicoot character and bounce, slide, jump, spin, and sprint your way to saving Crash's sister, Coco, from her kidnapper, the evil Dr. Neo Cortex. Prepare to battle giant robots and mutants. You can buy Crash Bandicoot Mutant Island for $6.99 from BlackBerry App World or CrackBerry App Store.

Air Traffic Control

Have you ever dreamed about becoming an air traffic controller? Maybe not. But the Air Traffic Control game gets you closer to becoming one, only in a small package. Take the game for a test run and start landing airplanes safely. When you're ready, you can buy Air Traffic Control for $4.99. Search for *Air Traffic Control* in BlackBerry App World or in CrackBerry App Store.

World Poker Tour 2—Texas Hold 'Em

Crave a game of Texas Hold 'Em while away from your buddies? Practice your bluff with World Poker Tour 2. When you're ready, play live online with other players. You can buy the game for $6.99 from BlackBerry App World or CrackBerry App Store.

Bubble Army

You have bubbles and fight with other bubbles. Sounds crazy and simple? Tell it to the many players who swear this game is addictive. Get Bubble Army from BlackBerry App World for $4.99. You can download a Bubble Army demo for free if you just want to try it first.

Aces Mahjong

Aces Mahjong is a based on the classic Chinese game of mahjong. It comes with 50 unique layouts. Buy Aces Mahjong for $3.99 from BlackBerry App World.

Next Dual Pack

Next Dual Pack is a highly rated game with 128 puzzles. You can save your solution and even undo your moves. You can get Next Dual Pack for $4.99 from BlackBerry App World or CrackBerry App Store.

Chuzzle

Do you love a game of Tetris, but you're tired of the same old thing every time? Try Chuzzle. You are controlling not blocks, but googly-eyed little balls of fur that giggle, squeak, and sneeze as you poke them across the board. A friendly warning: This game is simple yet addictive. And you'll get trophies too. For $6.99, you can download Chuzzle. Get it from BlackBerry App World or CrackBerry App Store.

Chapter 21

Ten Important Types of Web Sites

In This Chapter

▶ Weather

▶ News

▶ Search engines, directories, and portals

▶ Business

▶ Travel

▶ Sports

▶ Advice and self-help

▶ Social and virtual networking

▶ Shopping and shipping information

▶ Other browsing categories

*W*eb surfing with a BlackBerry has improved dramatically with the newer models. With higher screen resolution and bigger real estate, your BlackBerry Storm should give you one good mobile Web-browsing experience. And with a 3G connection, your Web browsing should be faster. Remember that by using Page view on your BlackBerry, where the Web page displays like it does in your PC Web browser, you can maintain the browsing habits you have on your PC, but in a smaller package.

The Web site recommendations in this chapter are based on reviews in the public domain and sites that help when you're on the go.

Weather

You can keep up with weather changes at these sites:

✔ **AccuWeather.com** (www.accuweather.com): AccuWeather.com provides the local weather forecast.

✔ **Weather.com** (www.weather.com): Weather.com is smart enough to know that you're using a mobile device and displays a nice, trim version of its page with a few links to non-weather–related information.

If these two sites aren't enough, check out the "Search Engines, Directories, and Portals" section, later in this chapter. Major portals have weather information as well as traffic alerts and airport delays.

News

Most major news companies have mobile versions of their sites. This section gives you a sampling of what's out there. We list the same Web address you'd expect when browsing from your desktop. These sites detect that you're using a smart phone and redirect you to the mobile-friendly version of their sites:

- **ABC News** (www.abcnews.com): Get ABC News on your BlackBerry.

- **BBC News** (www.bbc.com): Read the BBC News right from your BlackBerry, even if you're not in the United Kingdom.

- **CNN** (www.cnn.com): This is CNN's mobile-friendly Web site.

- **Reuters** (www.reuters.com): This is a mobile-friendly version of the Reuters site.

- **The New York Times** (www.nytimes.com): This automatically points you to *The New York Times* mobile-friendly Web site, a site that's clean and easy to navigate, without a lot of advertisements.

- **USA Today** (http://usatoday.com): *USA Today,* one of the most popular newspapers, is now available for free from your BlackBerry.

- **Wired News** (http://mobile.wired.com): Wired News is the mobile version of this tech-news Web site.

Search Engines, Directories, and Portals

In this section we list *Web portals,* which are sites that contain various information or links to other sites:

- **Google** (www.google.com): The king of search engines works like a charm on your BlackBerry.

- **MSN** (www.msn.com): You can access MSN Hotmail, MSN Messenger, and an online calendar. MSN has all the features that you can find in a Web portal, such as Web search, weather lookup, sports information, and news. Plus you get MSN's finance-related pages, which give you up-to-the-minute stock quotes.

✔ **RIM mobile home page** (http://mobile.blackberry.com): This is the default home page setting for most BlackBerry browsers. The service provider can customize it, though, so your BlackBerry browser may point to your service provider's home page. RIM's home page is definitely a place to start browsing the Web.

You should definitely bookmark this site.

✔ **Yahoo! Mobile** (www.yahoo.com): Yahoo! is a smart portal because it knows you're using a mobile device and formats the page accordingly — meaning a smaller page with no advertisements. The portal site allows BlackBerry users to employ regular Yahoo! functions, such as Yahoo! Mail, Messenger, Finance, and Games, as well as driving directions and weather.

This is another site you should bookmark.

Business

You can keep up with the latest news in the finance world from your BlackBerry. Visit the following sites for finance-related articles and news:

✔ **BusinessWeek Online** (www.businessweek.com): This is a place to get great finance information.

✔ **Fidelity** (www.fidelity.com): Fidelity is an online investment brokerage firm.

✔ **Yahoo! Finance** (http://finance.yahoo.com): This is a great site for checking the performance of your stocks.

Travel

Every site in the following list of BlackBerry-accessible travel sites features flight status and gate numbers. Some allow you to log in (if you're part of the airline's frequent-flier program) to access frequent-flier benefits:

✔ Air Canada: www.aircanada.ca

✔ American Airlines: http://aa.flightlookup.com/omnisky

✔ British Airways: www.britishairways.com

✔ Cathay Pacific: www.cathaypacific.com

✔ Continental Airlines: www.continental.com

✔ Delta: www.delta.com

- ✔ JetBlue: `http://jetblue.com`
- ✔ Northwest Airlines: `http://nwa.com`
- ✔ United Air Lines: `http://ua2go.com`
- ✔ Any airline: `http://flightview.com`

Also check out these travel sites:

- ✔ **TripKick** (`www.tripkick.com`): Don't be so excited about getting a good deal on a hotel only to end up in a crummy room. TripKick tells you who has the best rooms and who doesn't.
- ✔ **WikiTravel** (`www.wikitravel.com`): This is one of the most up-to-date and complete travel guides on the Web.

Sports

Tired of missing updates on your favorite sport while on the go? You don't have to. Visit the sports-related sites that follow and you'll get the scoop on what's happening with your favorite team:

- ✔ **CBS Sports Mobile** (`www.cbssports.com/mobile`): If you're active on CBS Fantasy Team, you'll be happy to know that you can log on and view your stats from this Web site. Popular U.S. sports are covered here.
- ✔ **ESPN** (`http://mobileapp.espn.go.com`): Everyone knows ESPN. This is the mobile version of its Web site.

Advice and Self-Help

Looking for ways to save time and get your questions answered? Check out these sites:

- ✔ **HowCast** (`www.howcast.com`): With a dose of humor, this site is a world of how-to videos.
- ✔ **Omiru** (`www.omiru.com`): This site offers practical fashion advice for the common person.
- ✔ **Yahoo! Answers** (`http://answers.yahoo.com`): Here, you can get all sorts of creative, amusing, and helpful responses to your questions — advice that's free.
- ✔ **Zeer** (`www.zeer.com`): No need to stand in the supermarket comparing nutritional labels; do it here.

Social and Virtual Networking

For those of you who are (or aren't yet) addicted to social networking sites, we list a few of the most popular ones here. If your favorite site isn't listed, don't fret; just search for it with a search engine:

- **Friendster** (www.friendster.com): This site is popular in Southeast Asian countries and is open to people 16 and older.

- **LinkedIn** (wwwlinkedin.com): LinkedIn caters to professional and business relationships. You'll find people publishing their bios on their profile.

- **Multiply** (www.multiply.com): This site claims to focus on real-world relationships and is open to anyone 13 and older. It's a popular site for teenagers.

- **Orkut** (www.orkut.com): Orkut is a social networking site run by Google. It's open to anyone 18 and older, and it requires Google login credentials. This site is popular in Latin America and in India.

- **Windows Live Space** (home.spaces.live.com): This is a social networking site run by Microsoft. It's open to everyone and requires a Hotmail or Windows Live login.

MySpace and Facebook both have an application you can download from RIM's Web site. Point your browser to mobile.blackberry.com and navigate to IM & Social Networking.

Shopping and Shipping Information

Shopaholics can keep it up online even when they're not in front of the PC. Check out these sites:

- **Amazon** (www.amazon.com): With Amazon Anywhere, you can shop and check your account information right from your BlackBerry.

- **eBay** (www.ebay.com): You can bid on goods from the convenience of your BlackBerry.

- **FedEx tracking** (www.fedex.com): This mobile version of the FedEx Web site allows you to track packages from your BlackBerry.

- **Gas Buddy** (www.gasbuddy.com): You can find the nearest gas station that sells the cheapest gas.

- **ILikeTotallyLoveIt.com** (www.iliketotallyloveit.com): This is shopping with a twist. Shoppers post things they like, from wasabi gumballs to DeLorean cars, and solicit opinions on posted sale items from other members.

- **UPS tracking** (www.ups.com): Like FedEx, UPS has a mobile version of its Web site that allows you to track packages from your BlackBerry.

Other Browsing Categories

You can visit the following sites from your BlackBerry to get more information on various topics:

- **BlackBerry Cool** (www.blackberrycool.com): A competitor to CrackBerry (see the upcoming bullet), BlackBerry Cool is one of the pioneers in providing great reviews of BlackBerry applications.

- **CrackBerry** (http://mobile.crackberry.com): Go here to discover the latest BlackBerry news, communicate with other BlackBerry users, find BlackBerry accessories, and read application reviews and BlackBerry-related articles. Without a doubt, this site is one of the most active BlackBerry communities.

  If you visit crackberry.com on Browser, you'll be directed to the mobile version of crackberry.com. Click through to Downloads and Mobile Links Directory, and you'll find a massive list of Web sites that offer up a solid mobile-viewing experience. While you're in the Downloads section, you may want to spend a few minutes finding some free wallpapers and ring tones to dress up your device!

- **MiniSphere** (www.minisphere.com): You find useful links designed for mobile devices here.

- **MizPee** (www.mizpee.com): When you gotta go, you gotta go. This site locates the nearest clean public bathroom.

- **Starbucks Locator** (www.starbucks.com): This site helps you locate the nearest Starbucks so you can meet your buddies or get a dose of caffeine.

Index

• A •

abbreviations
  AutoText feature, 29–31
  for texting, 130–131
ABC Amber BlackBerry Converter, 287
accessories, 309–313
Aces Mahjong game, 317
ACT! sync setup for, 249–253
actions
  Calendar Options for, 74
  for Contacts, 55–56
  for filtered e-mail messages, 115
Activity Log, opening, 55
address book. See Contacts
advice and self-help sites, 322
Agenda view (Calendar), 70
Air Traffic Control game, 317
alarms. See also Clock
  downloading sounds, 219–220
  options, 85–86
  wake-up, setting, 87–88
alerts. See also alarms
  Bedside mode settings, 87
  Calendar Options for, 74
  downloading sounds, 219–220
  LED, BerryBuzz application for, 39
  profiles for, 36–38
  reminder time for appointments, 77–78
  Ring Tones application, 205–206, 209
  ring tones for contacts, 49–50
  types of reminders and alerts, 35–36
all-day appointments, creating, 77
animations, repeat limit in Browser, 174
AOL Instant Messenger (AIM), 138, 140. See
    also instant messaging (IM)
Application Loader (Windows)
  accessing, 296–297
  described, 244
  installing applications using, 297–299
  OS upgrade using, 303–305
  uninstalling applications using, 301–302
Application Memory, freeing up, 50–51

applications. See also installing;
    specific applications
  alerts for, 35–38
  BlackBerry App World store for,
    291–294, 315
  cancelling a selection, 24
  closing when not using, 18
  convenience keys for opening, 18, 25
  described, 14
  games, 315–318
  Google apps, 81
  GPS, 222–225
  for instant messaging, 136
  opening Browser from, 159
  returning to Home screen from, 18
  returning to previous page, 18, 24
  switching, 25, 159
  third-party, 273, 291–295, 315
  Twitter clients, 138
  uninstalling, 301–303
  viewing list of, 18, 24–25
appointments (Calendar)
  all-day, 77
  information possible for, 76
  meetings versus, 80
  multiple per time slot, 77
  one-time, 76–77
  options, 74
  recurring, 78–79
  reminder time for, 77–78
ASCII Text File Converter, sync setup for,
    249–253
attachments to e-mail
  attaching a file, 110–111
  contacts, 56
  editing, 108–109
  types supported by BlackBerry, 107
  viewing, 107–108
Audio Boost option, 211
Auto Answer Call option, 229
Auto Correction option, 31
AutoText feature, 29–31

• *B* •

background
  for Home screen, 34–35, 166, 196
  for Web pages, 173
Backlight Brightness setting, 33
Backlight Timeout setting, 33, 223
backlighting feature, 211–212
backup, wireless, 280, 289
Backup and Restore
  accessing, 280
  automatic backup, 283–284
  described, 244
  full restore, 284–285
  importance of using, 279–280
  manual backup, 281–282
  reading backup files, 287
  selective backup, 285–287
  selective restore, 285, 287–288
  selectively deleting databases, 288–289
barcodes, scanning in BlackBerry
        Messenger, 147, 148
battery
  car charger for, 312
  charging, clock behavior during, 85
  charging, frequency for, 15
  charging pod for, 89, 312
  extra, 312
  turning off backlighting to preserve, 212
BCC (blind carbon copy) e-mails, 110
Beach Party game, 316
Bedside mode (Clock)
  charging pod for, 89
  entering, 88
  exiting, 89
  options, 86–87
Bell, BIS login address for, 101
belt clips, 311
BerryBuzz or BeBuzz application, 39
BES. *See* BlackBerry Enterprise Server
BIS. *See* BlackBerry Internet Service
BlackBerry App World
  BeBuzz application from, 39
  described, 291
  games from, 315
  installing applications using, 293–294
  navigating, 292–293
BlackBerry Application Center, 295
BlackBerry Browser. *See* Browser

BlackBerry community online, 220
BlackBerry Desktop Manager (Mac)
  automatic sync, 269
  Calendar options, 262–263
  Contacts options, 263
  deleting all music files from BlackBerry,
        267–268
  Device Options, 261–262
  installing, 259–260
  installing applications using, 299–300
  introduction of, 258–259
  manual sync, 268
  Music options, 266–267
  Notes options, 263–264, 265
  OS upgrade using, 305–306
  running the first time, 260–261
  Tasks options, 264–266
  uninstalling applications using, 302
BlackBerry Desktop Manager (Windows).
        See also specific programs
  Application Loader, 244, 296–299, 301–
        302, 303–305
  Backup and Restore, 244, 279–289
  connecting to your BlackBerry, 246–247
  deleting databases selectively, 288–289
  Device Switch Wizard, 244, 271–277
  installing in Windows, 244
  Media Manager, 214–218, 244
  opening, 245–246
  OS upgrade using, 303–305
  overview, 12
  running the first time, 247–248
  suite of programs with, 244
  Synchronize, 53–54, 248–257
BlackBerry Enterprise Server (BES)
  Browser connected to, 158
  Browser on, 178, 179–180
  Desktop Redirector for, 101–102
  synchronization over the air with, 243
  wireless application installation, 299
BlackBerry Internet Service (BIS)
  accessing, 98–99
  adding e-mail accounts, 99–101
  creating your account, 99, 100
  deleting e-mail from BlackBerry, 104–105
  features overview, 98
  filtering e-mail messages, 113–116
  login addresses for, 101
  signature for e-mails, 102–103

BlackBerry Maps, 55, 223
BlackBerry Media Sync, 218–219
BlackBerry Messenger. *See also* instant
    messaging (IM)
  accessing, 144
  adding categories, 145
  adding contacts, 147–149
  adding contacts to, 56
  adding symbols to your name, 152
  backing up contacts, 147
  broadcasting a message, 145, 155–156
  contacts list, 144–145
  creating custom groupings, 147
  deleting a contact, 146
  deleting backup files, 147
  disabling reception in Bedside mode, 86
  forwarding contact info, 145
  group conversations, 145, 150–152
  initiating a conversation, 145, 150
  inviting contacts, 145
  menu items, 145–147
  moving a contact, 146
  My Profile settings, 146
  opening Contacts from, 44
  PIN-to-PIN technology as basis of, 143
  restoring contacts from backup, 147
  saving the conversation history, 154–155
  scanning barcodes, 147, 148
  sending a file, 154
  sending a picture, 152, 153
  sending a Voice Note, 152–154
  sending a Web page address, 164
  sending pictures, 194–195
  subject for messages, 151
  viewing contact info, 145
BlackBerry OS 5.0, 15
blind carbon copy (BCC) e-mails, 110
Bluetooth
  BlackBerry support for, 14
  external speaker, 312–313
  headset, 235–236
  keyboards, 310
  Music Gateway, 313
bookmarks (Browser)
  adding a bookmark, 166–167
  adding subfolders for, 169–170
  Available Offline option, 168
  changing, 168
  deleting, 170–171
  going to, 167
  moving between folders, 170
  organizing, 168–171
  renaming folders, 170
Bookworm game, 316
brightness settings, 32–33, 87
broadcasting a message, 145, 155–156
Browser. *See also* Web surfing
  accessing, 158–160
  alerts for, 36
  bookmarking sites, 166–171
  cache settings, 174–176, 177
  configuring, 172–173
  default browser, 180
  default view for, 174
  in enterprise environments, 178, 179–180
  full screen view, 174
  Gears settings, 176
  General Properties screen, 173–174
  icons on top-right corner of screen, 164
  menu options, 161–163
  multiple personalities of, 158
  navigating Web pages, 161–163
  opening a Web page, 160–161
  options, 171–177
  saving a Web page address, 164–165
  saving Web images, 166
  sending a Web page address, 164, 166
  speeding up browsing, 175
  stopping a page from loading, 164
Bubble Army game, 317
business cards, virtual. *See* vCards
business environments. *See* enterprise
  environments
business sites, 321

• C •

cache settings (Browser), 174–176, 177
Calendar
  accessing, 69–70
  all-day appointments, 77
  creating appointments, 76–79
  going to a specific date, 73
  going to today's date, 73
  meetings, 80–82
  moving between time frames, 71–73
  multiple appointments per time slot, 77
  multiple calendars, colors for, 75–76

one-time appointments, 76–77
opening Contacts from, 44
options, 73–74
phone conference dial-in number setting, 81–82
recurring appointments, 78–79
reminder sounds for, 36
reminder time for appointments, 77–78
responding to meeting requests, 80–81
sending meeting requests, 80
switching views, 71
sync setup for (Mac), 262–263
sync setup for (Windows), 249–253
synchronizing Facebook profiles with, 67–68
synchronizing with Google, 81
views available, 70–71
call forwarding, 231–232
Call Log, 238–239
Caller ID, setting pictures as, 195–196
Camera
accessing, 183
default folder for pictures, 209
deleting pictures, 191
filename format for pictures, 190
flash settings, 188
focusing before taking shots, 184
geotagging pictures, 189
holding the camera steady, 187
listing filenames versus thumbnails, 191
locations for captured photos, 189
opening, 25
organizing pictures, 192–194
picture properties, 191–192
picture quality (resolution) settings, 186–187
picture size settings, 188–189
preparing to take a picture, 183–184
screen indicators, 185
sharing pictures, 194–195
shutter speed improvements with Storm2, 184
slide shows, 190–191, 212
viewing pictures, 189–190, 191
white balance settings, 188
zooming, 187–188
car charger, 312
car mount, 222, 313
cases, 311

categories, Filter feature using, 57, 59–61
CC (carbon copy) e-mails, 110
charging the battery
car charger for, 312
charging pod for, 89, 312
clock behavior during, 85
frequency of, 15
Chuzzle game, 318
Clipboard, 95
Clock
accessing, 83–84
alarm options, 85–86
Bedside mode settings, 86–87
behavior when charging, 85
countdown timer, 87, 90–91
face types for, 85
options, 84–87
stopwatch, 87, 89–90
time and time zone settings, 85
wake-up alarm setting, 87–88
closing applications, 18
colors
LED alerts, 39
for multiple calendars, 75–76
conference calls, 81–82, 233–234
configuring Browser, 172–173
Confirm Delete option, 53, 62, 95
confirming changes during sync, 255
connecting to BlackBerry Desktop Manager, 246–247
Contacts
actions for, 55–56
adding extra numbers after phone numbers, 46, 228–229
adding Facebook friend info, 66–67
adding from Messages, 50–51, 112
adding your own contact information, 28, 50
assigning PINs to names, 127–128
calling card numbers in, 228–229
categories for, 57, 59–61
copying from desktop applications, 53–54
creating a contact, 45–50
Custom Dictionary options for, 23–24
deleting a contact, 52–53, 142
duplicate names, allowing, 62
Edit mode for, 60
editing a contact, 51–52
Filter feature, 57, 59–61

finding a contact, 54–56
groups, 57–59
Notes field for, 46
opening, 44
options, 61–62
phone calls from, 228
phone extensions in, 46, 228–229
pictures for, 48–49, 195–196
renaming User fields for, 46–47
ring tones for, 49–50
separators for list, 62
sharing, 62–64
sorting, 62
sync setup for (Mac), 263
sync setup for (Windows), 249–253
synchronizing Facebook profiles with, 67–68
usefulness of, 43–44, 45
vCards for, 62–64, 154
viewing, 51
contacts (BlackBerry Messenger)
adding, 147–149
backing up, 147
categories for, 145
creating custom groupings for, 147
deleting, 146
forwarding info for, 145
inviting, 145
moving, 146
restoring from backup, 147
sending info as a file, 154
viewing info for, 145
convenience keys
described, 18, 25
programming, 33–34, 211
converting media files, 218
cookies, Browser cache settings for, 176
copying
chat history from BlackBerry Messenger, 154
contacts from desktop applications, 53–54
e-mail messages (CC and BCC), 110
media files to and from computer, 213–214
media files with Media Manager, 217–218
passwords from Password Keeper, 94–95
Web page address, 164

corporate environments. *See* enterprise environments
countdown timer, 87, 90–91
CrackBerry On-Device App Store, 295, 315
CrackBerry.com
BerryBuzz application from, 39
CrackBerry App Store client from, 295
icon for tips from, 4
tutorials on freeing up Application Memory, 51
Web site, 4, 5, 324
Crash Bandicoot Mutant Island game, 317
Custom Dictionary
adding words to, 23
options for, 23–24
for SureType keyboard, 21
using, 22
customizing. *See* options; personalizing your BlackBerry

● *D* ●

databases
deleting selectively, 288–289
outside Contacts, finding people in, 64–65
date, AutoText for, 31
Day view (Calendar), 70
deleting
automatic, for old e-mails and phone log entries, 50
bookmarks, 170–171
clearing the Clipboard, 95
Confirm Delete option, 53, 62, 95
contacts, 52–53
databases selectively, 288–289
e-mail, options for, 103
e-mail, purging on BIS client from BlackBerry, 104–105
e-mail, synchronizing deleted messages, 104
e-mail messages individually, 112
e-mail prior to a date mark, 113
IM contact or buddy, 142
music files (Mac), 267–268
pictures, 191
uninstalling applications, 301–302
desktop computer. *See also* BlackBerry Desktop Manager (Windows)

adding e-mail accounts to BIS, 101
BlackBerry Desktop Manager (Mac),
   258–269, 299–300, 301–302, 305–306
copying contacts from applications,
   53–54
copying media files to and from, 213–214
uninstalling applications, 301–302
Desktop Redirector, 101–102, 244–245
Device Switch Wizard
   described, 244
   switching from a non-BlackBerry device,
      274–277
   switching to a new BlackBerry, 271–274
digital zoom (Camera), 188
directories, 320–321
distribution lists, groups for, 59
Documents to Go, 108–109
Domino, finding people in database, 64–65
downloading
   BlackBerry Desktop Manager (Mac), 259
   Google Maps, 224
   instant messaging apps, 136, 137
   iSkoot for Skype for BlackBerry, 297
   Media Manager, 214
   OS upgrade, 303
   over the air (OTA) download, 299
   podcasts or videocasts, 218
   sounds, 219–220
   themes, 34
   wallpaper, 35
driving safety, 14, 135, 221–222
duplicate contact names, allowing, 62

• E •

earphones, 14
editing
   attachments to e-mail, 108–109
   contacts, 51–52
   entering Edit mode in Contacts, 60
e-mail. *See also* Messages
   adding sender to Contacts, 51, 112
   attaching a file, 110–111
   BCC recipients for, 110
   CC recipients for, 110
   chat history with BlackBerry Messenger,
      154–155
   Delete On options, 103
   deleting messages individually, 112

deleting messages prior to a date mark,
   113
deleting on BIS client from BlackBerry,
   104–105
editing attachments, 108–109
filtering messages, 113–116
forwarding e-mails, 109–110, 115
forwarding phone notes, 239–240
groups for distribution lists, 59
out-of-office messages, 105
receiving messages, 106
redirecting from Outlook, 244–245
reusing saved searches, 120
saving a draft, 110
saving messages, 106
saving search results, 119–120
searching for messages, 116–119
sending a Web page address, 164, 166
sending pictures, 194
sending to multiple people, 110
sending to one person, 109
separating text messages from, 136
shortcut for accessing incoming mail,
   120–121
signature for, 102–103
spell-checking outgoing messages, 111
storage time for, 121–122
Synchronize Deleted Item option, 104
viewing attachments, 107–108
viewing saved messages, 107
wireless e-mail reconciliation, 98, 103–105
e-mail accounts. *See also* BlackBerry
      Internet Service (BIS)
   adding to BIS, 99–101
   availability on BlackBerry, 97–98
   calendars for, 75–76
   filtering messages for, 113–116
   native e-mail client for, 81
   out-of-office messages for, 105
emoticons or smileys
   for BlackBerry Messenger, 152
   for instant messaging, 141
   for texting, 132–133, 135
emulation type for Browser, 173
End/Power key, 18
enterprise environments. *See also*
      BlackBerry Enterprise Server (BES)
   Browser in, 178, 179–180
   Code of Silence in, 125

Desktop Redirector for, 101–102, 244–245
PIN-to-PIN messaging in, 56, 125
receiving enterprise e-mails, 101–102
smiley and shorthand use in, 133
synchronization over the air in, 243
erasing. *See* deleting
escape key, 18, 24
etiquette for texting, 135
Exchange, finding people in database,
      64–65
Explore, 209
external speaker, 312–313

• *F* •

Facebook
   adding friend info to Contacts, 66–67
   synchronizing profiles with Contacts,
      67–68
features overview, 12–14, 17–19
file types supported
   converting media files, 218
   music formats, 201
   picture formats, 204
   ring tone formats, 206
filenames for pictures
   format for, 190
   listing when viewing folders, 191
   renaming, 192–193
Filter feature (Contacts), 57, 60–61
filtering e-mail messages, 113–116
finding contact information
   actions for found contacts, 55–56
   categories for, 60–61
   in Contacts, 54–56
   in databases outside Contacts, 64–65
finding messages. *See* searching Messages
Fine picture quality, 186
finger-scroll, defined, 20
finger-swipe, defined, 20
Firefox, Browser emulation of, 173
flash (Camera), 185, 188
flash drive, using BlackBerry as, 213–214
focusing the camera, 184, 187
folders
   for bookmarks, 169–170
   excluding from Pictures display, 212
   Explore for navigating, 209

for pictures, 193–194, 209
   saving messages to, 106
fonts
   Browser settings for, 173–174
   Media options for, 212
   settings, 31–32
   themes, 34
formatting options (Calendar), 74
forwarding
   BlackBerry Messenger contact info, 145
   e-mail, 109–110, 115
   phone calls, 231–232
   phone notes, 239–240
   SMS or MMS messages, 135

• *G* •

games, 315–318
Gears settings (Browser), 176
General Properties screen (Browser),
      173–174
generating passwords randomly, 93–94
geotagging pictures, 189
Global Address Lists (GAL), 64–65
Gmail, Gears settings for, 176
Google
   applications, 81
   Sync for BlackBerry, 81
Google Maps, 224–225
Google Talk, 138, 140. *See also* instant
      messaging (IM)
GPS (global positioning system)
   BlackBerry Maps for, 223
   car kit for, 222
   disabled, 221
   driving safety with, 221–222
   Google Maps for, 224–225
   requirements for, 222
   TeleNav GPS Navigator for, 225
group conversations (BlackBerry
      Messenger), 145, 150–152
groups of contacts
   in BlackBerry Messenger, 147
   in Contacts, 57–59
GroupWise, finding people in database,
      64–65
GT Blackjack game, 316
GT Slots game, 316

• *H* •

Handango app store, 295
headset, 235–236, 310–311
Headset Equalizer option, 211
Hidden pictures, finding, 209
Home screen
  background for, 34–35, 166, 196
  jumping back to, 18
  opening Browser from, 158, 160
Hover Period setting, 19, 33

• *1* •

IBM Domino, finding people in database,
    64–65
IChat AV. *See* instant messaging (IM)
ICQ Instant Messenger, 138, 140. *See also*
    instant messaging (IM)
IM. *See* instant messaging
images. *See* Camera; pictures
importing media files. *See* media files,
    acquiring
installing
  applications from BlackBerry App World,
    293–294
  applications from the Web, 177–178
  applications using Application Loader
    (Windows), 297–299
  applications using Macs, 299–300
  BlackBerry Desktop Manager (Mac),
    259–260
  BlackBerry Desktop Manager (Windows),
    244
  Desktop Redirector, 244–245
instant messaging (IM).
    See also BlackBerry Messenger
  adding a contact, buddy, or friend,
    140–141
  deleting a contact or buddy, 142
  disabling reception in Bedside mode, 86
  downloading apps for, 136, 137
  emoticons or smileys for, 141
  getting a user ID/password for, 138
  initiating a conversation, 141
  logging on/signing in, 138–139
  overview, 136–137
  popular services for, 137
  requirements for, 137
  SMS versus Internet for, 142
  tips for using, 141–142
Internet Browser. *See* Browser
Internet Explorer, Browser emulation of,
    173
Internet resources. *See also* downloading;
    Web surfing
  ABC Amber BlackBerry Converter, 287
  accessories, 309–313
  accessories list, 309
  advice and self-help sites, 322
  BIS login addresses, 101
  BlackBerry App World, 291–294, 315
  BlackBerry community, 220
  BlackBerry Desktop Manager (Mac)
    download, 259
  Bluetooth keyboards, 310
  business sites, 321
  car kits, 222
  CrackBerry.com, 4, 5
  directories, 320–321
  finding locations of geotagged pictures,
    189
  games, 315
  Google applications, 81
  Google Maps, 224
  informational sites, 324
  instant messaging apps, 136, 137
  instant messaging user ID/password, 138
  iSkoot for Skype for BlackBerry, 297
  Media Manager download, 214
  news sites, 320
  OS upgrade providers, 303
  Palm user guide, 275
  portals, 320–321
  search engines, 320–321
  shipping information, 323–324
  shopping sites, 323–324
  SmrtGuard for BlackBerry, 289
  SMS shorthand, 130
  social networking sites, 323
  sounds for downloading, 219, 220
  sports sites, 322
  TeleNav GPS Navigator, 225
  themes, 34
  for third-party applications, 295
  travel sites, 321–322
  tutorials on freeing up Application
    Memory, 51

virtual networking sites, 323
wallpaper, 35
weather sites, 319–320
Web sites for this book, 5
iSkoot for Skype for BlackBerry
  downloading, 297
  installing (Mac), 299–300
  installing (Windows), 297–299
iTunes
  deleting all music files before sync,
    267–268
  synchronizing with, 218–219, 266–267

● J ●

Jabber. *See* instant messaging (IM)
JavaScript, Browser options for, 172, 174

● K ●

Ka-Glom game, 316
Key Rate setting, 19
keyboard, full, 310
keyboards, virtual. *See* QWERTY keyboard;
  SureType keyboard
keywords
  searching for messages using, 117–119
  for your PIN, 125–126

● L ●

language settings, 28–29, 30
LEDs, 39, 86
lock key, 18, 39
Lotus Notes and Lotus Organizer, sync
  setup for, 249–253

● M ●

Mac. *See* desktop computer
map applications for GPS, 222–225
mapping fields to sync, 253–255
Maps, 55, 223
Media
  accessing, 198
  capabilities of, 197
  closing when inactive, 211
  Explore application, 209

icons on opening screen, 198–199
Memory Use application, 210
Music application, 199–203, 209
navigating menus in, 208–209
options, 210–212
personalizing wallpaper using, 34–35
Pictures application, 204–205, 208
Ring Tones application, 205–206, 209
Video Camera application, 199, 203–204
Videos application, 199, 203–204, 209
Voice Notes application, 199, 207–209
Voice Notes Recorder application, 199,
  206–207
volume buttons and slider, 208
media files, acquiring
  downloading sounds, 219–220
  methods for, 212
  synchronizing with iTunes, 218–219,
    266–267
  using BlackBerry as a flash drive, 213–214
  using Media Manager, 214–218
media formats supported, 201, 204, 206
Media Manager
  accessing, 215
  converting media files, 218
  copying media files to BlackBerry,
    217–218
  described, 244
  downloading the latest version, 214
  features overview, 216
  importing media files to, 216–217
  interface, 215–216
meetings
  appointments versus, 80
  enterprise e-mail notification for, 102
  phone conference dial-in number setting,
    81–82
  responding to requests, 80–81
  sending requests, 80
MemoPad, sync setup for
  Mac, 263–264, 265
  Windows, 249–253
memory
  checking card's with Memory Use, 210
  freeing up Application Memory, 50–51
  tutorials on freeing up, 51
  types of, 51
  viewing info for, 50
menu key, 18, 24–25

menu layout, themes for, 34
menus
  in BlackBerry Messenger, 145–147
  Browser options for, 161–163
  in Media applications, 208–209
Messages. *See also* e-mail; e-mail accounts
  accessing incoming phone calls from, 50
  adding contacts from, 51, 112
  alerts or ring tones for, 35–38, 49–50
  attaching a file to e-mail, 110–111
  automatic deletion of, 50
  deleting messages individually, 112
  deleting messages prior to a date mark, 113
  disabling reception in Bedside mode, 86
  editing attachments, 108–109
  e-mail ease with BlackBerry, 12
  filtering e-mail, 113–116
  forwarding e-mail, 109–110
  opening, 105
  opening Contacts from, 44
  PIN-to-PIN messaging, 55, 56, 123–129
  receiving e-mails, 106
  receiving enterprise e-mails, 101–102
  reusing saved searches, 120
  saving a draft e-mail, 110
  saving messages, 106
  saving search results, 119–120
  searching for messages, 116–119
  sending e-mail, 109, 110
  shortcut for accessing incoming e-mail only, 120–121
  signature for e-mails, 102–103
  sorting the message list, 106
  spell-checking outgoing messages, 111
  storage time for e-mail, 121–122
  synchronizing Facebook profiles with, 67–68
  types of messages listed by, 105
  viewing attachments, 107–108
  viewing saved messages, 107
Messenger. *See* BlackBerry Messenger
Michulak, Kevin (CrackBerry tips provider), 1
microSD card, 310
microSD slot, 18, 25

Microsoft Exchange, finding people in database, 64–65
Microsoft Internet Explorer, Browser emulation of, 173
Microsoft Outlook. *See* Outlook
Microsoft Schedule, sync setup for, 249–253
Microsoft Windows Mobile device, switching to a BlackBerry from, 275–277
MMS (Multimedia Messaging Service). *See also* SMS (Short Message Service)
  contact action for, 55
  described, 129
  emoticons or smileys for, 132–133, 135
  etiquette and cautions for, 135
  sending a message, 133–134
  sending a Web page address, 164
  sending pictures, 194–195
  shorthand for, 130–131
  viewing a message, 135
Month view (Calendar), 70
moving items
  bookmarks between folders, 170
  contacts in Messenger, 146
  pictures between folders, 193–194
Mozilla Firefox, Browser emulation of, 173
multitap mode, 22, 24
Music application
  accessing, 199
  creating playlists, 201–202
  formats supported, 201
  menu navigation in, 209
  opening screen, 199–200
  playback interface, 199–201
  playing playlists, 203
mute key, 18
muting phone calls, 230
My Profile settings (BlackBerry Messenger), 146

navigating
  BlackBerry App World, 292–293
  to media files, 209

Media menus, 208–209
Web pages, 161–163
network service provider
  branding by, 12, 158, 180
  need for, 10–11
news sites, 320
Next Dual Pack game, 318
NikkiSoft QuickLaunch application, 44, 213
Nintaii game, 316
Normal picture quality, 186
note-keeping programs. *See also* phone
    notes; Voice Notes
  sync setup for Mac, 263–264, 265
  sync setup for Windows, 249–253
Notes (IBM), finding people in Domino
    database, 64–65
notifications. *See* alarms; alerts

• O •

offline content (Browser), 168, 176
one-time appointments, creating, 76–77
opening e-mail attachments, 108
operating system (OS)
  BlackBerry OS 5.0, 15
  upgrading, 303–306
options
  alerts, 35–38
  Auto Answer Call, 229
  Auto Correction, 31
  automatic backup, 283–284
  AutoText, 29–31
  backlight, 33, 223
  BlackBerry Messenger, 147
  brightness, 32–33
  Browser, 171–177
  Calendar, 73–74
  Camera, 186–187, 188–189
  Clock, 84–87
  conference dial-in number, 81–82
  Confirm Delete, 53, 62, 95
  Contacts, 61–62
  convenience keys, programming, 33–34
  Custom Dictionary, 23–24
  Delete On (for e-mail), 103
  e-mail storage time, 121–122

fonts, 31–32
Home screen background, 34–35
language, 28–29
language settings, 30
Media, 210–212
Owner, 28
password for BlackBerry, 38
Password Keeper, 95
screen look and feel, 31–33
signature for e-mails, 102–103
SmartCase, 30
Specified Case, 30
Spell Check, 111
SurePress touch screen settings, 19,
    32–33
text shortcuts, 31
themes, 34–35
wallpaper, 34–35
Word Completion, 31
OS (operating system)
  BlackBerry OS 5.0, 15
  upgrading, 303–306
Outlook
  finding people in Exchange database,
    64–65
  redirecting e-mail from, 244–245
  sync setup for, 249–253
Outlook Express, sync setup for, 249–253
out-of-office messages, 105
over the air (OTA) download, 299
over the air (OTA) synchronization, 243
Owner Options, 28

• P •

Palm device, switching to a BlackBerry
    from, 274–277
Password Keeper
  changing your password, 96
  copying and pasting passwords from,
    94–95
  creating password entries, 92–93
  need for, 91
  options, 95
  password for, 92
  random password generation, 93–94

random password options, 95
using master password for, 96
passwords
  for instant messaging, 137–138
  for Password Keeper, 92, 96
  Password Keeper for, 91–96
  PIN versus, 125
  for your BlackBerry, 38, 96, 279
PC. *See* BlackBerry Desktop Manager
    (Windows); desktop computer
personal digital assistant (PDA)
  BlackBerry capabilities for, 10, 13
  defined, 2
  history of, 11
  switching to BlackBerry from, 274–277
personal identification number. *See* PIN
personalizing your BlackBerry. *See also*
    options
  alerts and ring tones, 35–38, 49–50
  AutoText feature, 29–31
  convenience keys, 33–34, 211
  need for, 27
  screen look and feel, 31–33
  text shortcuts, 31
  themes, 34
  wallpaper, 34–35
  with your name and contact information,
    28, 50
Phone
  alerts or ring tones for, 36, 49
  Auto Answer Call feature, 229
  automatic deletion of log entries, 50
  Bluetooth headset for, 235–236
  call forwarding, 231–232
  Call Log, 238–239
  conference calls, 233–234
  disabling reception in Bedside mode, 86
  making a call, 227–229
  muting, 230
  notes, 237–240
  opening Contacts from, 44
  receiving a call, 229–230
  speaker phone function, 235
  switching between conversations, 234
  Voice Dialing application, 236–237
  voice mail setup, 231
  volume adjustment, 230
phone logs, 50

phone notes
  accessing, 238–239
  forwarding, 239–240
  taking, 237–238
phone numbers. *See also* Contacts
  AutoText for yours, 31
  conference dial-in number, 81–82
  extra numbers after, adding to Contacts,
    46, 228–229
  voice mail access, 231
Picasa, Gears settings for, 176
pictures. *See also* Camera
  adding to contacts, 48–49, 195–196
  Browser background, 173
  Browser options for displaying, 172–173,
    174
  as Caller ID, 195–196
  deleting, 191
  filename format for, 190
  formats supported, 204
  geotagging, 189
  Hidden, finding, 209
  Home screen background, 34–35, 166, 196
  locations for captured photos, 189
  moving between folders, 193–194
  organizing, 192–194
  Pictures application for, 204–205, 208
  properties, 191–192
  quality settings (Camera), 186–187
  renaming files, 192–193
  saving Web images, 166
  sending with BlackBerry Messenger, 152
  sharing, 194–195
  size settings (Camera), 188–189
  slide shows, 190–191, 212
  viewing, 189–190, 191, 205
  zooming, 205
Pictures application, 204–205, 208, 212
PIN (personal identification number)
  assigning PINs to names, 127–128
  AutoText for, 31
  defined, 124
  finding yours, 125–126
  keyword for yours, 125–126
  passwords versus, 125
  PIN-to-PIN messaging, 55, 56, 123–129
  switching to a new BlackBerry, 272–273

PIN-to-PIN messaging. *See also* BlackBerry Messenger
  assigning PINs to names, 127–128
  BlackBerry Messenger based on, 143
  contact action for, 55
  discovering your PIN, 125–126
  in enterprise environments, 56, 125
  history of, 124
  overview, 123–125
  privacy of, 124–125
  receiving a message, 129
  sending a message, 128–129
  sending a Web page address, 164
Pixelated game, 316
podcasts, downloading, 218
portals, 320–321
power. *See* battery
Power/End key, 18
preferences. *See* options
profiles
  Bedside mode settings, 87
  for Calendar reminders, 78
  categories of alerts in, 36
  customizing, 37–38
programming convenience keys, 33–34, 211
prompt options (Browser), 174
properties
  Browser, 173–174
  viewing for pictures, 191–192
pushed content, 36, 176

• Q •

QuickLaunch application, 44, 213
QWERTY keyboard
  AutoText feature, 29–31
  described, 17
  displaying, 20
  hiding, 21
  in portrait orientation, 24
  using, 21

• R •

radio, disabling in Bedside mode, 86
random password generation, 93–94, 95

Really Simple Syndication (RSS), 218
recharging. *See* charging the battery
recipient, searching for messages by, 116–117, 119
recurring appointments, creating, 78–79
redirecting e-mail from Outlook, 244–245
reminders. *See* alarms; alerts
removing. *See* deleting
renaming
  bookmark folders in Browser, 170
  picture files, 192–193
  User fields for contacts, 46–47
restoring from backup
  BlackBerry Messenger contacts, 147
  full restore, 284–285
  selective restore, 285, 287–288
ring tones. *See also* alarms; alerts
  for alarms, 85
  assigning to contacts, 49–50
  for countdown timer, 87
  creating your own, 206
  downloading, 219–220
  formats supported, 206
  listening to available tones, 205–206
  profiles for, 36–38
Ring Tones application, 205–206, 209
ripping, defined, 214
RSS (Really Simple Syndication), 218

• S •

saving
  BlackBerry Messenger conversation history, 154–155
  message search results, 119–120
  message to folder, 106
  reusing saved searches, 120
  Web page address, 164–165
scalable vector graphics (SVG), 173
scanning barcodes in BlackBerry Messenger, 147, 148
screen brightness settings, 32–33, 87
screen protector, 311
Screen/Keyboard options, 19, 31–33
scripts, terminating slow running, 172
search engines, 320–321

searching for contacts. *See* finding contact information
searching Messages
  methods for, 116
  reusing saved searches, 120
  running a general search, 117–119
  saving searches, 119–120
  by sender or recipient, 116–117, 119
  shortcuts for, 117
  by subject, 117
security. *See also* passwords
  BlackBerry strengths for, 15, 279
  locking your BlackBerry, 38–39
  password setup, 38
send key, 18
sender, searching for messages by, 116–117, 119
Sensitivity settings, 19, 33
settings. *See* options
sharing
  Contacts, 62–64
  pictures, 194–195
shipping information sites, 323–324
shopping sites, 323–324
shortcuts
  accessing incoming e-mail, 120–121
  AutoText feature, 29–31
  navigating Web pages, 161
  QuickLaunch application for, 44, 213
  searching messages, 117
  text, 31
shorthand for SMS, 130–131
signature for e-mails, 102–103
SIM card, viewing contacts saved on, 56
size
  of Application Memory, 50
  for fonts, 32
  number of pictures (Camera), 185
  of pictures (Camera), 188–189
skins or skin cases, 311
slide shows, 190–191, 212
SmartCase option, 30
smileys
  for BlackBerry Messenger, 152
  for instant messaging, 141
  for texting, 132–133, 135

SmrtGuard wireless backup and restore, 280, 289
SMS (Short Message Service)
  challenges for beginners, 130
  contact action for, 55
  disabling reception in Bedside mode, 86
  emoticons or smileys for, 132–133, 135
  etiquette and cautions for, 135
  instant messaging using, 142
  maximum message size, 130
  sending a message, 133–134
  sending a Web page address, 164
  separating e-mail messages from, 136
  shorthand for, 130–131
  viewing a message, 135
Snooze Time setting, 86
social networking applications, 65–66. *See also* Facebook
social networking sites, 323
sorting
  contacts, 62
  message list, 106
  pictures, 212
sounds. *See* alarms; alerts
speaker, external, 312–313
speaker phone, 235
Specified Case option, 30
speeding up browsing, 175
spell-checking outgoing messages, 111
splitting a conference call, 234
sports sites, 322
Status screen, PIN on, 126
stereo headset, 310–311
stopwatch, 87, 89–90
storage time for e-mail, 121–122
streaming music using Bluetooth, 313
subject, searching for messages by, 117
Sudoku Lite game, 316
SuperFine picture quality, 186
SurePress touch screen
  described, 17
  settings for, 19, 32–33
  using, 20
SureType keyboard
  AutoText feature, 29–31
  Custom Dictionary for, 21, 23–24

described, 18
displaying, 21
multitap mode, 22, 24
using, 21–22
surfing. *See* Browser; Web surfing
SVG (scalable vector graphics), 173
switching
applications, 25, 159
to new BlackBerry, 271–274
from non-BlackBerry device, 274–277
between phone conversations, 234
Synchronize (Windows)
applications that can be synchronized, 249
automatic sync, 258
configuring PIM synchronization, 249–253
confirming record changes, 255
copying contacts from desktop applications, 53–54
data that can be synchronized, 250
on-demand sync, 257–258
mapping fields for synchronization, 253–255
resolving update conflicts, 255–257
Synchronization Configuration view, 249
Synchronize view, 248
synchronizing. *See also* BlackBerry Desktop Manager (Mac); Synchronize (Windows)
Facebook profiles and Contacts, 67–68
with iTunes, 218–219, 266–267
over the air (OTA), 243
wireless e-mail reconciliation, 98, 103–105

• T •

tap, defined, 20
Tap Interval setting, 19, 33
tasks, sync setup for
Mac, 264–266
Windows, 249–253
TeleNav GPS Navigator, 225
Telus, 12, 101
Texas Hold 'Em game, 317
text shortcuts, 31
texting or text messaging. *See* SMS (Short Message Service)

themes, 34
third-party applications
BlackBerry App World store for, 291–294, 315
defined, 273
other stores for, 294–295
switching to a new BlackBerry, 273
time
setting for Clock, 85
storage time for e-mail, 121–122
time zone, setting, 85
timer, 87, 90–91
to-do lists
reminder sounds for, 36
sync setup for, 249–253
touch screen. *See* SurePress touch screen
touch-press, defined, 20
travel sites, 321–322
Twitter clients, 138

• U •

Unify AV Solution, 309
uninstalling applications, 301–303
updating contacts, 51–52
upgrading the Storm OS, 303–306
user ID for instant messaging, 138, 140–141

• V •

vCards, 62–64, 154
Vegas Pool Shark Lite game, 316
Verizon, BIS login address for, 101
Verizon, BlackBerry branding by, 12
vibration. *See also* alarms; alerts
for alarms, 86
for Calendar appointments, 77–78
for countdown timer, 87, 91
customizing profiles for, 37–38
Video Camera application, 199, 203
videocasts, downloading, 218
videos
closed captions for, 212
playing, 203
recording, 203–204
Videos application, 199, 203–204, 209
views (Calendar), 70–74

virtual keyboards. *See* QWERTY keyboard;
   SureType keyboard
virtual networking sites, 323
Vodafone, BIS login address for, 101
voice command application, opening, 25
Voice Dialing application, 236–237
voice mail setup, 231
Voice Notes
  playing, 207–208
  recording, 206–207
  sending with BlackBerry Messenger,
    152–154
Voice Notes application, 199, 207–208, 209
Voice Notes Recorder application, 199,
   206–207
volume
  for alarms, 86
  for alerts, 38
  buttons for, 208
  for countdown timer, 87
  Media controls for, 208
  for phone calls, 230

• W •

wallpaper, 34–35, 166
WAP (wireless application protocol), 158
weather sites, 319–320
Web resources. *See* Internet resources
Web Sites, 319–324
Web surfing. *See also* Browser
  alerts for channel push, 36
  BlackBerry capabilities for, 13
  bookmarking sites, 166–171
  navigating Web pages, 161–163
  opening a Web page, 160–161
  Password Keeper for e-commerce sites,
    91–96
  saving Web images, 166
  speeding up, 175
  stopping a page from loading, 164
Week view (Calendar), 70
white balance settings (Camera), 188
Wi-Fi connection, Browser for, 158
Windows Live Messenger, 138, 140. *See
   also* instant messaging (IM)

Windows Mobile device, switching to a
   BlackBerry from, 275–277
wireless application installation, 299
wireless backup, 280, 289
wireless e-mail reconciliation, 98, 103–105
Word Completion option, 31
World Poker Tour 2 game, 317

• Y •

Yahoo! Messenger, 138, 140. *See also*
   instant messaging (IM)
YouTube, Gears settings for, 176

• Z •

zooming
  Camera, 185, 187–188
  when viewing pictures, 205

Business/Accounting & Bookkeeping

Bookkeeping For Dummies
978-0-7645-9848-7

eBay Business
All-in-One For Dummies,
2nd Edition
978-0-470-38536-4

Job Interviews
For Dummies,
3rd Edition
978-0-470-17748-8

Resumes For Dummies,
5th Edition
978-0-470-08037-5

Stock Investing
For Dummies,
3rd Edition
978-0-470-40114-9

Successful Time
Management
For Dummies
978-0-470-29034-7

Computer Hardware

BlackBerry For Dummies,
3rd Edition
978-0-470-45762-7

Computers For Seniors
For Dummies
978-0-470-24055-7

iPhone For Dummies,
2nd Edition
978-0-470-42342-4

Laptops For Dummies,
3rd Edition
978-0-470-27759-1

Macs For Dummies,
10th Edition
978-0-470-27817-8

Cooking & Entertaining

Cooking Basics
For Dummies,
3rd Edition
978-0-7645-7206-7

Wine For Dummies,
4th Edition
978-0-470-04579-4

Diet & Nutrition

Dieting For Dummies,
2nd Edition
978-0-7645-4149-0

Nutrition For Dummies,
4th Edition
978-0-471-79868-2

Weight Training
For Dummies,
3rd Edition
978-0-471-76845-6

Digital Photography

Digital Photography
For Dummies,
6th Edition
978-0-470-25074-7

Photoshop Elements 7
For Dummies
978-0-470-39700-8

Gardening

Gardening Basics
For Dummies
978-0-470-03749-2

Organic Gardening
For Dummies,
2nd Edition
978-0-470-43067-5

Green/Sustainable

Green Building
& Remodeling
For Dummies
978-0-470-17559-0

Green Cleaning
For Dummies
978-0-470-39106-8

Green IT For Dummies
978-0-470-38688-0

Health

Diabetes For Dummies,
3rd Edition
978-0-470-27086-8

Food Allergies
For Dummies
978-0-470-09584-3

Living Gluten-Free
For Dummies
978-0-471-77383-2

Hobbies/General

Chess For Dummies,
2nd Edition
978-0-7645-8404-6

Drawing For Dummies
978-0-7645-5476-6

Knitting For Dummies,
2nd Edition
978-0-470-28747-7

Organizing For Dummies
978-0-7645-5300-4

SuDoku For Dummies
978-0-470-01892-7

Home Improvement

Energy Efficient Homes
For Dummies
978-0-470-37602-7

Home Theater
For Dummies,
3rd Edition
978-0-470-41189-6

Living the Country Lifestyle
All-in-One For Dummies
978-0-470-43061-3

Solar Power Your Home
For Dummies
978-0-470-17569-9

Internet

Blogging For Dummies,
2nd Edition
978-0-470-23017-6

eBay For Dummies,
6th Edition
978-0-470-49741-8

Facebook For Dummies
978-0-470-26273-3

Google Blogger
For Dummies
978-0-470-40742-4

Web Marketing
For Dummies,
2nd Edition
978-0-470-37181-7

WordPress For Dummies,
2nd Edition
978-0-470-40296-2

Language & Foreign Language

French For Dummies
978-0-7645-5193-2

Italian Phrases
For Dummies
978-0-7645-7203-6

Spanish For Dummies
978-0-7645-5194-9

Spanish For Dummies,
Audio Set
978-0-470-09585-0

Macintosh

Mac OS X Snow Leopard
For Dummies
978-0-470-43543-4

Math & Science

Algebra I For Dummies
978-0-7645-5325-7

Biology For Dummies
978-0-7645-5326-4

Calculus For Dummies
978-0-7645-2498-1

Chemistry For Dummies
978-0-7645-5430-8

Microsoft Office

Excel 2007 For Dummies
978-0-470-03737-9

Office 2007 All-in-One
Desk Reference
For Dummies
978-0-471-78279-7

Music

Guitar For Dummies,
2nd Edition
978-0-7645-9904-0

iPod & iTunes
For Dummies,
6th Edition
978-0-470-39062-7

Piano Exercises
For Dummies
978-0-470-38765-8

Parenting & Education

Parenting For Dummies,
2nd Edition
978-0-7645-5418-6

Type 1 Diabetes
For Dummies
978-0-470-17811-9

Pets

Cats For Dummies,
2nd Edition
978-0-7645-5275-5

Dog Training For Dummies,
2nd Edition
978-0-7645-8418-3

Puppies For Dummies,
2nd Edition
978-0-470-03717-1

Religion & Inspiration

The Bible For Dummies
978-0-7645-5296-0

Catholicism For Dummies
978-0-7645-5391-2

Women in the Bible
For Dummies
978-0-7645-8475-6

Self-Help & Relationship

Anger Management
For Dummies
978-0-470-03715-7

Overcoming Anxiety
For Dummies
978-0-7645-5447-6

Sports

Baseball For Dummies,
3rd Edition
978-0-7645-7537-2

Basketball For Dummies,
2nd Edition
978-0-7645-5248-9

Golf For Dummies,
3rd Edition
978-0-471-76871-5

Web Development

Web Design All-in-One
For Dummies
978-0-470-41796-6

Windows Vista

Windows Vista
For Dummies
978-0-471-75421-3